Beyond Employment

Beyond Employment

*Changes in Work and the Future
of Labour Law in Europe*

ALAIN SUPIOT

with
María Emilia Casas
Jean de Munck
Peter Hanau
Anders L. Johansson
Pamela Meadows
Enzo Mingione
Robert Salais
Paul van der Heijden

A report prepared for the European Commission

OXFORD
UNIVERSITY PRESS

OXFORD

UNIVERSITY PRESS

Great Clarendon Street, Oxford OX2 6DP

Oxford University Press is a department of the University of Oxford.
It furthers the University's objective of excellence in research, scholarship,
and education by publishing worldwide in

Oxford New York

Athens Auckland Bangkok Bogotá Buenos Aires Cape Town
Chennai Dar es Salaam Delhi Florence Hong Kong Istanbul Karachi
Kolkata Kuala Lumpur Madrid Melbourne Mexico City Mumbai
Nairobi Paris São Paulo Shanghai Singapore Taipei Tokyo Toronto Warsaw

and associated companies in Berlin Ibadan

Oxford is a registered trade mark of Oxford University Press
in the UK and in certain other countries

Published in the United States
by Oxford University Press Inc., New York

British Library Cataloguing in Publication Data

Data available

Library of Congress Cataloging in Publication Data

Data available

ISBN 0–19–924305–0
ISBN 0–19–924304–2 (pbk.)

1 3 5 7 9 10 8 6 4 2

Typeset by Hope Services (Abingdon) Ltd.
Printed in Great Britain
on acid-free paper by
T.J. International Ltd., Padstow, Cornwall

PREFACE

As a group of experts[1] we were assigned a very ambitious task by the European Commission: 'to conduct a prospective and constructive survey on the future of work and labour law within a Community-wide, intercultural and inter-disciplinary framework, culminating in a conference and subsequent report on the subject'.[2] The nature of the objective was therefore legal—to attempt to define the future evolution of the basic categories of labour law in European countries—but it could only be achieved by undertaking a cross-disciplinary analysis of the changes taking place in the actual practice of labour relations. Any such analysis, moreover, had to be comparative and take account of national diversity. Finally, the purpose of this analysis was not to deal with the present state of labour law, but rather to consider the question in the context of its historical dynamic, which calls for a diachronic, as opposed to a synchronic, approach to the issues at hand. There are three difficulties associated with this task.

First, there are difficulties associated with a cross-national approach. In the last fifteen years, the building of Europe has encouraged comparative social research. That experience has revealed clearly the extreme difficulty involved in such comparisons.

Secondly, there are difficulties associated with a cross-disciplinary approach. The legal issues which we have been invited to consider both determine and express conditions prevailing in society, sociologically, economically, politically, and culturally. Such legal matters cannot therefore be addressed without some reference to actual practice. This, in turn, calls for a dialogue between legal theorists and social scientists.

Finally there are difficulties associated with a diachronic approach. Such an approach aims to break down the motives underlying change into their component parts in an attempt to understand the course it takes.

In view of these difficulties, any expert group undertaking such a task must be extremely cautious, both when defining the scope of its work and when setting out the results. Caution is called for in defining the scope of the survey, because the solutions to the major problems which are emerging from today's changed background to work will definitely not

---

[1] See p. xiii for group membership.
[2] Definition of the mission of the group of experts. Note dated 18 July 1996.

be provided. Rather, the solutions will emerge from actual practice; it is the action and imagination of those who work, at whatever level, to make the world the way it is. The most researchers can do is to help formulate the problems and identify the pitfalls with which the possible avenues of change are strewn.

Caution is needed as well in the wording of the results, because the foremost experts in labour relations are the parties to such relations: workers, employers, and their organizations. No matter how scrupulous the researcher may be, his or her work necessarily consists of abstracting syntheses from the diversity of individual experience; syntheses that are always questionable, and can always be improved.

Of necessity therefore, our understanding of changes in the circumstances surrounding work on the European scale is incomplete, and the most we have been able to do in applying a rational approach to change in labour law has been to expand and diversify our sources of information as far as possible and subject our analyses to discussion and critique.

The group's deliberations on the future of labour law have been organized around five major themes, which are addressed in the first five chapters of this report:

- work and private power;
- work and membership of the labour force;
- work and time;
- work and collective organization;
- work and public authorities.

The following procedure was employed in the analysis of each of these areas. A special rapporteur was appointed to draw up a questionnaire to which the group members replied in the form of written reports. Such special reports were compared and discussed during a working session. The special rapporteur then drafted an initial synthesis based on the written and oral contributions. Outside experts were also heard and their opinions incorporated.[3] One of these interviews provided the material for Chapter 7 of the report on what is at stake, economically speaking, in the future of labour law. An interim report was drafted halfway through the survey. That report provided material for an extensive discussion among social partner leaders and Community institutions, as well as among experts in the various European Union countries, at a conference held in Nantes on 25 October 1997.[4] In response to one of the conclusions of that conference,

---

[3] See Appendix p. 230 for the list of experts interviewed.
[4] See Appendix p. 230 for a list of the participants at that conference.

it was decided to expand the initial programme to include a chapter addressing the problems of gender equality. Although the principle of equality is a line of thought developed throughout our study (in particular in the chapter dedicated to work and time), it was felt that a synthesis of the expert group's position on the issue would prove to be useful. Finally, a total of forty-five national reports and seven first draft syntheses per subject were compiled. The general rapporteur has drafted the present report on the basis of that body of fifty-two texts and the conclusions of the ten working sessions to which they gave rise. The report is, therefore, the result of the endeavours of the expert group as a whole. The diversity of nationalities, disciplines and opinions represented in the group did not in any way prevent us from reaching a joint analysis; quite the contrary, it proved to be a stimulant for individual contributions and enhanced the final result of our work.

Alain Supiot

PREFACE TO THE ENGLISH LANGUAGE EDITION

The publication of the French language edition of this book *Au-delà de l'emploi* in 1999 generated a great deal of interest and debate in the French media. That has tended to create the impression that the analysis and the diagnoses it contains apply mainly to France. However, the members of the group which produced the book come from eight different European countries—Germany, the Netherlands, Sweden, Italy, the UK, Spain, and Belgium as well as France. We found it striking to observe the extent to which trends in the labour market were common to most, if not all of them. There are two key limitations which are worth drawing to the attention of the reader. Although it draws comparisons between different European Union member states, it does not, except occasionally in passing, compare the EU with other parts of the world. The analysis is also restricted to countries that are members of the European Union, which means that it does not cover other countries in central Europe. These omissions are accounted for by the book's origins. The specific brief for the expert group was a review of the European Union regulatory regime in the light of labour market developments.

The original report was produced for a conference in the summer of 1998, which means that in some places it has been overtaken by events. A very limited number of changes have been made to reflect events that have happened (for example the introduction of the euro) since the report was written but which were forthcoming at that time. But inevitably some sections will not reflect the most up-to-date position.

The members of the expert group were both multi-disciplinary and multi-lingual. The general working practice was for written comments to be submitted in whichever language the contributor felt most comfortable working in. Similarly contributions referred to references in several different languages. However, most of the final report was drafted in French and this book is translated from that original. The English text still carries much of the French style. It has only occasionally been paraphrased into a more typically English style in order to make it more readily understood. One of the challenges in preparing the English text for publication has been to ensure that abstract concepts which are clear and well understood in French speaking countries can be conveyed clearly into concepts which can be similarly understood by the English speaking reader. The most problematic concept was that of *statut professionel*, the subject of Chapter 2. The underlying idea is the recognition that an individual is a member of the labour force even if he or she does not currently have a job. *Professional status*, does not carry the same connotation in English, as it would generally refer to professional occupations—medicine and the law, for example. After some discussion we have used the phrase *membership of the labour force* in the English text. This and other instances where there were translation challenges have been indicated with a footnote.

I would particularly like to thank Paul van der Heijden and Hetty van der Meij for their support in preparing the English text for publication. However, as the only native English speaker among the group of authors, I have to accept responsibility for any remaining errors.

Pamela Meadows
London
July 2000

CONTENTS

MEMBERS OF THE EXPERT GROUP

María Emilia Casas, Complutense University of Madrid

Jean De Munck, Louvain University (College Thomas More)

Peter Hanau, Cologne University

Anders Johansson, National Institute for Working Life, Stockholm

Pamela Meadows, National Institute of Economic and Social Research, London

Enzo Mingione, Padua University

Robert Salais, Laboratory *'Institutions et Dynamiques Historiques de l'Economie'* (CNRS-Ecole Normale Supérieure de Cachan)

Alain Supiot (General Rapporteur), Nantes University; Wissenschaftskolleg zu Berlin

Paul van der Heijden, Amsterdam University

1

Work and Private Power

In labour law, the notion underlying labour relations is both hierarchical and collective. The employment contract is basically defined here by the bond of subordination it establishes between the worker and the party to whom his services are delivered. A business is conceived as a community of workers with different trades contributing a single economic activity under the supervision of a single employer.

This concept corresponds to what in the language of industrial relations is called the 'Fordist' model, that is a large industrial business engaging in mass production based on a narrow specialization of jobs and competencies and pyramidal management (hierarchical structure of labour, separation between product design and manufacture). This model has been largely dominant throughout Europe in various different forms (in fact sociologists and political scientists speak of 'models of welfare capitalism or of welfare systems' (Esping-Andersen 1990, Ferrera 1998) which, as we shall see, are also reflected in certain differences in the legal and institutional structures (ranging from the particular features of the Nordic or Scandinavian model, based on the provision of universal welfare services by the state to citizens independently of employment, to the Southern European variants, based on the continued importance of self-employment, micro-firms, and emigration). However the core feature of the model, present everywhere to some extent, is the crucial importance of standard full-time non-temporary wage contracts (particularly for adult men), centring around the trade-off between high levels of subordination and disciplinary control on the part of the employer and high levels of stability and welfare/insurance compensations and guarantees for the employee (extended to family members as a result of the high, homogeneous existence of stable forms of nuclear households).

It is hardly a novelty today to point out that these standardized patterns of social and economic regulation of employment are fast losing ground, and this fact is also reflected in various changes in labour law throughout Europe. Under the three influences of the rising level of employee skills and qualifications (and the consequent increase in the levels of professional autonomy enjoyed by workers, irrespective of their contractual subordination),[1] the increasing pressure of competition on more open markets, and the ever speedier evolution of technical progress (especially in the areas of information and communication) other patterns of work organization have developed (European Commission 1997d). Moreover, the massive entry of married women into the labour market and important social and demographic transformations (like the ageing of the population and increasing divorce, instability and heterogeneity in household structure) have helped to erode the power of the standard model based on the trade-off between subordination and stability in the social sphere as well.

The problem is that there are several of these patterns, the features are mostly different in particular countries, even if deriving from the same global processes of transformation, and the new patterns have not brought about change in the various forms assumed by the Fordist regime of employment and welfare throughout Europe. Under current economic and social circumstances, a single pattern of work relationships cannot be expected to emerge because of the many different kinds of environment existing today (Salais and Storper 1993). The use of self-employed workers, sub-contracting or outsourcing of labour, for instance, may simply be strategies to evade labour regulations and reduce costs in traditional lines of business where there is little added value. But it may also tie in with strategies designed to implement an innovative approach in sectors requiring high levels of expertise. In the former case, the aim is to reduce the costs of human resources; in the other, the opposite aim is pursued, so as to enhance the impact of human involvement (in terms of initiative, competencies and expertise). A new distribution of power and new balances between autonomy of work and socio-legal and welfare protection may arise in labour relations under a wide range of circumstances, which call for an equally wide variety of legal approaches in addition to the awareness that the diversity which was typical of the Fordist regimes is not disappearing at present but is, on the contrary, fostering a large and complex set of trends.

[1] Beretta (1995) documents with survey data how the number of workers feeling in full control is increasing and is particularly high (nearly half) in countries like the Netherlands and Italy.

From the legal point of view, these changes can be identified essentially at three levels:

- fostering or development of self-employment as opposed to waged employment;
- evolution of the principle of subordination which defines the nature of the employment contract;
- outsourcing or sub-contracting of labour to businesses that are economically dependent on a principal.

TRENDS IN SELF-EMPLOYMENT

Employment contracts have never been the only means of engaging in remunerated work (or even the only type of dependent work, since in most European countries civil servants are not subject to standard labour law). Many civil or commercial contracts concern work in exchange for a fee. Self-employment prevailed at the turn of the nineteenth century, when most workers were farmers (or farm labourers), tradesmen, craftspeople or freelance professionals. Throughout the twentieth century, dependent work rose steadily, with a concomitant drop in the number of self-employed workers. In most countries, this trend, which went hand-in-hand with the rise in the Fordist model, was fuelled by the development of social rights attributed to wage-earners, especially with respect to social security. The law or jurisprudence has aimed to extend the scope of social protection by likening certain circumstances to those of wage-earners or through the presumption of employee status.

Our working hypothesis was that the employment crisis and management changes would reverse the trend, increasing the number of self-employed compared to the number of employed workers. Although the results of our research do not fully support this hypothesis, it has proved useful because it has enabled us to highlight the main features of today's changing circumstances. This trend is encouraged at Community level by the guidelines on employment adopted by the Council of Ministers on 15 December 1998, which link the development of self-employment to that of the entrepreneurial spirit.

Quantitative Stability and Qualitative Changes

Measuring current changes is no easy task in view of the heterogeneity of the notion of self-employment. The statistical studies that are available do, however, provide evidence of the dual phenomena at work with respect to self-employment, namely, quantitative stability and qualitative change.

According to the statistics published by the ILO in 1990,[2] self-employed and unpaid family workers in France accounted for 14 per cent of total employment (82 per cent in agriculture, 9 per cent in industry and 11 per cent in services), compared to 8 per cent in the USA (44/6/8), 6 per cent in Sweden (54/3/5), 11 per cent in the United Kingdom (46/11/11), 9 per cent in the West Germany (36/5/9), 21 per cent in Italy (49/15/25), 9 per cent in the Netherlands (50/4/10), and 18 per cent in Spain (48/14/22).

A more recent survey carried out in Europe on the proportion of non-wage-earners yielded very different results. The overall rate for 1994 was 24.1 per cent in Italy, 22.1 per cent in Spain, 12.9 per cent in the United Kingdom, 11.8 per cent in France, 9.3 per cent in Germany, and 8.4 per cent in Denmark (Eurostat 1995). This confirms the importance of non-wage-earning work in the Southern European countries. In the 1990s the proportion of self-employed workers outside agriculture increased in the Union but at slower pace compared with the second half of the 1980s. The only Member States where there has been a decrease are Belgium, France, and the UK. In contrast, self-employment has been disproportionately important for the net creation of new jobs both in the Southern European countries and in Germany, the Netherlands, and Denmark (European Commission 1996a).

The general trend is not therefore an increase in self-employment but rather stabilization with respect to total employment. However, this quantitative stability masks some important qualitative trends: self-employment is increasing in the services sector (especially in services to companies, which are thus able to outsource some of their functions), whereas the number in agriculture continues to fall.

Where self-employment is growing, such growth may be associated with either of the two opposing strategies mentioned above, that is lowering or enhancing the value of labour:

- the value is lowered where the use of self-employed workers is often intended to exclude unskilled and casualized workers from the

[2] ILO (1990) table A1, p. 108.

protection afforded by labour law; self-employment under such circumstances may sometimes be regarded as an illegal method of deregulation whereby firms engaging in such practices avoid the burden of non-wage labour costs incurred by their competitors (especially with respect to social insurance costs);

- the value is enhanced where the use of self-employed workers gives free rein to the capacity of genuinely autonomous and often highly qualified workers for innovation and adaptation. This brighter side of self-employment is an ideal/typical form of post-Fordist labour. Flexible in terms of time, place, type of service and cost, it meets the needs of the most advanced economic sectors in which the innovation and quality they require depends on the quality and creativity of the people performing the work.

Legislative or Jurisprudential Expansion of the Scope of Self-employment

First, it must be stressed that no European country allows the parties to an employer–employee relationship alone to define the legal status of this relationship, since this would make labour law optional. The general principle, applied everywhere, is that ascertaining whether or not a given worker is self-employed is contingent not upon the existence of a conventional arrangement, but rather on the circumstances actually prevailing. And this principle must be firmly maintained if action is to be taken against fraudulent self-employment and the resulting unfair competition.

In several European countries, however, the presumption of employee status has tended to recede and an effort has been made to provide a legal framework for genuine self-employment. Until the 1980s, both to protect workers and to guarantee the basis for social security contributions, law and jurisprudence generally interpreted the notion of a contract of employment for a wage in the broadest sense of the term, rendering self-employment more difficult to practise. The opposite is now true and the present tendency is to refrain from obstructing the development of genuine self-employment.

This concern has been expressed in the most recent Spanish case law which seeks alternatives to the employment contract (*vías alternativas al contrato de trabajo*) by allowing some leeway for the express will of the parties involved, providing they are not then contradicted by observation of their respective behaviour.[3] In Germany, the Federal Labour Court admitted—in a controversial ruling—that an employer was free to re-organize his company by resorting to self-employed workers rather than hiring employees.[4] In France, the Madelin Act of 11 February 1994 on Initiative and Individual Enterprise established the presumption of non-wage-earning status for persons registered under social security as self-employed workers.[5] This presumption is in principle a simple presumption that can be reversed if it is found that the activity of the workers concerned places them 'in a situation of permanent legal subordi-nation' with respect to a principal. Such extension of the scope of self-employment risks depriving these workers of any social protection and of excluding them from labour law without offering them any other employ-ment status. Unfair situations of this nature are to be found in most coun-tries.

In France, for example, some taxi companies have replaced their wage-earning drivers with drivers who rent the vehicle and are expected to assume all the risks of this 'business'; the company owners thus ensure themselves a secure income whereas the brunt of the financial risk is borne by the workers. In the Swedish forestry industry, employed wage-earners have often been replaced by self-employed workers who rent or own the forestry machine or tractor.

Two conditions must be met to avoid these risks. First, the principle of reclassifying false self-employment as wage-earning work must be firmly enforced and, secondly, genuine self-employment must be endowed with true employment status, primarily to guarantee social protection.

Pursuit of an Appropriate Legal Framework for Self-employment

The wide range of specific situations prevailing in self-employment makes it difficult to formulate such a framework. This diversity is not always fully grasped, legally speaking. Certain countries, such as France or Sweden, make no distinction between a self-employed worker and a capitalist

[3] Supreme Court Judgment, Sala de lo Social, 13 April 1989; see also Rodríguez-Piñero (1996).

[4] Bundesarbeitsgericht, 9 May 1996, *Der Bertrieb*, 1996, 2033 (Weight Watchers case). The employer wanted to change his network of establishments into a network of franchises. His right to dismiss his staff for this purpose and to offer his dismissed workers the status of free agents (*freie Mitarbeiter*) was recognized.

[5] *C. trav.*, Art. L120-3; *C. sécurité.social*, Art.L311-11; see: Teyssié (1994), Barthélémy (1994), Laroque *et al.* (1995).

entrepreneur. In others, on the other hand (Germany, Italy), a distinction is made between completely independent entrepreneurs subject to civil or commercial law and self-employed professionals who are financially dependent on one or more principals.

These situations of semi-independence have given rise to legal provisions that vary from country to country, but in all of them the labour relations of such semi-independent workers are subject to at least some of the rules or principles of standard labour law.

German law, for instance, identifies three categories of independent workers. The first two cover entrepreneurs who may either work under a business contract (*Werkvertrag*) or under a free contract for services (*freier Dienstvertrag*). The difference between these two categories is that the purpose of a free contract for services is the mere obligation to perform a task (as with most liberal professions), whereas a business contract also calls for delivery of some result (as with craftspeople or traders). The third category is that of 'quasi-employees' (*arbeitnehmerähnliche Personen*) who work under a free contract for services or business contract but for a main principal on whom they depend financially. The law applies certain provisions of labour law to these legally independent workers relating to time off, labour disputes or collective bargaining. Workers working alone (without the help of other employees), owing over half their income to the services rendered to their main principal, and whose need for social protection is similar to that of employees are deemed to be financially dependent.[6]

In the Italian notion of 'para-subordination', the approach is slightly different though practically the results are the same. The notion of para-subordinate workers was introduced by Act No. 533/1973 (Art. 409 c. proc. civ.), which extended the act on individual labour disputes to agents, commercial representatives and other similar relationships involving continuous, co-ordinated and personal work, even if there is no subordination ('*altri rapporti di collaborazione che se concretino in una prestazione d'opera continuativa e coordinata, prevalentemente personale anche se non a carattere subordinato*'). This is therefore an 'open' category, which in practice includes such widely differing professions as corporate attorneys or doctors in the national health service. What distinguishes them from German quasi-employees is that the need for social protection is not included in the definition. The debate in Italy turns on whether the criterion of economic dependence must be included in this notion, in which case labour law would, in principle, be applicable to 'para-subordinate'

---

[6]   See: sect. 12 a of the 1974 Act on collective bargaining (*Tarifsvertragsgesetz*).

workers, or whether, on the other hand, the latter must maintain self-employment status—in which case they would not be entitled to any rights under labour law except those in areas expressly covered by the act, that is primarily in legal action involving health and safety (Mengoni 1986, Ballestrero 1987). It is this second approach that has prevailed in doctrine and in case law.

In the Netherlands, a draft law currently under debate aims to guarantee financially dependent workers protection equivalent to that of employees. In Spain, the Workers' By-laws provide for the partial extension of labour legislation to self-employment.

Countries where there is no generic category covering such semi-independent workers have proceeded case by case and made certain professions subject to partial enforcement of labour law. This is the case for example for certain professions covered by Book 7 of the French labour code (commercial representatives, managers of commercial branch offices, etc.), or Spanish wage-earning managers, who are subject only to part of the provisions of the Workers' By-laws, or brokers (*likställda uppdragstagare*), considered by Swedish law to fall under the scope of the laws on collective agreements. There therefore seems to be a clear need for an intermediate legal category between employee and entrepreneur.

In this respect, it is interesting to note the intention of the ILO to introduce a convention on work under contract. The ILO has clearly identified the existence of a large category of workers who are dependent but do not have employment contracts, at least not yet. According to the draft Convention, the expression 'work under contract' designates the work done for a natural or artificial person (the user firm) by a person (a worker employed under contract) when the work is carried out by the sub-contracted worker personally under conditions of actual dependence or subordination with respect to the user firm, similar to those characterizing labour relationships as defined by national law and practice and when either the work is carried out under a direct contractual arrangement other than an employment contract between the sub-contracted worker and the user firm, or the sub-contracted worker is made available to the user firm by a sub-contractor or intermediary. A first round of discussions was held on this Draft Convention on Subcontracting Work at the ILO conference in June 1997. A Recommendation was attached to the Convention with a view to developing several matters in greater detail.

This new category of workers has yet to be clearly defined so that they can be afforded a coherent and sufficiently attractive employment status. Seen in this light, both the German and Italian initiatives seem to leave a great deal of room for improvement. The status of German 'quasi-employees' is hardly a model of legal simplicity. In Italy, the heated debate around the notion of 'para-subordination' was kindled by the development of a new type of relationship called 'co-ordinated, continuous collaboration'. This relationship was first defined in fiscal terms in 1986,[7] before Act 335/1995 introduced a mandatory 10 per cent social contribution for old age, invalidity and death benefits (Lagala 1997, Vianello 1997). It focuses on the use of labour involving a new form of subordination but forming part of a stable relationship in terms of both the work performed and the remuneration received in exchange.

These recent developments are indicative of the key role played by social protection issues in this debate. Fostering self-employment is inconceivable if its aim or effect is to drain social security systems of their revenue;[8] nor is self-employment status attractive if, in addition to the inevitable financial ups-and-downs, it also entails inadequate social protection.

Ultimately, the rise in self-employment or semi-independent work involves handling the transition from one employment status to another. There has been some experience in this area, especially in France, where efforts have been made to assist employees to set themselves up as self-employed workers, mostly where they have been the victims of redundancies (support mechanisms for the creation of businesses or the exercise of a freelance profession) or of restructuring processes within their companies (technically called *essaimage*, or hiving off, where the company receives tax relief for helping its employees to set up on their own). Recognition of the rights of people taking such initiatives is emerging, albeit sketchily, not only in labour law but also as regards social security, vocational training, tax law, etc. Freedom to work is now considered a specific liberty which the law must not only allow but also facilitate. One of the major features of this freedom is that citizens should be entitled to embrace different employment statuses throughout their working lives (employee, entrepreneur, self-employed, or semi-independent worker) without forfeiting the continuity of their social rights.

---

[7] '*Si considerano tali (rapporti di collaborazione coordinate e continuata) i rapporti aventi poer oggetto la prestazione di attività, non rientranti nell'oggetto dell'arte o della professione esercitata ai sensi del comma 1 dell'Art. 49 del texto unico que pur avendo contenuto intrinsecamente artistico or professionale sono svolte senza vincolo di subordinazione a favore di un determinato soggetto nel quadro di un rapport unitario e continuativo senza impiego di mezzi organizzati e con retribuzione periodica prestabilita*' (*Testo unico delle imposte sui redditi*, decree of 22 December 1986, Art.49-2-A).

[8] The Länder of Hesse and North-Rhine-Westphalia alone, in connection with a draft law to combat false self-employment (see below), estimated at DEM 10 billion per year the losses in social contributions resulting from false self-employment.

TRENDS IN THE CONCEPT OF SUBORDINATION

Important changes are taking place in the way power is exercised in companies. Such changes make it more difficult to deal with subordination as a criterion, even though it remains the major criterion in the definition of employment contracts. Discussion is under way in various countries on the question of broadening such criteria.

Trends in Practice

Here developments are ambivalent. In certain respects, workers are allowed greater independence with regard to the organization of their lives and work. In others, however, the preponderance of subordination in working relations is growing.

Advances in greater on-the-job autonomy constitute the bright side of current trends. They are the result of the development of new technologies, enhanced worker training, new participative management methods, etc. Wherever horizontal management tends to replace pyramidal management, power is wielded differently, on the basis of an evaluation of work performance rather than on the specification of job content. Pay is linked more to results than to methods. This affords employees much greater freedom in performing their work and encourages initiative. Constraint does not disappear—it is internalized. A growing number of wage-earners thus work under conditions that do not differ substantially from the terms for sub-contracted self-employed workers. Management avails itself of the contractual metaphor to conceptualize this new kind of working relationship between wage-earners in the same company.

This trend, which can be observed in all European countries, involves both the manufacturing sector and services. In Sweden, worker participation in everyday organization is a common practice in most companies with more than fifty employees. In Swedish firms, 85 per cent of workers' job descriptions define responsibilities. These trends lead to a revaluation of the collective dimension of work. Workers are not, under these new arrangements, confined to a specialized task, but involved in collective production (Lundgren 1996). Greater on-the-job independence should not, then, be taken to be a corollary of individualization, since more often than not independence is collective; it is group dynamics that are sought.

This aim may also ultimately cast some doubts on the viability of individualized pay policies that flourished in the 1980s.

The growing weight of subordination is felt most directly in the new kinds of casualized employment, such as on-the-job training contracts offered to young people, or fixed-term contracts. In these cases, employers indeed acquire, in addition to their usual power, the power inherent in the ability to extend at their discretion the employment contract upon expiry. This gives employers a powerful tool to influence worker behaviour, particularly in the case of young adults who more often than not begin their careers under this kind of contract.

Studies conducted in Italy indicate the importance of such informal pressures brought to bear on young adults hired under the terms of a *contratto di formazioni e lavoro* (on-the-job training contract) or a *contratto a tempo determinato* (fixed-term contract). Management is in a position to dissuade them from joining a union, participating in strikes, refusing to take on extra work, etc.

But even outside casual employment, employer power is strengthened by two factors. The first, obviously, is the high unemployment rate, which prompts employees to accept working conditions that they would refuse if they knew that they could readily find a job elsewhere. The second is the shift of large numbers of jobs from large to small and medium-sized businesses. This trend is encouraged by the rising incidence of the business networking model, whereby firms are interrelated by means of subcontracting or outsourcing arrangements. In most EU countries, the figures show that small (under fifty employees) or very small (under ten employees) companies account for most jobs. The regulation of employer power by labour law in such businesses is limited both for legal (employee thresholds) and sociological (ineffectiveness) reasons.

Broadening of the Concept of Legal Subordination

The changes observed in the exercise of power in labour relations have not, to date, led to the questioning of the notion of subordination as the primary consideration in the legal definition of what constitutes an employment contract. Consequently, the treatment of subordination is growing more and more complex, rendering the definition of the term 'employee' all the hazier.

The general trend in case law, at least until recently, has been to prevent the autonomy enjoyed by certain employees in the performance of their

work from excluding them from the scope of labour law. Such jurisprudential policy goes hand-in-hand with the evolution of the legal notion of
subordination, a concept which is no longer defined only in terms of submission to orders in the performance of work itself, but also in terms of
the integration of workers in a collective organizational scheme designed
by and for others. This broadening of the concept of subordination has
made dealing with it more uncertain and, above all, more complex.
Hence, when workers are afforded a certain degree of autonomy in the
performance of their duties, other indications of their possible subordination must be sought to establish the legal status of their contracts. This
technique, called 'indication clustering', has become a common feature in
labour law in European countries. Rather than verifying that all indications conform to the situation under consideration, it consists of inferring,
from the existence of several such indications, that the resulting relationship involves subordination.[9]

The items on such indication clusters vary from one country to another.
By way of illustration, the following are drawn from the list (not exhaustive) established under Swedish case law as set out during the preparatory
work on that country's 1976 act on co-determination:[10]

- the party concerned is hired to undertake the work personally;
- the means to do the job are furnished by the other party;
- professional expenses are defrayed by the other party;
- the work is remunerated;
- the worker's economic and social status is equivalent to that of an
  employee.

It is understandable, then, that the changes observed in labour relations in
practice have not entailed any change in the legal notion of subordination:
indication clustering, initially formulated to extend the scope of labour
law to professions whose nature calls for a certain degree of independence
(doctors, journalists, teachers), can today be used to *maintain* employees
affected by 'post-Fordism' and greater on-the-job independence within
the limits of the definition of an employee. As is often the case, the law has
evolved more slowly than the events it is intended to regulate.

The broadening of the concept of subordination has made it possible to
convert a large number of jobs into employee positions. Labour law,
rather than worker or employee law, has become the common law for all

---

[9] See in this regard the Bundesverfassungsgericht (German Federal Constitutional Court)
decision of 20 May 1996 (1 BvR 21/96), according to which the definition of employee is an
ideal, the various elements of which are simply indications of that status.

[10] Act (1976: 580); cf. SOU 1975: 1, p. 722.

working relations. The result of such trends, prompted primarily by social security considerations, is the growing heterogeneity of the employee population. Such heterogeneity, in turn, promotes the fragmentation of labour law, which must adapt to a variety of occupational situations. Another effect, less often noted, is the inclusion of rules characteristic of self-employment in labour law, such as the no-competition clause covenanted by sales agents (Gaudu 1996).

Generally speaking, the loosening of the bonds between subordination and employee status has enabled workers with a high degree of independence (company managers, for instance) to benefit from the protection afforded by labour law, whereas workers in weaker positions are deprived of all or part of such protection because of the casual nature of their jobs or are even excluded from labour law altogether as a result of their false self-employment status.

These perverse effects, added to the legal uncertainty deriving from the dilution of the concept of subordination, explain why the definition of the term 'employee' has again become a topic of intense discussion in several European countries.

The Debate on the Definition of Employee Status

Two opposing tendencies are emerging in this new debate on the definition of employee status in several European countries.

Reducing the Scope of Labour Law

The first tendency is to reduce the scope of labour law and return to a strict interpretation of the notion of subordination. This tendency is the corollary of legislative and jurisprudential policies designed to allow self-employment a broader scope for development.

In France, for example, the Madelin Act of 11 February 1994, mentioned above, introduces into the labour code reference to permanent legal subordination as an indication of the existence of employee status; French law had, until then, ignored such a requirement, although it exists in other legal systems such as the British system and can lead to the exclusion of temporary or intermittent employment from the definition of protected employee status. Case law, in turn, which for the last twenty years had

included the notion of integration in an organized company in the definition of what constitutes an employment contract, has recently re-affirmed
that subordination to the orders of an employer is the primary criterion
for such a definition.[11] Integration in a company belonging to someone
else, which had gradually become the main characteristic of subordination, is now relegated to being merely one of a number of indications of
such a relationship.

Broadening the Scope of Labour Law

The second tendency, by contrast, is to broaden the scope of labour law,
by resorting to other criteria in addition to legal subordination. The two
avenues currently being explored in this regard have given rise to doctrinal or legislative proposals.

Financial Dependence

To begin with, some authors propose replacing the notion of legal subordination with that of financial dependence. This idea had already been
put forward early on in the establishment of labour and social security law
(that is 'social' law in the French context) in various European countries.[12]
The problem at that time was already a question of matching the scope of
labour law to the actual need for protection. From this standpoint, technical submission to someone else's orders in the performance of work is less
important than depending on that other person for one's livelihood. This
notion of financial dependence could have led to extending the scope of
labour law to cover all those in a weaker position in working relations. The
target population at the time, in addition to employees, essentially com-
prised workers in 'pre-Fordist' situations (agents or sales staff on commission, small tradesmen, or homeworkers) who practised their trade for the
exclusive account of a single contractor, who was, therefore, in a position
to impose his terms. The problem was eventually solved either by the
disappearance of such semi-independent workers, who were absorbed
into Fordist model enterprises, or by the effects of *ad hoc* legal provisions,
whereby such workers were covered by special arrangements (integration
contracts in farming) or likened to employees (sales agents, home
workers).

[11]   Cass. Soc. 13 Nov. 1996 (Société Générale), in: *Droit Social*, 1996, 1067, obs. Dupeyroux.
[12]   See the articles by Paul Cuche in France in the 1930s, for instance.

This issue, which had been thought to be definitively settled, has reappeared with the advent of new kinds (post-Fordist) of working arrangements, which have given rise to a new generation of home workers (with computer and telecommunications links to the worksite) and technically self-employed professionals who are none the less financially dependent. These are the reasons behind the renewed interest in financial dependence.

It is in Germany where this debate seems to be most fully developed. One doctrinal argument proposes to extend the notion of employee to eliminate the loopholes in labour law. This position has been defended primarily by Professor Rolf Wank,[13] according to whom submission to orders can no longer be considered the most characteristic feature of employee status. Under this argument, the need for protection is not linked to such submission but rather to financial dependence on a single employer, which may be characterized as follows:

- work performed personally, without the help of assistants;
- work performed for the account of a single employer;
- work performed essentially without any personal capital outlay;
- work forming part of someone else's organizational scheme.

Workers meeting the above qualifications can still choose to keep self-employment status, wherever the market risks they incur seem to be consistent with their opportunities.

This thesis has been accepted by certain jurisdictions, in particular by the *Landesarbeitsgericht* (Labour Appeals Court) in Cologne in an important decision dated 30 June 1996.[14] Under the terms of that decision 'the traditional notion of employee used by the Federal Labour Court, based essentially on the degree of worker subordination and taking account primarily of the existence of specific employer-imposed working hours, no longer suffices to guarantee respect for fundamental rights'. Applying Prof. Wank's criteria, the Court ascertained whether the worker brought his skills independently to market, assuming business risks and opportunities. The Nuremberg Labour Court also adopted the financial dependence criterion in a case involving an 'outsourced' insurance employee.[15] Deeming that such an employee was in no position to operate on the

---

[13] In a publication titled *Arbeitnehmer und Selbständige*, 1988; see: *Der Betrieb*, 1992, 90 for a summary of this position.

[14] Published in *Entscheidungssammlung zum Arbeitsrecht* §611 BGB Arbeitnehmerbegriff no. 29.

[15] Decision of 31 July 1996, published in *Entscheidungssammlung zum Arbeitsrecht* §611 BGB Arbeitnehmerbegriff no. 57.

market with his own capital and organization, the court considered that he qualified for employee status. This interpretation nevertheless risks clashing with the legal existence of 'quasi-employees' (see above) in Germany: this intermediate category between entrepreneur and employee obviously limits the extension of the scope of employee status as such.

A bill introduced in 1996 by the *Länder* of Hesse and North-Rhine-Westphalia to curb the tendency to resort to false self-employment is relevant to this discussion. This draft legislation concerns social security rather than labour law. None the less, it contains a precise definition of financially dependent workers, understood to be:

- not employing others in the course of their work, with the exception of family members;
- generally working for a single person;
- performing work that can be likened to the work done by an employee;
- not marketing their services as a business.

Under this bill, the existence of two of the above elements would suffice to support the presumption of employee status.

In the Netherlands, the issue of flexibility and security has been under discussion in recent years. The outcome has been a bill stipulating that, unless the employer can prove the contrary, persons working under 'conditions similar to those that characterize employment relations' would be considered to be holders of an employment contract. This is what is meant by the expression 'rebuttable presumption of the existence of an employment contract'. The essential aim is to guarantee the group in question protection equivalent to that enjoyed by holders of employment contracts.

In Sweden, the debate on employment changes is still very much seen from a Keynesian, cyclical perspective, due to the deep recession between 1991 and 1996. The discussion about self-employed, temporary workers and even part-time workers is therefore very much related to the recession of the 1990s, rather than to the 'third industrial revolution' and structural changes on the labour market.

Integration in Someone Else's Company
Another possible avenue for broadening the scope of labour law would consist of replacing the concept of legal subordination with that of integration in someone else's company. The idea in this case is not new, either, as it is already used in the indication clustering technique, in particular under French case law. Such integration could plausibly be consid-

ered to be the main criterion for establishing the existence of a wage-earning relationship.

This approach has firm supporters in Spain, in particular in the works of Prof. Alonso Olea (Olea 1994). According to him, dependence or subordination are both merely the result of a characteristic feature of wage-earning work: the fact that the party concerned works for someone else instead of being self-employed. The party who pays for the work and markets the results is thus vested with the power to direct and control the work and to co-ordinate it with work performed by other persons remunerated in the same way. The forms that such supervision, control or co-ordination may adopt are therefore essentially irrelevant. Insistence on the concept of subordination can, from this standpoint, lead only to unsolvable contradictions, since the power of the party for whom the work is performed can be wielded in a variety of ways and with different degrees of intensity, whereas the fact that the work is performed for someone else remains unchanged.

This criterion of work performed for someone else is not, however, unanimously accepted. The most notable objection is that it covers workers who are not currently considered to be employees (freelances, for instance). This weakness might be considered a strength where the objective is to extend the limits of employee status to ensure that new forms of working relations—those arising in and around business networks—remain covered by labour law. It is nevertheless unlikely that a single criterion will one day suffice to characterize employee status. This is not a given, something which exists in itself, but rather a legal construct continually in the making.

DEPENDENT BUSINESSES

Fordist companies performed all the functions required to manufacture their products. One advantage of that solution was that it eliminated the transaction costs involved in dealing with suppliers and also made it possible to control the entire working process, including both core and peripheral aspects. Labour law was adapted to such a model to the extent that it was built around vertical unionism (as opposed to horizontal unionism, as in pre-Fordist days) and the collective bargaining it supported in turn targeted a business sector (industry-wide agreements) or a company in that sector (company-wide agreements) rather than a trade that could be practised in various sectors.

Several factors have cast doubts on this model. The tendency to cut back on costs and business overheads (so-called flexibilization policies) have certainly played an important role and may explain the outsourcing of tasks requiring little skill (cleaning, gardening, catering, transport, etc.). But outsourcing tasks calling for higher qualifications has essentially been the result of two other factors. First, technical progress (specifically, the role of new information and communications technologies), which has, simultaneously, raised the level of skills required for certain tasks and encouraged outsourcing. Secondly, the evolution of contracting techniques, which today afford clients a fair knowledge of their suppliers, thereby eliminating the risks inherent in outsourcing or sub-contracting certain tasks (in particular, by requiring conformity with ISO 9000 quality standards).

The drawbacks to this new model have only just begun to become apparent (loss of skills in the user firm; higher transaction costs; vulnerability to sub-contractor failure, etc.). Certain large firms seek to reduce such risks by establishing stable co-operative relations with their sub-contractors, occasionally standardized under 'Sub-contracting Charters'.

This trend has generally led companies to fall back on their core businesses and outsource auxiliary tasks to other concerns. As in the tendency to resort to self-employment, this poses two different types of problem with respect to labour law: one is labour fraud, consisting of the establishment of a 'front' company between a worker and his/her actual employer; the other relates to genuine outsourcing or sub-contracting, in cases where the company is placed in a position of technical or financial dependence with respect to its principal. The risk of fraud is particularly common where the supply of labour constitutes the main or only service that one company provides another. The purpose of the legislation on temporary work in effect for twenty years in most European countries (Italy was the last country to adopt such legislation) was to regulate this kind of service and separate the wheat (flexibility of the temporary work market) from the chaff (trafficking in labour).

Temporary Work and Traffic in Labour

Sub-contracting and outsourcing labour constitute a return to old (pre-Fordist) forms of work organization. It was common practice in the nineteenth century for workers to be subject to labour hire arrangements (as opposed to service contracting); such contracts could be signed by the workers themselves (who were hired for a specific task, hence the term piecework) or by a '*marchandeur*' or sub-contractor of labour who agreed terms with a client on the work to be done and then proceeded to have it performed by workers he remunerated and paid directly (hence the generic term '*marchandage*' to designate that practice, which covered a variety of situations: from team hiring, where the '*marchandeur*' was the workers' representative, to labour sub-contractors where he appeared as their employer).

Virtually eliminated by Fordist work organization, some of these old forms were actually outlawed. Today in several countries the law draws a distinction between banned subcontracting or trafficking in labour and sub-contracting or rendering services that constitute lawful contracts.[16]

Labour trafficking (*tráfico de mano de obra*) is prohibited by Spanish law, which defines it as the illegal exercise of temporary work (Art. 43 of the Workers' By-laws). It is none the less no easy task to distinguish it from the practice, legal in Spain, of team hiring—whereby an employer engages a group of workers as such and thereafter represents them as their team leader (*jefe del grupo*). The Spanish Penal Code calls for penalties of six months to three years in prison and fines of six to twelve months for 'those engaging in illegal labour traffic', and adds that the same penalty is applicable to 'whoever recruits persons or prevails upon them to leave their jobs, promising deceitful or false employment or working conditions' (Art. 312).

In Italy, the *caporalato* hiring system is still quite common, especially in agricultural southern regions and in the building sector. This is in fact a kind of illegal labour trafficking in which workers (illegal immigrants, women, etc.) in the 'black economy' are placed in their extremely precarious jobs by a *caporal*, who takes part of their wages for this 'service'. This kind of labour placement is illegal and is almost always controlled by local criminals. Nevertheless, it is quite widespread in certain regions of southern Italy. The lower labour costs, the lack of controls, and the rare

---

[16] In France, the prosecution of trafficking in labour is based on two distinct but largely overlapping crimes (concurrent infringements): (i) the crime defined in article L 125-1 of the labour code as: any *profit-making* operation involving labour, the *effect* of which is to impair employee interests or to evade enforcement of the law. Defined then in terms of its effects, this crime is committed wherever the sub-contracting or rendering of services conceals what is actually the mere supply of labour; (ii) the crime defined in article L 125-3 as: any *profit-making* operation whose *sole purpose* is to supply labour under terms outside the provisions of the law on temporary work. This infringement applies both to temporary work agencies that do not abide by the law and to transactions which purport to be sub-contracts for services, but which actually place third party labour under the authority of the presumed principal. The court investigates the actual facts rather than the wording of the contract to ascertain whether what is actually being sub-contracted is a service or merely an illicit supply of labour.

prosecution of the firms who use this kind of recruitment system can help to explain how widespread it is.

The rules against labour trafficking seem to be essential to the fair functioning of the labour market. Just as a company should not be allowed to make use of a front to evade tax or environmental obligations, competition would be distorted if certain companies were able to evade labour law by setting up a front employer between themselves and the employees whose only function would be to permit such fraud. Domestic legislation can do very little in this regard, in view of the potential offered by the ability to render services freely throughout the European Union. The recent directive on the delivery of services on a European scale is a clear indication that, in line with the principle of subsidiarity, it is at the Community level that this issue must be addressed.

Sub-contracting and Labour Law

Genuine sub-contracting poses problems of a very different nature, which are still poorly handled in European legislation. The sub-contracting of former in-house activities entails obvious consequences for the workers concerned, who will no longer benefit from the working conditions deriving from collective agreements with the company in question and will be subject to different working conditions under their new employer, which are usually less advantageous than the ones to which they were initially entitled. The only protection offered them lies in the possible use of the Directive on Transfers and any national legislation applicable to their situation. Such protection is notoriously limited, in terms both of the scope of its application (requirement that the economic unit survives and preserves its identity) and the effects (no transfer of collective benefits).

But the main problem consists of regulating the triangular relations between the user firm, the sub-contractor and the employees of the latter. Under legal sub-contracting, there is in principle no legal relationship between one company and the employees of another. And yet the employees' lot may depend more on decisions made by the principal than on those of their actual employer. This is particularly true where the sub-contractor is financially dependent solely on the principal, whose decisions may determine not only the number of jobs, but also vocational training policies, work organization, etc. In such situations, most labour law provisions are ineffective. In particular, representation, negotiation, and bargaining structures provide no access to the most relevant party, that is the principal. Although this problem has been clearly identified in the case of groups of companies, it still remains essentially unsolved for networked companies co-operating on a routine basis to manufacture a product or deliver a service.

Regulations on temporary work provide some idea of the kind of link that may be established between one company and the employees of another; but that model involves simple outsourcing of labour, in which the work is in fact performed on the user company's premises.

With respect to sub-contracting *per se*, only a few provisions here and there can be cited that are relevant to labour arrangements. Community Directive 92/57 of 27 June 1992 (Temporary or Mobile Worksites) calls for companies conducting work on the same building site or engaging in the same civil engineering project to co-ordinate all measures relating to worker health or safety.[17] Such co-ordination involves the appointment of a co-ordinator, whose task and powers are defined by contract, the possible creation of a joint inter-company body whose membership includes employees working on the site in an advisory capacity, and the extension of certain provisions of the labour code to self-employed workers. Such provisions make 'co-activity'—a concept that many authors consider to be particularly fertile for labour law—more consistent with social reality (Morin 1994 and 1996).

In certain cases (in particular as regards health and safety), French law obliges companies in the same network or working on the same worksite to share or co-ordinate responsibility (British law is similar). The labour code similarly makes both companies involved jointly and severally liable for undercover (Art. L324-10 and L324-13-1) or sub-contracted (Art. L125-2) work, or the infringement of working hours in road transport.

In Spain, labour regulations on contracts for hiring labour for piecework and sub-contracting do not specify that the principal should be considered the employer of sub-contractor workers, but they do make the former guarantee the employer's solvency. Such guarantees are applicable only to worker hire contracts or sub-contracts 'involving the principal's core business' (Art. 42 of the Workers' By-laws).

The issue for the future, and one that is already being posed in labour law, is, therefore, the impact of (functional or regional) networking arrangements on the status of the workers employed in such networks. Barring extreme cases (*de facto* management of the sub-contractor by the principal), the legal and financial independence of the sub-contractor

[17] Act No. 93-1418 of 31 December 1993 and Décr. 94-1159 of 26 December 1994, transposing the Community Directive on Temporary and Mobile Worksites, No 92/57 of 24 June 1992: *C. trav.* Art. L. 235-2 s. and R. 238-3 s.

prevents the establishment of a direct legal link between the principal and the sub-contractor's employees. But in certain cases the sub-contractor's financial dependence on the principal may call that principle into question. Further in-depth research into the triangular relations developing in practice between principals, dependent firms and wage-earners in the latter would be welcome. Generally speaking, labour law should be made more effective in the context of networking. Attention may be drawn to the importance of ISO standards in this regard, as they favour employee access to training in such networked companies.

CONCLUSIONS

There is a growing diversity in the kinds of contract covering paid work, which may initially be classified into three categories:

- traditional wage-earners working under an employment contract in which subordination is an essential feature;
- other contracts stipulating the performance of work in exchange for remuneration;
- self-employed entrepreneurs.

The second category may be expected to develop further, although such development is still modest, quantitatively speaking. Such growth in free contracts for services, subject here to social security, there to labour, elsewhere to commercial legislation, poses a crucial question for the future of labour law. The traditional view is that labour law applies only in situations where the worker is strictly subordinate. However, the expert group supports the view that it is appropriate to extend coverage in some circumstances to other kinds of work contracts and relationships. The approach, then, is to favour the establishment of a common, broadly-based labour law, certain branches of which might, in turn, be adapted to cover the many and varied kinds of labour relations (subordinate work in the traditional sense; 'para-subordinate', that is financially dependent work). The European Union may possibly have a role to play in the formulation of a framework of rules to ensure basic protection for all financially dependent workers.

Generally speaking, the group believes that it is advisable to prevent a gulf from forming between employees protected under contract and persons working under other kinds of arrangements that afford less protection. One of the historical functions of labour law has been to ensure social cohesion. It will only be able to continue to fulfil that function if it is able to accommodate new developments in the way that work is organized in contemporary society and does not revert to covering just the situations it was originally intended to address, which are becoming less typical.

Work and Membership of the Labour Force

The whole concept of membership of the labour force[1] as built up over the years by labour and social security law reflected the Fordist production regime, as articulated in the different variants already mentioned in Chapter 1. It was a relatively homogeneous and stable status whose ideal model was the male head of household (the breadwinner) who would typically undergo a relatively short period of initial vocational training before working on a permanent basis in the same job or same type of job in the same company or at least in the same occupation before taking well-deserved retirement just a few years before his death. However, working career arrangements varied depending on the importance of self-employment and micro-firms (typical of Southern European countries and reflected in the persistence of 'long' family arrangements protecting young adults from a more difficult entry into the world of work), or, alternatively, the presence of an increasing number of foreign guest workers (particularly in Germany) along with clearly diversified training-entry-career paths for native youth (reflected in the importance of the dual training system).

As mentioned, it was in Southern Europe where the family-oriented patterns inherent in that model were strongest. We refer here to data on Italy in particular, which more or less also reflect the situation in the other

---

[1] The phrase 'membership of the labour force' is used in this chapter to translate the French phrase *statut professionel*. This concept is readily understood in French, being akin to marital status or civil status. However, in the common law systems common in English speaking countries the concept of civil status does not exist. An individual is a citizen or a subject of the sovereign. The most direct translation in English might be the idea of someone having the status of 'worker' even though they might not currently have a job. However, the word worker still has political connotations which mean that the concept might be misinterpreted if it were used in this context.

member countries of the area, particularly as regards the youth and female nature of unemployment and the consistent protection of the male breadwinner. In 1991, heads of households accounted for only 12 per cent of all unemployment and only 4 per cent of long-term unemployment. Unemployment seems in a way to preserve the father's traditional bread-winner role, which also makes the family responsible for supporting unemployed women and young adults. Italy is one of the countries in Europe with the smallest percentage of public spending on employment policies (1992/93: 1.84 per cent compared to 2.99 per cent in France, 3.95 per cent in Spain, 4.19 per cent in Germany, 6.77 per cent in Denmark).

The homogeneous nature of membership of the Fordist labour force, from the point of view of both labour law and social security legislation, arose from the common interests of employees, with trade unions as their natural representatives. The fact that this status really only benefited a proportion of the workforce has not prevented it becoming a benchmark for all those who did not enjoy its advantages. Quite the contrary. Whole professional categories of workers (civil servants, self-employed workers, farmers, etc.) have all claimed for themselves either the direct application (through their becoming part of the body of employees) of this status or at least some or all of the collective benefits arising from it (trade union rights, the right to strike, collective bargaining rights), along with its advantages for the individual (income security, social protection). This has been the central reference point around which all employment relations have tended to revolve and it is not so much a benchmark for workers *per se* as for employees: the employee whose loyalty to the company has been secured and who devotes his whole life to the company, which guarantees him a steady job in return.

This same stability is what has been missing in post-Fordist models of labour organization. Companies still demand a great deal from their employees—certainly much more than before—when it comes to their level of training, adaptability, ability to work on their own, etc. (see Chapter 1), but they no longer guarantee these same employees any job security in return. As a result, the terms of the trade-off on which employee status was always based—that is subordination in return for security—are now turned on their head without any new ones taking their place. Companies cannot ask workers to become even more involved if they do not guarantee them any kind of future, either inside the company or outside it. The State, which has to address the question (and the costs) of managing the lengthy professional life of workers, is not really in the best position to find an answer. Its heavy intervention, causing a huge drain on public finances, can serve only to alleviate the situation without getting to the very heart of the problem, which is the creation of a labour force membership adapted to the new models prevailing in the employer–employee relationship.

Where the Fordist model hinged on the stable organization of groups of workers, these new models are based on the opposite idea of the co-ordination of mobile individuals. Essentially, they deal with the necessity (and the difficulty) of defining a membership of the labour force that integrates individualization and the mobility of professional careers. If this individual mobility is to become the dominant characteristic in tomorrow's world of work, labour law will come up against some rather formidable problems. In fact, not only the impact but also the goal of this law has been to ensure employment stability and thereby guarantee workers real recognition as labour force members. This latter aim has not lost any of its value, but the problem to be solved today is how to adapt labour law rather than sacrifice it to change.

Management has readily understood this new pressing need for mobility and has therefore demanded 'flexibility' in the employer–employee relationship. From a legal point of view, this whole idea of flexibility—a management term—does not have much meaning. It really only makes sense when referring to the principle of professional freedom as understood from its two sides: the freedom to set up a business and the freedom to work. The claim for flexibility can then be understood in law as a demand for professional freedom to be enhanced within work organization. Labour law should take this demand into account and not stand in the way of the evolution of work organization methods. However, the fundamental question to be resolved today is not about increased flexibility (something that has already widely been taken up in legislation in a number of European countries), but about bringing the new imperatives of greater work freedom into line with the equally pressing need of every worker to enjoy a long-lasting real membership of the labour force which actually enables him to exercise individual initiative.

Even if no European country today seems to have managed to set up a new model of labour relations that meets these very different demands, there are some important experiences with a transition towards new trends in labour relations. It is crucial to mention that, contrary to the media stereotypes of the incompatibility between welfare arrangements, on one hand, and job creation and flexibility, on the other, some of these experiences combine high levels of innovative welfare protection with low and decreasing unemployment and extremely dynamic economies. Denmark and the Netherlands provide particular examples, but within the Union Portugal, Northern Italy, Southern Germany and Austria too have persistently maintained low levels of unemployment, below the highly publicized levels accompanying the neoliberal experiences of the UK and the USA.

The United Kingdom cites a reduction in unemployment: around one million jobs have been created over the last four years. The drop in unemployment in Great Britain has largely been prompted by factors unrelated to labour law, particularly by the fact that employers had not maintained available work capacity during the previous recession. For the moment, there is no real evidence that the British culture of easy hiring and firing really does bring about growth in average employment over the cycle, even if we think it may be one of the factors responsible for the drop in unemployment.

But the British example also throws up a problem. The growth in female employment has actually been double that of male employment and male unemployment mainly affects heads of households, which has implications for household income. The explanation provided for this phenomenon is that male unemployment remains high because women seem more ready and willing to accept non-standard employment and provide management with a pool of people who will take up such jobs. Then, when the employer turns these temporary jobs into permanent posts, the worker (usually female) continues in the same post.

It is interesting to see the absence of any significant shift in the United Kingdom away from permanent jobs and towards temporary jobs, even where there are no legal restrictions on this. Whereas temporary work used to account for 5 per cent of total jobs, this figure has risen only to around 7 per cent in the 1990s. A study explains this slight increase by the fact that large companies prefer to use temporary employees to cover staffing problems when employees are on sick leave, holiday or maternity leave rather than over-size their workforce. There has certainly been an increase in the number of temporary workers, but the number of people actually working for temporary employment agencies is still under 0.5 per cent. In addition, these agencies are focusing more and more on permanent jobs as they strive to find competent employees for their clients. Spain lies almost at the opposite end of this positive trend seen in the United Kingdom. The high rate of unemployment in Spain is combined with a very high percentage of temporary work (42 per cent in the private sector). In Sweden, which by contrast has a highly regulated labour market with a high rate of unemployment, the group of temporary workers rose from roughly 250,000 persons in 1990 to approximately 325,000 persons in 1995. Self-employed persons without employees rose from roughly 230,000 persons in 1988 to 270,000 in 1995.

It seems, therefore, that no member country is in a position to propose any sort of credible alternative to the employees' status which still remains the reference point in labour law. However, every country is attempting to adjust this status by reorganizing the transitions within a working life that is no longer guaranteed to follow a straight line. We have, therefore, looked into how the law stands with regard to these major transitions. This survey detects the emergence of new laws and legal categories indicating the development of a status for workers that no longer hinges on the holding of a job but rather depends on the continuity of labour force membership that goes beyond the number of different jobs held. This new status is original in the way it adds the dynamic organization of the transitions between successive employment situations to the static organization of the employer–employee relationship. The common aim in organizing these transitions is for employee status not to be linked to a stable job.

Three main situations can be distinguished:

- first of all, job-seeking, which may apply to young people who have finished their initial training or to the unemployed: a law on access to employment has emerged in response to this particular situation;
- next, job discontinuity, which may be the result of both internal flexibility policies (job modification or transformation) and external flexibility policies (the use of casual employment contracts): labour law today tends to associate the principle of continuity of membership of the labour force with this job discontinuity;
- finally, job cuts: this is the traditional domain of legislation on redundancies, whose aim is no longer just to defend employees against the loss of existing jobs, but also to offer them new opportunities with the emergence of a right to redeployment.

This overview opens up new perspectives for the design of a labour force membership that combines both freedom and security.

MEMBERSHIP OF THE LABOUR FORCE AND ACCESS TO EMPLOYMENT

From Initial Training to Employment

Initial training is provided both in educational institutions and in companies. Its conditions vary between the different EU Member States but all countries are committed to implementing reforms to improve initial vocational training and to smooth the transition from initial training to professional life.

Bridging the Gap between School and Employers

Initial training for young people is the subject of debates that directly concern labour law. One of the main issues in these debates is the priority to be given respectively to academic training at school or university and to on-the-job training. Academic training is mainly aimed at the general job market whereas in-company training gives workers the skills they need for a particular company or similar kinds of companies. These two aims should be borne in mind when talking of a systematic strategy. The development of youth unemployment has led several countries to place the emphasis on practical training given in companies and to try and bridge the gap between schools and employers.

In Sweden, a recent proposal from the Ministry of Education has sparked off a real debate. The idea is to allow students to receive practical rather than theoretical training in their third year at university. This apprenticeship would form an integral part of the education system. The social partners seem to back the proposal, which would allow for more extensive contact and better communication to be developed between schools and industry and would make education more flexible.

In France, too, initial vocational training was mainly of an academic nature whereas apprenticeship was something only followed by people learning a trade or craft. More recently, however, efforts have been made to encourage a more practical style of training. In 1990, France enacted a law setting out the right of each worker to obtain a vocational qualification and, in 1993, the right of every young person to specialized training. A number of different types of employment contract now exist to ensure that in-company training alternates with theoretical training (*contrat de qualification*; *contrat d'insertion professionnelle*). Some of these contracts arc subsidized by the State. A proposed bill to integrate in-company training into the final part of university courses (called '*stages diplômants*') is at an equally advanced stage. However, it is still facing serious opposition and it is not certain whether it will be implemented in the near future.

In the United Kingdom, the government has introduced the idea of modern apprenticeship, although very few young people actually take part in this programme. With the national vocational qualifications, the emphasis is placed on the specific levels or standards that must be reached rather than on their particular duration. However, employers are generally unwilling to train more young people than they actually plan to employ in the long term. There has nevertheless been a rapid growth in the numbers of young people enrolled in further education colleges, often on vocational courses.

The same problem of a lack of employers keen to train young people arises in Spain too. In that country, training contracts, which have been given a variety of names and been the subject of successive legal regulation, have never satisfactorily served their purpose as training platforms, but rather have been used essentially as contractual devices for first jobs, for which young people are underpaid and hired under casual conditions, with no prospect of eventually securing steady employment. Despite all this, and due to their similarity to other temporary contractual formulae intended to foster employment, their use has been relatively infrequent. A very low percentage of these kinds of employment contracts actually result in real employment.

In Germany, the traditional apprenticeship system is also going through a difficult time. The fact is that employers are less and less inclined to train young people. They are seeking shorter apprenticeships. Some collective agreements signed recently try to encourage companies to train young people by providing for lower wages, which for instance might be as much as 15 per cent less in companies training young people for the first time or training more than before. Furthermore, many German companies are no longer willing to offer all their apprentices a permanent employment contract at the end of the training period.

Where Italy is concerned, the deregulation of work can be said to apply mostly or almost exclusively to new entrants, that is young people. This is the case with the *contratti de formazione e lavoro* (CFL), introduced at the beginning of the 1980s (Acts No 79/1983 and No 863/1984). This kind of fixed-term contract (maximum length two years) applies only to young people (initially under 29, now under 32) and they can stipulate wage and employment conditions inferior to those agreed for the rest of the workforce, even in the same plant or firm. Their aim was explicitly to introduce a sort of trade-off on the labour market between more work opportunities on the one hand and more labour flexibility on the other for younger people (with tax benefits for enterprises). When the contract expires, the employers can decide to hire these young people on regular employment contracts. Currently, Italian labour laws require of firms to hire a quota of 50 per cent (that is 50 per cent of the *contratti di formazione e lavoro* must be turned into regular employment contracts upon expiry) before they can introduce new *contratti di formazione e lavoro*. By 1994, the rate of CFLs confirmed as regular contracts was around 60 per cent.

As a factor in work insecurity, however, it must be underlined that the young workers hired on these contracts are not considered to form part of the minimum number of employees legally required for the application of the wider system of labour laws and worker protections known as the *Statuto dei Lavoratori* (Act No 300/1970), which in Italy applies only to firms with more than fifteen employees. Apprenticeship contracts have recently been supported and subsidized by the Italian government to improve the chances of young people entering the labour market.

There is a tendency developing in Europe whereby companies are no longer seen as simple *production* centres but as *training* centres as well. A nation cannot be trained in the classroom alone as training needs to take place in companies too. This concept should be recognized in all sectors of social security and labour legislation.

Initial Employment Contracts

One way of building a bridge between vocational training and employment is to use contracts that have no educational aim but take into account the lower productivity of young people who are hired in their very first job. This type of contract authorizes employers to pay such young people a wage under the statutory or normal minimum wage.

In Spain, some collective agreements have made provision for lower wages for new contracts: this leads to problems resulting from the 'double wage standard', which distinguishes between workers hired previously and those joining the company after the entry into force of the new collective agreement. The question is whether or not such regulations by agreement conform to the constitutional principle of equality. Legal doctrine is not unanimous on this point and the issue has not yet been settled by the Constitutional Court. In 1993, the French Government also tried to introduce a special contract to combat youth unemployment by providing for optional training and pay lower than the minimum wage. However, student protests put a stop to this initiative. In the German chemicals industry, a collective agreement has been reached allowing for a 10 per cent reduction in the wages paid to the long-term unemployed during the first phase of their new job. The regulations for the national minimum wage in Britain exclude many trainees.

From Unemployment to Employment

While unemployment was not widespread and was of short duration, it could be considered as a small risk in a linear career. This risk was covered by an insurance system guaranteeing workers an income, often indexed to their wages, until they found another job matching their skills. As mass, long-term unemployment has taken hold today, this model of unemployment needs to be rethought. The duty to work has now emerged as the other side of the equation where the unemployed are guaranteed an income. This new element in labour force membership means that a worker must be prepared to change his occupation or to take up a job less well-paid than the one he has lost. This new pressure put on the unemployed has gone hand-in-hand with recruitment incentives offered to employers in the form of subsidized jobs. The aim of this new type of work is to bridge the gap between unemployment and employment, although its many detrimental effects have not yet been fully assessed.

The Duty to Work

The explicit aim of the policies implemented by European Union Member States is to increase employment levels as far as possible. But what should employment priorities be? Is it a question of guaranteeing a certain level of income or guaranteeing membership of the labour force at the same time? The analysis of current changes shows a shift in the idea of an occupation, as defined by qualification, towards that of a job for which the only benchmark is money.

This trend is clearly visible in the analysis of the criteria governing the right to unemployment benefit and to a pension, which are increasingly emphasizing the recipient's earning capacity and less and less his previous occupation. This indicates how any guarantee of continuing in the same occupation is partly or wholly sacrificed to a quantitative and monetary assessment of people's position in the job market. In the past, in all countries, the decision on whether an unemployed person was suitable or not for a job partly depended on their occupation. Now, more and more importance is placed on potential earnings.

In the United Kingdom, a certain period of grace (usually three months for skilled workers) was traditionally granted to the unemployed to allow them to find a job in their own professional field. Now, however, they are being forced to accept any job—even a non-skilled one—if they do not want to lose their unemployment benefit.

In Sweden, in the past an unemployed person (particularly a white-collar worker) would not be asked to accept a job that did not correspond to his previous profession. This practice has changed and that same person now has to accept any job whose wages equal at least 90 per cent of unemployment benefit. The critical aspect, however, is to find a new balance between those in the labour force who are in training and those in jobs on the regular labour market. One of the big challenges is, in other words, to prevent the risks of inflation that follow from a shortage of labour due to broad training and education programmes. Short and relatively rapid cyclical changes on the labour market make it very difficult to find a consistent balance between demand for and supply of labour. As we know, training and education programmes are often long-running tasks.

This trend is observed in all countries, the only difference being the level of acceptable earnings. In Spain and France, the pay must be the normal wage paid in that particular sector. In Spain, previous pay levels and the amount paid in unemployment benefit are not taken into account. In France, the proposed pay must be at least 80 per cent of previous earnings. In Germany, a person can turn down a job during the first period of unemployment if the proposed pay is under 80 per cent of previous earnings. This falls to 70 per cent during a subsequent period of unemployment and, after six months of unemployment, they must take any job that pays at least the amount paid in unemployment benefit.

In the case of disability benefits paid in the event of reduced earning capacity, the trend seems a little more uneven.

In France, people with a disability making them unfit for work are not subject to any kind of control when seeking a job. The mechanisms used to calculate the benefit, however, take into account the residual work capacity of the person, whether or not this is actually put into practice. A person with a disability, an incapacity to work, is one who cannot obtain a wage *in any occupation* that is more than one third of the normal remuneration paid in his previous occupation. Disabled people who are still able to obtain a paid job despite this two-thirds incapacity are paid a benefit equivalent to only 30 per cent of their previous remuneration.

In Spain, different degrees of disability are established depending on the disabled person's ability to do his or her usual job, or any job. The recent act consolidating and rationalizing the social security system, adopted in 1997, sets out the degrees of permanent disability—with the percentage reduction in the working capacity of the disabled person assessed in line with an approved statutory list of illnesses—and widens the concept of the usual occupation on which these assessments are based. In fact, the act defines this occupation as 'the occupation held previously by the person in question or the occupational group in which he worked before the event causing his permanent incapacity took place'.[2]

Employment Subsidies

Most European countries seem to have tried out the policy of using public finances for employment. The idea is to use public money—unemployment insurance funds first of all—to finance employment rather than to support the unemployed. In practice, this leads to subsidizing employment. Two different methods have been tried. The first is to encourage employment in the business sector by giving financial aid to companies that hire people. The second is to support the emergence of new types of employment in the non-business sector.

As a result, the number of subsidized jobs has grown significantly in most countries, although the importance of these subsidies and the number of people that benefit from them vary greatly. Subsidies sometimes come from unemployment insurance and sometimes from public funds.

Subsidized Contracts in the Business Sector
The aim of this first type of subsidy is to lower labour costs for employers likely to hire new workers. These subsidies were initially thought of as temporary measures, but have now become firmly established in labour law and in some cases have become firmly tied to certain types of jobs which the public authorities are keen to encourage because they result in a greater reduction in the number of people unemployed (for example, part-time jobs).

In Germany, financial aid for recruiting unemployed workers is mostly targeted at the non-business sector. However, this method is increasingly criticized because such work lies outside the normal economic cycle and may even compete with it and prompt the disappearance of non-subsidized jobs. Another option now being tried is to promote recruitment

---

[2] Article 8 of the Bill consolidating and rationalizing the Social Security System (*Official Journal of the Spanish Parliament*, 26 December 1996). The Bill is the result of the agreement on the consolidation and rationalization of the Social Security System reached between the Government and the majority trade unions (Trade Union Confederation of Workers' Commissions and General Workers Union), on 9 October 1996, against the opposition of the employers' association, the CEOE.

by companies of unemployed workers who are finding it difficult to re-enter the job market (such as the disabled or older age groups) by means of subsidies that may be equivalent to as much as 50 per cent of pay over a period of twenty-four months. These amounts are paid to the employers.

In Spain, until the appearance of the *Acuerdo para la Estabilidad en el Empleo* (Agreement on Steady Employment), negotiated by the most representative trade unions and management in April 1997 and later enacted as RDL 8/1997, annual employment assistance programmes have been developed for companies. These are targeted at the disabled, the long-term unemployed (more than one year out of work) or older people (aged over 45). The term of these employment contracts is one to three years and the advantage for the employer is that they pay lower social security contributions than normal. Subsidies are also given when a company takes on its first employee or makes temporary employees into permanent employees. However, these contracts are rarely used.

Spanish employment policy is continuing with temporary contracting programmes for the disabled. In addition, the intent of the above *Acuerdo para la Estabilidad en el Empleo* is to eliminate temporary employment by subsidizing—while reducing certain severance indemnities—employment on permanent terms of unemployed workers and workers with temporary contracts by creating a new contractual device known as the 'contract to foster open-ended employment'.

The same type of subsidized contracts also exist in France (through a reduction in the social security contribution paid or the payment of a subsidy to employers equal to the unemployment benefit that the worker would have received), but over time they have led to a shift in unemployment from one category of worker to another and have not brought about any real rise in employment. French unemployment insurance also helps the unemployed who want to set up their own business or become self-employed. It is also possible in France to do voluntary work, undergo training or take up temporary or part-time work whilst still being paid unemployment benefit. This measure has been designed to improve the chances for the unemployed of finding permanent jobs in the future. This opportunity is available in Germany only with very strict constraints.

In Belgium, since the beginning of the crisis, a number of employment promotion plans provide for subsidies for recruiting new employees. Such plans offer either lower social security contributions or co-funding schemes in which public money is involved. Such plans are usually applied selectively to target populations (the long-term unemployed or young adults, for instance).

In the United Kingdom, there have until recently only been a few local examples of employment subsidies. However, from 1 April 1998 a new programme of guarantees for young people under 25 has subsidized employment as one of its options, as does a similar scheme for people aged over 25 who have been unemployed for more than two years. Previous experience with job subsidies suggests that they become less effective at creating additional job opportunities the larger the number of subsidized jobs. The most effective schemes have provided one new job for every three jobs subsidized, with typical outcomes closer to one new job for every five subsidized.

Sweden is an example of yet another country that has designed a great many programmes for the job market without any signs as yet of an improvement in the employment situation. Under the Swedish system, unemployed workers are paid benefit for 300 days and then they are obliged to participate in one of the labour market programmes for six months in order to be able to claim a further 300 days of unemployment benefit. Training allowances are equal to unemployment benefit. A government proposal for the social security system to take responsibility for payments after a certain period of time has been withdrawn following strong opposition. Some notable Swedish programmes are: work experience systems, employment training, on-the-job training, temporary public work, computer centres, programmes for young people run by local councils, wage benefits, recruitment benefits, protected employment with public employers, start-up grants and all sorts of training programmes. However there has been a positive trend in Swedish employment figures since 1998.

Direct employment subsidy policies in the job market are now seen to have a number of adverse effects (deadweight and substitution) and to be ineffective in reducing unemployment in the long term. From a legal point of view, public subsidies for employment could also turn out to be contrary to the principles of Community competition law.[3] Therefore, it is reasonable to think that direct aid to companies is unlikely to be the way forward in the future. Public aid should, on the other hand, lead to the building of real professional career paths as part of a policy of equal opportunities in the job market, and to the creation of opportunities for the workers themselves. The policy of directly targeting these subsidies on the basis of socio-economic criteria can therefore be questioned. Such targeting helps to divide wage and salary earners into two groups and to develop second-rate jobs. It would be much better to start off from a

---

[3] See the case-law of the European Court of Justice in Luxembourg in this regard and especially ECJ September 1996, *Droit Social* 1997, 185, obs. A. Lyon-Caen.

dynamic basis of the freedom to work and to offer all workers new opportunities. Public money to help finance special leave—particularly for
training, family circumstances, or setting up businesses—could both
create new activity opportunities for their recipients and provide opportunities for the unemployed to secure a job.

Subsidized Contracts in the Non-business Sector
The general idea here has been to explore new forms of employment.
These are jobs that meet collective needs which are wholly or partly
ignored by the business sector. Public money helps to prime the pump for
the creation of this type of job, in the expectation that it will then stand on
its own in the voluntary sector, public sector, or business sector.

In the United Kingdom, there is growing interest in the role of the vol-
untary-sector intermediate labour market in providing a route back to
market employment for those who have been out of work for some time.
Its key features are the undertaking of socially useful work (energy-saving
projects in public housing for example) and wages rather than unemployment benefits. The most successful schemes seem to rely on the ability of
talented social entrepreneurs to bring together funding from a variety of
sources, including the European Social Fund, to make them viable.

In Spain, the unemployed must carry out voluntary work if they are not
to lose their unemployment benefit. Specific agreements exist between
the national employment agency and public bodies or charitable foundations offering temporary work in the public interest. Unemployed persons
working under such arrangements are not subject to an employment contract and can continue to receive their unemployment benefit.

In Belgium, Local Employment Agencies (ALE) have been created to
promote jobs for the long-term unemployed. All workers wholly unemployed for over three years are automatically enrolled. Unemployed workers may be called upon to provide services at 150 BEF per hour, without
forfeiting their unemployment benefits, up to a total of 45 hours per
month. This work consists of tasks that would not otherwise be done and
are characteristic of the primary labour market. It covers such jobs as
helping people in their homes, gardening, child care, helping volunteer or
educational organizations, local authorities—particularly in the area of
environmental conservation—and seasonal agricultural work. In practice,
such local employment agencies (system generalized under the act of 30
March 1994) are meeting with limited success, with enormous differences
from one place to another. Whereas the ultimate objective is to place the
long-term unemployed back on the labour market, in reality most of these
people remain in this subsidized work system.

In France, the experience with work for the benefit of the general public under employment-solidarity contracts has been similar. Social security or tax advantages have also encouraged the development of personal services, notably domestic jobs. A new step was taken in this direction with the announcement in August 1997 of the creation of new general-interest jobs for specific occupations in the field of education, the environment, etc. The novel aspect of this scheme is that they are full-time, long-term (5 year) jobs. It is thereby hoped that some of the adverse effects of previous schemes (casualization of public employment; advantages obtained for high income brackets) will be avoided.

In Italy, there are what are known as *Lavori socialmente utili* (LSU) or jobs with very short working hours almost entirely paid for by the State. Initially limited to social service work, this kind of subsidized employment was extended to State-owned companies and Government under a law enacted in 1996.

The emergence of this non-business sector, which some people see as a 'second job market', is one of the biggest issues of the moment. It is not clear who is to set the rules and to run this second job market on a day-to-day basis. This question has already been answered in the United States with the creation of a Workfare system run by private companies and public authorities as the project managers. The United Kingdom seems to have opted for the same solution. The trend in Belgium is more towards rejecting compulsory work for the unemployed and allowing the social partners (trade unions and management) to run the second job market, working together with the local authorities. This option may seem an interesting one provided that the second markets can act as a nexus between *new* supply and demand in employment. In this latter sense, the second job markets could be used to promote economic solidarity and become part of a dynamic social process in a co-ordinated project. In this case, it would not mean setting up a cheap market to compete with the primary market but rather a new market within a dynamic framework of co-operation that aims to meet collective needs that the primary market does not satisfy.

JOB DISCONTINUITY AND CONTINUITY OF MEMBERSHIP OF THE LABOUR FORCE

Policies designed to introduce greater flexibility lead to an increase in situations of job discontinuity, where the employee periods in work are followed by periods of inactivity. This tendency generally takes the form of a series of employment contracts each of a specified length or involving temporary assignments, or work on a sporadic basis. Such contracts may be either with the same employer or with different employers.

Provisions are now emerging in the legislation of certain countries with the aim of ensuring a certain degree of continuity in employment relationships, in an effort to overcome this job discontinuity.

The Italian experience with the *Cassa Integrazione Guadagni* constituted one of the first legal devices designed to combine corporate restructuring with continuity of the status of the employees involved. Formally, the bond between employees covered by this Fund and their former employers is not broken, but their wages are paid (80 per cent replacement rate) with public funding (from the National Social Provision Institute). We have to note, however, that this Fund has operated like an unemployment fund for just a very small part of the 'primary sector' labour force over the last two decades. Some authors have stressed, in fact, that the CIG mechanism has introduced a form of macro-flexibility for firm downsizing.

There are now plans to replace it with a system comprising three levels:

- income insurance in the event of temporary redundancies; this insurance would also be available for self-employed workers;
- unemployment insurance for employees who have lost their jobs; and
- social support for unemployed with no insurance coverage. (However, we have to stress that this third type of unemployment subsidy, unconnected to previous work status, is still under evaluation in Italy.)

The idea advocated today is to allow the employee to alternate between working periods and training or holiday periods, whilst enjoying good, secure economic conditions. This is the idea on which the 'activity contract' proposal, put forward in the Boissonnat report (Commissariat général du Plan 1995), is based. Research into the continuity of membership of the labour force can be viewed differently, depending on whether the mobility in question is within the same company or involves movement between a number of different companies.

From One Job to Another within One Company

Within the same company, the model of the linear career can be thrown off course in two different ways. The first case is where, for technical or economic reasons, the position occupied undergoes substantial change. In this type of case, labour law can favour what are known as policies of internal flexibility, which consist of arranging for employees' in-house mobility rather than making them redundant and hiring others in their place. A second scenario is where, in the context of an external flexibility policy, a series of casual employment contracts are offered within the same company, thus raising the question of whether such contracts could entitle the employee concerned to certain rights.

Job Modifications

The next step was to examine the influence of those models using internal flexibility (for example, the Japanese model), which consists of adapting to economic constraints whilst maintaining an employment relationship rather than making employees redundant. Two contrasting situations have developed in the EU. In those countries which are traditionally more flexible, the implementation of European legislation has reduced, or will slightly reduce, the amount of flexibility, whereas in systems which are traditionally less flexible, there is a tendency to ease up on legal restrictions.

In the United Kingdom, contractual freedom has been the dominant factor determining working hours and conditions. It is, for example, quite rare to find agreements on the number of working hours per year. This freedom will be restricted by the implementation of the directive on working time, due in October 1998. Despite this flexibility, there are seldom cases in which modification of the terms and conditions of employment avoids redundancies. In some firms, employees have agreed to reduce the number of working hours to avoid redundancies. Unemployment insurance, which does not recognize partial unemployment, is an obstacle to this type of agreement. Furthermore, in view of the fact that employers have no obligation to train their employees to meet changing employment needs, redundancies are very often due not only to a surplus of workers, but also to the unsuitability of their skills. This is a further obstacle to avoiding redundancies.

In Sweden, there is little scope for individual agreements, and the unilateral modification by an employer of the terms of employment contracts is not permitted. However, collective agreements stipulate that manual workers must carry out all the tasks they are obliged to perform and which are covered by the agreement in force. The implementation of European legislation has basically strengthened the fundamental individual rights of employees in employment relationships and has done so to the detriment of Swedish collective legislation on employment.

German legislation has not yet been adapted to the model of internal flexibility. For example, there is a regulation under which part-time jobs must always stipulate a certain number of hours, while the pattern, but not the conditions, of a part-time job may be modified. However, a range of collective agreements has led to greater freedom. They enable workers, together with their representatives in the company, to agree on a reduction of working hours and/or wages, within certain limits and for a certain period, if the employer neither hires nor fires during that time. Certain collective agreements have also introduced flexibility in working patterns in such a way that labour can be adapted to the firm's needs without either reducing wages or paying overtime.

In France, it is now possible to introduce a great amount of flexibility in the organization of working hours through collective agreements. Moreover, the law has encouraged the review of collective agreements, and judicial precedents greatly favour any action aimed at internal flexibility; an individual employee is not entitled to refuse to accept modifications of the collective workers' status as determined by common practice or collective agreement. On the other hand, individual employment contracts are not possible without the employee's consent and the employer is under an obligation to train the employee to deal with changes in his or her job. However, if the modification proposed is for a legitimate reason, an employer may dismiss an employee who refuses it. Recent case law establishes:

- that in ascertaining the collective agreement most favourable to the employee account should be taken of the interests of employees in general and not just a particular individual; and
- that such appraisal should take account of possible guarantees of maintaining employment levels.

Therefore, an amendment to a company agreement calling for lower pay in return for a commitment to maintain employment levels may be considered to be more favourable for employees.[4]

Legislators tend to encourage job sharing and part-time work. A 1996 law, the so-called Robien Act, permits a reduction in social security contributions if there is an agreement to reduce working hours which will help

[4] Cass. Soc. 19 Feb. 1997 (Cie. générale de geophysique), *Droit Social*, 1997, 432, obs. critiques G. Couturier.

create new jobs or preserve old ones. New job creation equivalent to 10 per cent gives the firm the right to a 40 per cent exemption in the first year and a 30 per cent exemption for the next six years. If the proportion of new jobs increases to 15 per cent, this exemption will be 50 per cent and 40 per cent, respectively. This law has been a huge success, although it has given rise to considerable debate, which has grown more controversial following the act establishing the 35-hour working week (see Chapter 3). A 30 per cent reduction in social security contributions is also granted for each part-time job created, or for the transformation of any full-time job into a part-time job, providing this results in the creation of a new post.

In Spain, a 1994 law also introduced greater flexibility in working hours, wages and contractual modifications. Contracts may now be substantially modified without administrative authorization. These modifications must be justified by economic, technical, production-based or organizational reasons and the workers' representatives must be consulted where collective modifications are involved. Conditions concerning the place of work, working days or hours, shift work or wage systems or employees' duties may now be modified without the employee's consent. If an employee disagrees, he will be asked to leave.

The Italian system of industrial relations, while providing a valid system of labour protection against the risks of downsizing, making it more difficult for the firms to proceed with individual firings, has at the same time allowed a very large degree of functional flexibility within the production processes. In fact, even in larger plants with internal labour markets, seniority rules have never constituted a constraint in work relations, as in the United States, for example. On the contrary, internal mobility has always been regarded in Italy as a form of upskilling, both by workers and trade unions. During the 1970s, most collective labour agreements enshrined the principle that job rotation among different work positions was a pre-condition for career advancement within the company.

Recently, the so-called *legge Bassanini*, which reformed the employment status of public employees, introduced a new regulation governing the job mobility of such employees. This is a major innovation for the Italian public employment system, as the law states that public servants, if redundant, can be moved to other jobs and duties in the public administration sector, even in a different territorial area. The law gives workers the right to refuse such moves, but after three refusals they can be fired.

Successive Jobs

We were interested to know whether there were any provisions for calculating the number of years of service, regardless of any discontinuity there may have been between successive working contracts with the same employer.

The law in Sweden stipulates that parental leave, military service, education, and training do not interrupt the employment relationship (the situation of 'atypical workers' is more difficult). Part-time work is considered in the same light as a normal job and the same rule is applied. Similar provisions are found in French and Belgian legislation.

In the United Kingdom, by contrast, employees must reach an agreement with their employers if they wish to interrupt their work for parental leave, public service or charitable work whilst retaining their job continuity. The exception is for maternity absence where a gap of up to forty weeks does not interrupt continuity of service. Needless to say, such agreements are few and far between.

In some cases in Sweden, France, and Britain, once certain limits have been reached, consecutive contracts of specific duration may be reclassified as a single contract for an unlimited period. In France, however, several contracts of specific duration may follow on one after another if there is a minimum period of inactivity between them. In this case, all the contracts are considered to be different contracts of specific duration (with service discontinuity).

In Spain, if there are a number of consecutive contracts with the same employer, these are not generally included in the calculation of years of service, although there are some exceptions to this rule. These include jobs that subsequently become permanent, training contracts, subsidized contracts, or fraudulent contracts in breach of the law.

From One Job to Another with a Variety of Employers

Single Job with Several Employers

Under some circumstances, where a single job has been performed for employers constituting different legal entities, the law may consider this to represent a single employment relationship.

Groups of Companies
Some Member States do not consider these to represent different employers, whilst others partially or completely accept this to be the case.

In Germany, employment by different companies within the same group is generally treated separately. In Spain, however, although the same rule exists, there are a number of exceptions. These include workers working for all group companies simultaneously, those cases where there is a single set of assets and where there is external unity or a single management structure.

French case law has also established certain exceptions in cases of dismissal for economic reasons. The seriousness of the economic motives is examined in the context of the general sector of activity to which the group belongs. There is also consideration of the possibility of offering the person concerned an alternative position in any of the group companies whose activities and organization would allow transfer of all or part of the personnel. More commonly, French law permits continuity of the employment contract within a group that forms part of the same economic and social unit.

British legislation considers that companies with the same shareholders are linked and represent a single employer. This makes transfers within the group easier and allows continuity of service.

Networked Companies which Share Employment of the Same Workers
The French report illustrates a number of examples of companies which share employment of the same workers. This may involve legitimate, shared systems organized in the conventional way, whereby, say, several companies form an association of employers whose aim is to take on workers who will then work for all of the association's different members. The law has developed a number of similar solutions to encourage businesses to take on the unemployed. The French government has announced in its action plan for employment implementing the Community guidelines that, where plural employment is concerned, consideration will be given, in an initial stage, to the establishment of provisions that will be to enable workers holding several different jobs to take their holidays at the same time, to take into account the refusal to work additional hours when this is due to the concomitant conduct of an activity with another employer, and to permit a single medical examination if certain requirements are satisfied. Moreover, the government undertakes to examine ways of removing the obstacles to the development of groups of employers. This may, on the other hand, involve an unlawful operation,

in which case the law makes all the employers involved liable. Charges of illicit employment can then be brought not only against the direct employer, but also against other indirect employers who have used illegal workers, provided they were aware of the illegality involved.

Consecutive Employment with Several Employers

Labour law may, under certain circumstances, make a connection between consecutive jobs held with different employers. This is the case where there are rules prescribing job continuity when a company changes hands. This continuity principle is recognized at Community level by the Transfer of Undertakings directive. The same is true for temporary employment in the national legislation of certain countries. There are forerunners of the 'activity contract' in the field of temporary work, where the law or collective agreements guarantee the workers concerned a certain continuity in their status which overrides the discontinuity of the tasks actually assigned to them.

The national legislation of a number of countries makes the employer of temporary staff responsible for, or the guarantor of, certain obligations towards the workers, particularly health and safety at work or payment. However, there are many countries where the situation of temporary workers is still extremely precarious, income is irregular, and access to continuing vocational training is difficult. The tendency in several Member States is to facilitate the continuation of such temporary assignments. In Belgium, some so-called 'atypical' contracts are used to fight unemployment. A law passed in 1994 allows certain exceptions to the ban on repeated successive temporary contracts. Below a certain wage level, there is no longer any legally binding period of notice and this may be stipulated in the employment contract. The danger is that an employee will accept a very short notice period simply to obtain the coveted job. Sweden has also abolished certain restrictions on the use of temporary work. Since January 1997, temporary contracts no longer depend on the type of job to be performed and are permitted, for any reason, for up to twelve months in any three-year period or for up to eighteen months for companies taking on staff for the first time. The only restriction is that no more than five temporary workers may be employed at any one time. In Britain, there is and has never been any restriction on temporary employment.

It seems appropriate to consider methods which would make it possible to reconcile the discontinuity of temporary assignments with a true status as full members of the labour force which would guarantee that workers could really exercise their individual and collective rights. Some collective agreements in this sector already contain interesting provisions in this respect, particularly in the field of training. This is a direction that could be encouraged at Community level.

Under the Italian industrial district model, the human resources in the district are pooled informally. The weak point of the model, however, is the absence of any co-ordinated management of what is clearly a common good, namely, the vocational training provided by the companies involved in this kind of network.

Given their limited size, vocational training in such companies is often non-existent apart from simple on-the-job training, whereas for specific or particularly highly skilled occupations, the normal solution is to resort to the skilled labour market, often attempting to attract a competitor's skilled workers. Considering, moreover, that nearly 85 per cent of the Italian workforce is employed in small enterprises, in which the job turnover rate is over 40 per cent, it is readily understandable that vocational training remains a minor concern for these companies and therefore for much of the productive sector in Italy.

MEMBERSHIP OF THE LABOUR FORCE AND JOB LOSS

Labour law first tackles what happens before redundancy, by imposing a procedure that must be observed and requiring a review of the reasons behind the dismissal. The aim in this case is to safeguard existing jobs. However, jobs can also be protected after the dismissal. This does not protect the employee from the redundancy decision itself, but against the consequences of this redundancy, permitting the person concerned to find a new job within a short space of time.[5]

Protection against Dismissal and Safeguarding Existing Jobs

A debate has opened up in a number of countries on the effectiveness of this protection. Some argue that protection against dismissal is more of a barrier to employing people than it is a help in safeguarding existing jobs.

---

[5] For a comparison of national legislations, see European Commission (1997a).

In Italy, one of the proposals that has aroused greatest controversy is for the elimination of the restrictions that currently make it difficult to dismiss individuals for justified, objective reasons. This is in line with a deregulatory and liberal interpretation of the labour market (Ichino and Ichino 1994) which, freed of the rigidity inherent in the rules and constraints intended to protect labour, would then be able to expand freely. Under the proposal, it would essentially be possible for a company to dismiss an employee whenever the cost of maintaining the job is higher than the productivity deriving from it. It should be noted that this cost is understood to be an opportunity cost and therefore also as the possibility of increasing profits as a result of eliminating the job.

In Italy, there are two main insurance unemployment benefits. Both are granted to workers who have been dismissed or have lost their jobs. Unlike with the *Cassa Integrazione*, these labour market measures interrupt the continuity of the status of the employees involved, breaking any bond between employees covered by these schemes and their former employers.

Since 1994, the *Tratamento ordinurio di disoccupazione* has been equal to 30 per cent of the worker's remuneration during the three months preceding unemployment and can be obtained for a maximum of 180 days. To qualify for this benefit, a laid-off worker must have been employed for at least two years and must register with the state employment service. (These benefits are also used to compensate seasonal workers.)

The mobility benefit (*Indennità di mobilità*) is 80 per cent of gross remuneration during the first year of unemployment, but there is a maximum amount payable, making it equivalent to about 65 per cent of the remuneration of the average worker. It lasts up to a maximum of three years for older workers in the South of Italy. To qualify for the mobility benefit, a worker must have an employment record of twelve months and be laid off in the course of collective dismissals due to restructuring or a company crisis. In addition, workers have to have been employed in industrial companies with more than fifteen employees, or in commercial companies with more than 200 employees. During the 1993–94 crisis, access to the *Cassa Integrazione Guadagni Straordinaria* and the mobility benefit was extended to some other service sectors.

Finally, it should be emphasized that in Italy disability pensions have frequently been used as assistance benefits for workers with difficulties in finding a job. In fact, in the 1970s it was decided that the degree of disability (and hence the pension amount) should be determined in part on the basis of the person's socio-economic environment, and in particular on his or her employment potential.

We are interested in discovering the influence this reasoning may have had on legislation in the EU Member States. The national reports show that European governments have generally tended to relax regulations on redundancy, although they have done so on very different levels.

In Britain, redundancies are generally authorized, provided there are economic reasons or changes in the nature of the work to be done. Compensation must be paid to the employee who has been made redundant and the choice of persons dismissed must be fair. The courts have taken it upon themselves to ensure that this requirement is met, although employers may choose among volunteers. The grounds must be clear. For example: the people concerned must be those last taken on, those able to receive pensions, the most expensive workers, those with least experience or the least productive. Where there is an intention to make workers redundant, it is also compulsory for their representatives to be notified and consulted in advance, so that attempts can be made to prevent redundancy. According to the British report, there is no pressure to strengthen protection from redundancy, as the view is that this would lead to more widespread recourse to temporary employment.

In Germany, protection from redundancy is equally weak, with the courts leaving employers to decide whether or not there must be downsizing of the workforce. Even labour selection criteria (younger rather than older employees) have recently been blurred. It is always compulsory to agree on a labour compensation plan in the event of collective redundancies. Protection against redundancy in small companies has been reduced still further (there is no protection in companies with fewer than eleven employees). The upshot is that there is no more than the mere appearance of protection against redundancy in Germany, although even this apparent protection is supposed to dissuade employers from taking more people on, because they fear they would then not be able to dismiss them.

In Sweden, dismissals must be based on material or staff-related circumstances. If the motives are economic, transfer possibilities must be examined. If the reasons are staff-related, employers must do everything in their power to find an alternative to redundancy. There is a fixed order of redundancy for employees, but the employer and the unions can agree on different selection criteria. There is a constant debate in Sweden as to whether the protection laws discourage employment.

In France, prior administrative authorization of redundancies for economic reasons was abandoned in 1986. It is still compulsory for workforce representatives to be consulted. Any workers dismissed for an economic reason must be offered a conversion agreement designed to help them find a new job. In the event of 'mass' redundancies (companies with more than fifty employees and dismissing at least ten at any one time), a labour compensation plan must be arranged. This will include alternatives to redundancy or new job creation. If this is not done, the dismissal is null and void. The judiciary strictly enforces the procedures and the content of the labour plan that accompanies dismissal.

In Spain, a law passed in 1994 has reduced the number of cases where administrative authorization is required for collective redundancies, although without abolishing this requirement completely. Judges now only deal with the admissibility of individual redundancies. In companies which employ at least fifty people, the employer must arrange a labour compensation plan, which offers financial compensation and may include training or other measures aimed at facilitating the search for a new job. At the same time, the new law has restricted temporary work still further. This law has been greatly criticized for not going far enough, in terms of both reducing barriers to dismissal and increasing the restrictions on temporary work. The scope of the problem becomes evident if we consider the number of dismissals declared illegal or null and void by the courts (61 per cent according to one study) and the very high level of temporary work. The subsequent legal reform of 1997, a result of the above Agreement on Steady Employment, restricts the terms of casual hiring while broadening the financial, technical, organizational, or production-related reasons justifying non-collective redundancy, and reduces, in certain cases, the compensation for such dismissal where declared wrongful by the courts.

Protection against the Consequences of Job Loss and the Right to New Placement

Traditionally, the manner in which an employment relationship is established is separate from the way in which this relationship is broken. Recent developments, however, show that the situation can be tackled in a different way: the employer's right to dismiss the worker can be linked to the worker's right to be placed in another job.

Member States have put considerable effort into this matter, mainly on a voluntary basis. In France, dismissed employees must be offered conversion agreements to assist their search for a new job. These agreements stipulate that the person concerned must receive remuneration for a certain period, an assessment of his or her professional qualifications and an offer of training. In the event of 'mass' redundancies, the accompanying labour plan must use every means at its disposal to offer a worker another post in the company or its group (new internal placement).

In Belgium, this kind of conversion is primarily negotiated by the social partners, although the resulting agreements may later be made legally binding. In Spain, labour plans particularly in large public corporations sometimes also include training measures and assistance in the search for a new job. In Britain, in those cases where redundancy affects thousands of employees, some employers have hired special organizations which help find the employees new jobs, set up in business on their own, retrain, or become involved in setting up new enterprises in the region. There are not many such agreements, but those that do exist appear to have met with some success. In Sweden, some collective agreements require employers to contribute to a 'security fund' designed to finance training activities to enable employees to remain in the company and to help them find a new job or set up a business. Many of these agreements have proved to be quite successful.

CONCLUSION: TOWARDS A NEW LABOUR FORCE MEMBERSHIP STATUS FOR INDIVIDUALS

Understanding the Change

Given increased flexibility, the major division in the area of labour force membership will now be the distinction between typical and atypical jobs. How should we interpret this trend?

An initial interpretation could be couched in the following conventional terms: the destabilization of the employment relationship demonstrates a revival of the class struggle, and more specifically the struggle between capital and labour. This interpretation assumes that the nature of labour has not undergone any fundamental change in post-industrial society. What has changed, on the other hand, is the relationship between the forces involved. Capital has reorganized in the course of the last twenty years. The changes include a marked increase in the autonomy of financial capital when compared to industrial capital; capital has spread throughout the world, opening the way for mass delocalization and relocation; capital is increasingly less fixed and is growing more and more flexible. These transformations in capital have brought about a management offensive which seeks to adapt workers to the new conditions of capital development. It is here where deregulation comes into play. Deregulation involves dismantling a certain number of barriers which capital faces on the labour market (regulations inherited from Fordism) and restoring to capital its discretionary power. And that involves the destruction of the protection associated with the employment relationship.

A second interpretation argues that it is not only capital which has changed, but that, in a partially autonomous way, labour has changed as well. We have moved from the job whose prototype was manufacturing (working on something material) to a new type of work, where the prototype is the service relationship; here work involves more interaction and manipulation of symbols than working directly on something material. This is one way of describing the movement to a tertiary economy and the new technological revolution. And just as the nature of work has changed, so have the rules for organization and co-ordination of that work. From this perspective, the employment relationship can be understood as an institutional form adapted to a certain prototype of work. Given the transformation undergone by this prototype, we gradually need to seek new institutional ways of protecting workers. In short, the destabilization of the employment relationship is due not only to the transformation of capital but also to changes in labour itself. It is this second, more complex type of interpretation which should, it seems, be the focus of our attention.

According to this interpretation of events, labour law and the social partners are faced with a strategic choice. If we follow the first of these two interpretations, labour law (the legislative powers and the judiciary) and unions will find themselves faced with a duty to resist. This resistance will involve defending the employment relationship whatever the cost. It would involve the utmost effort to maintain a stable status for the worker with a single employer for an indefinite period of time.

A second strategy would involve mere adaptation. This involves acknowledging a relationship of strength which is both strong and flexible and adapting this by uncoupling two different systems. On the one hand, there is a need to preserve the employment relationship as far and as extensively as possible. On the other hand, we must endeavour to alter the status of non-employment, guaranteeing a minimum amount of social protection. In this case, the unions would have to become more 'co-operative' and less confrontational. They would need to offer services for managing flexibility and human resources, rather than playing the part of the industrial rearguard in a post-industrial society.

Neither of the two strategies is really satisfactory. Both divide society in two. The first, in particular, could have the perverse effect of turning labour law into an elitist and corporatist form of protection for the happy few who enjoy the status of employees.

A third strategy may also be envisaged, that is active adaptation to avoid such risks: this would consist of re-institutionalizing the employment relationship. Re-institutionalization is used here to mean setting rules, allocating negotiating forums for these rules and enabling the collectives involved to intervene effectively. The comparative analysis presented shows that the basic outline for a re-institutionalization of this type is already in place in national legislation. Employee status, which makes security contingent upon subordination, should be replaced by a new labour force membership status based on a comprehensive approach to work, capable of reconciling the need for freedom and the need for security.

Mastering Change

The need to transcend the employment model is common to all European countries. Broaching this issue at the Community level is particularly difficult. To illustrate this difficulty, we need only to refer to the way the employment model has manifested itself throughout Europe: on the one hand employment has given rise to very different legal constructs in Europe (evidenced by the diversity of national labour law) (see Chapter 5 in this regard); on the other hand, the common theme is the creation, within the framework of a contract (the employment contract), of a status able to afford protection for the person so covered. The divergent and convergent forces at work in the evolution of the various national bodies of labour law must not be underestimated. Moreover, although there is no way at this time to predict what specific legal forms this superseding of the employment model will assume in each country, it is possible to define the conceptual framework in which it will take place. It is not the purpose of our endeavour here to anticipate the legal formulas that may eventually be applied in different countries. Rather, we have been called upon to explore the ideas that come from an analysis of current changes in employment status, ideas that are precise enough to be operational but general enough for each country to be able to adapt them to its own circumstances.[6]

---

[6] The following discussion draws heavily on analyses previously published in Supiot (1997).

Employment, Work and Activity

To escape the influence of employment in our understanding of people's occupational status, we have to start with a comprehensive review of working life which is not just limited to paid work. In building up the concept of employment, we have ignored all non-marketable forms of work, such as training on one's own initiative or unpaid work. The concept has also developed in contrast to self-employment, incorporating the split between the private and public sectors. The reason is because paid employment, as an occupational status, is merely the projection of employment as an exchange value on the labour market. Accordingly, the employment relationship is taken into account by labour law only in so far as work is the subject of a contract. The difficulty nowadays is to perceive the occupational status of persons as extending beyond the immediate contractual commitment to their work to cover the diverse forms of work experienced during one's life.

Non-marketable forms of work are in fact those most crucial to humankind. A general strike might bring the market to a temporary halt, yet it would not jeopardize the survival of a country (France regularly indulges in such pastimes). Nevertheless, society could not survive for more than a few days any disruption of the domestic work that secures everyday life. It is this unremunerated work which bears the real burden of economic life and markets. Japanese men could not work such long hours, for example, if their wives did not assume sole responsibility for the upbringing of their children at the cost of complete or partial withdrawal from the labour market on marriage. Disregarding these close ties between work inside and outside the market is tantamount to disregarding both the circumstances of people's lives and those of the market, and setting a course for disaster. Treating labour as an infinitely flexible resource compromises not only workers' living conditions but also the conditions under which their children are brought up.

Furthermore, the issue of occupational status must now include the requirements of equality between men and women, continuing training, the undertaking of activities of common benefit and career choice. That means that various forms of work must be perceived more through what they have in common than through their differences. It is along those lines that we can hope to define an occupational status which reconciles diversity and continuity in working life.

Very encouraging forward-looking considerations have been put forward in that direction in France, including the idea of the activity contract presented in the Boissonnat Report (Commissariat général du Plan 1995), and developed by Thierry Priestly (Priestly 1995; Gaudu 1995). The great merit of the proposed activity contract is to draw attention to the need to develop an occupational status which does not only refer to employment and makes enterprises seek viable alternatives to this model. Its weakness lies to some extent in the converse of its merits: its purely experimental and voluntary nature. Rather than any contract *per se*, it is legal status that should be at the core of the debate on seeking ways of redefining people's contractual arrangements in the labour market. Moreover, the notion of activity is too imprecise to be legally relevant. Activity is an integral part of life, the social rights connected with life are universal social rights. Accordingly, the reference to activity is not appropriate as a basis for specific rights.

The only concept which extends beyond employment without encompassing life in its entirety is the concept of work, which is therefore the only concept that can provide the basis for occupational status. The distinction between work and activity should not be made by the nature of the action accomplished (the same mountain walk is a leisure activity for the tourist but work for the guide accompanying him). Work is distinguished from activity in that it results from an obligation, whether voluntarily undertaken or compulsorily imposed. This obligation may result from a contract (employed person, self-employed person) or from legal condition (civil servant, monk). It may be assumed against payment (employment) or without payment (voluntary work, traineeship). But work always falls within a legal relationship. That is why we can speak of school work since school attendance is compulsory, work in the domestic sphere since bringing up children is a duty linked to parental authority, the work of elected representatives given that there are procedures for removing them from office if they fail to fulfil their remit properly, etc. It is necessary and sufficient for the effects of law to be attached to a commitment to act for such action to be described as work. This status depends ultimately either upon a voluntary commitment or on the law enshrining the social usefulness of certain tasks.

The Four Circles of Social Law

In considering the future of social law (in the broad sense: labour law and social security), some experts maintain that a recovery in employment is the only way of providing funding for social security once again and of giving everyone a genuine occupational identity. Others advocate, on the one hand, a complete break between social protection and work, with universal minimum social benefits and leaving the rest to market forces. The disadvantages of these theories is that they put all social rights on the same footing, whereas history has demonstrated that we must, on the contrary, distinguish between social security risks and degrees of dependency in employment relationships. They also confuse work and employment: they consider that there is nothing between employment and citizenship on which specific social rights could be based. This is broadly refuted by a scrutiny of positive law, where social rights fall within four concentric circles.

- The first circle covers 'universal' social rights, that is rights guaranteed to everyone irrespective of any kind of work. This universal coverage applies today in the case of family benefits. It applies more or less in the field of health care insurance. It remains a principle as regards entitlement to vocational training.
- The second circle covers rights based on unpaid work (care for other people, training on one's own initiative, voluntary work, etc.). Such work is in fact recognized under social law. Many texts attach rights or social benefits to the pursuit of socially useful activity (that is unpaid work: for example, retirement benefits linked to child rearing, accident coverage for certain kinds of volunteer work, etc.).
- The third circle covers the common law of occupational activity, which has a basis also in Community law (health and safety, for instance).
- The fourth circle covers the law relating to paid employment, which contains provisions directly connected with subordination only and provides for a scale of rights related to the degree of the subordination.

The principle of equal treatment for men and women, however, applies to all four circles.

This typology could provide a useful framework for defining a labour force membership status covering people from cradle to grave and covering both periods of inactivity proper and periods of training, employment, self-employment, and work outside the labour market. The paradigm of employment would thus be replaced by a paradigm of labour force membership for individuals, not defined by pursuit of an occupation or a specific job, but covering the various forms of work which anyone might perform during his or her life.

Social Drawing Rights

This labour force membership status for individuals must incorporate the need for freedom of work, understood as a practical freedom, and must facilitate change from one type of work to another. This is essential to rule out the risk of becoming stuck in a given work situation. Providing for individual freedom in the definition of social rights means departing from the prevailing perception of these rights, which have been regarded as a counterpart to risks or specific constraints. This perception is linked in part with the view of the employed person as passive and subject both to the risks of life and to the burden of subordination.

Here again, however, scrutiny of positive law reveals that a different legal figure has emerged: the worker entitled to switch from one work situation to another. The first measure introducing this right of initiative was doubtless the granting of time off to employees holding a position of collective responsibility (staff representative); in the same vein: special leave and the right to absence (which have increased in recent years), training leave, time saving accounts, assistance for the unemployed in creating or taking over companies, training vouchers, etc. We are surely witnessing here the emergence of a new type of social right, related to work in general (work in the family sphere, training work, voluntary work, self-employment, work in the public interest, etc.). Exercise of these rights remains bound to a previously established claim, but they are brought into effect by the free decision of the individual and not as a result of risk. This twofold feature can be seen in the terms frequently used for these rights: accounts, credits, savings, vouchers, etc. These new rights could be described as 'social drawing rights'.

They are *drawing* rights as they can be brought into effect on two conditions: establishment of sufficient reserve and the decision by the holder to make use of that reserve. They are *social* drawing rights as they are social both in the way they are established (different ways of building up the reserve) and in their aims (social usefulness). In contrast to the holder of a bill of exchange, the 'drawer' has a right only with a view to a specific social purpose. His personal right is a functional right which cannot be transferred to a third party at will. However, the social usefulness of the function provides for the undertaking or the community to build up the reserve. This concept should be clarified by distinguishing between the two facets of such rights.

They operate first by releasing time, and the procedures differ at present according to whether the rights are used under an employment contract, while it is suspended or outside such a contract (usually following termination). The problem of the continuity of the legal, labour force membership condition arises in different ways according to the above situations. Under an employment contract, such time may be regarded as working time for the purposes of the benefits connected with continuity of the contract. Outside that context, various techniques have been applied, including treating such time as working time under social security law.

Secondly, social drawing rights provide for work to be funded outside the market. Such funding is most frequently on a joint basis. The reserve can thus be built up by the State (this is the case for most tasks of general interest), by the social security services (for example: benefit subject to having a dependant), by joint mutual insurance bodies (training leave for example), by enterprises (continuity of employment contract, time off, parental benefits, etc.), or by the worker himself, who may supplement the other contributions (time-saving account, use of holiday entitlement, giving up part of previous income, etc.).

There is no general framework for this heterogeneous set of rules which could amalgamate all the consequences of the principles of continuity and mobility inherent in the labour force membership of individuals. Nevertheless, the employee subject to full-time, open-ended subordination is surely not the only model for working life. Another figure can be discerned on the horizon: a worker who can reconcile security and freedom.

Work and Time

INTRODUCTION

In pre-industrial labour relations, the question of time and its measurement never acquired the importance it has today. Since such relations were seen more in terms of a personal connection than an exchange of services, the issue of measurement, keeping detailed accounts of working time, simply made no sense.

This pre-industrial view still prevailed, for instance, in the relations between master and servant in the Swedish regulations of 1833. Servants were hired on a yearly basis (from October to October), the relation was tacitly renewed and could not be cancelled at just any time. Masters had to continue to attend to their servants' needs when they were ill or old, in view of their many years of loyal service. In return, servants did not count their working hours and were at their masters' permanent disposal. These regulations were not formally abolished until 1926.

The industrial revolution imposed another approach to time, in which the Taylor model for the organization of work was seen as the ideal. With the 'scientific organization of work' advocated by Taylor, 'the stop-watch made its way into the workshop' (Coriat 1994). Under this analytical view, the time line is divided into homogeneous and abstract moments, defined prior to any specific action, leaving no room for uncertainty. Such coding of work has both qualitative and quantitative aspects. Qualitatively, it provides a precise definition of the co-ordinates of optimum action, establishing a strictly frugal 'code of motion'. Quantitatively, it measures the productivity of movements and enhances their intensity. The latter calls for a control mechanism along the assembly line itself rather than a strictly centralized hierarchy. The pace of work is set from outside by the conveyor belt, that new technique which made it possible to keep workers at their individual work stations by mechanizing carriage of the parts on which they work. Machine settings constitute a way of controlling the productivity of effective working time. Moreover, meticulous and authoritarian supervision provides for strict monitoring of the adequacy of even the slightest movement.

This new approach to time became an integral part of a model of labour relations, whose major features were as follows:

- hierarchical dependence on the company manager;
- exclusive nature of the relationship with the employer, which lies at the root of the permanent nature of the employment contract, as well as the obligation to be loyal and discreet that many legal codes require of workers;
- integration in company organization;
- obligation of the worker to make his time available to the employer (within the limits of the employment contract);
- fixed work schedule and patterns for organizing the work to be done.

The above, broadly speaking, covers the basic characteristics of the model for regulating work in medium-sized and large enterprises. Obviously, that general outline leaves room for specific national or regional regulations. Similarly, the social security system has a substantial effect on women's participation in the labour market: in Europe social security has usually led to an employment model built around a primarily male family breadwinner. Recent historic analysis has shown that this model was unevenly and more or less belatedly disseminated and systematized, depending on the country. Today, Fordism seems more and more to have been a sort of widespread scale against which production patterns were interpreted, and which tended to tone down certain persistent differences (Sabel and Zeitlin 1997).

This male breadwinner model was the axis on which so-called Fordist productive entities turned, since with the success of standardized mass production, the patterns for organizing working time and work schedules tended to become more stable. The introduction of shifts (generally on the basis of two eight-hour shifts, five days a week) made it possible to increase production levels and therefore the level of utilization of equipment while technological innovation ensured higher productivity per work unit.

Labour law systematized that model. Time was conceived as an objective reference that could be used to regulate working relations, both individually and collectively. Doubts have been cast on this conception in view of recent changes leading to individualization and greater heterogeneity of working time. That, in turn, has called for new perspectives for labour law, in which time is perceived in a personal and subjective dimension.[1]

WORKING TIME AS AN OBJECTIVE REFERENCE

From the legal standpoint, the reference to time has played a dual role in labour relations: on the individual level, as a way of measuring subordination and therefore wages;[2] and, collectively, as a way of establishing discipline and therefore solidarity.

Measure of Subordination

In labour law, the reference to 'working time', on the one hand, limits the employer's hold on the worker's life and, on the other, allows the employer to evaluate his services. Time is simultaneously a limit to worker obligations and a standard against which to value what labour is worth. The legal limitation of working hours and the model for working life thus defined lead to 'working time' and 'free time' being regarded as contradictory terms and unpaid work being virtually ignored.

The Legal Working Week

With the exception of the United Kingdom, all European countries have a legally defined working week. (In the United Kingdom, the first regulations limiting the working week took effect in October 1998.)

This is the framework, in terms of time, within which the Fordist production model took root and developed. Its main characteristic is the formal standardization of working hours. Such standardization was

---

[1] The point of departure for this chapter was the summary report by Profs. Mingione and Barbieri. Certain of the analyses reworked here were taken from previous works by the members of the group of experts, where more thorough discussions of them can be found (De Munck (forthcoming), Supiot 1995*a*).

[2] On the advent, in Anglo-Saxon political economy, of the idea of 'Work is time', see Méda (1995).

Table 3.1. Regulation of working time

	Legal annual weeks	Contractual annual weeks	Legal weekly hours	Contractual hours	Maximum annual overtime (hours)	Restriction on night work (0–2)	Summary restrictions rank*
Belgium	46.14	44.14	38	38.0	200	2	5.0
Denmark	47.14	47.14	39	37.0	144	0	2.0
France	46.94	44.84	39	39.0	233	1	7.5
Germany	46.94	44.53	48	38.0	540	1	6.0
Greece	47.34	45.14	40	40.0	135	1	10.0
Ireland	47.54	46.34	48	39.0	300	0	3.5
Italy	48.14	48.14	48	39.0	363	1	3.5
Netherlands	46.74	45.64	48	38.0	540	2	7.5
Portugal	45.34	45.14	48	42.0	120	1	11.0
Spain	44.34	44.44	40	39.5	80	0	9.0
UK	n.a.	n.a.	n.a.	n.a.	n.a.	n.a.	1.0

* Summary restrictions on overtime, flexible, weekend, and night work (*Source*: Grubb and Wells, OECD Economic Studies, No. 21/1993).

directly linked to the organizational characteristics of the mass production of standard articles.

By contrast, the world of self-employment remained outside this aspect of the model. There was a dual system in which normal paid working time co-existed with other ways of organizing time (agriculture, small shops, family enterprises, or freelance professionals). Indeed, the only limitation that could be imposed on the working time of self-employed workers rose from the nature of the products and services offered (agriculture and other seasonal activities), market organization (for instance, rules on closing shops on Sundays), or provisions relating to health and safety (such as restrictions on driving time in road transport).

Inside large Fordist companies, the model is somewhat rigid, as regards both production and the organization of work, working time and schedules; in all others, with the exception of specialists and maintenance crews, it is the rigidity of the technological solutions in use that determine the rigidity of the ways in which time and working schedules are regulated, calling for regulations agreed with trade unions. The extreme rigidity of technological solutions makes them fragile and thereby enhances the negative power of organized labour. For this reason, the general flexibility of production times must necessarily be regulated via collective bargaining between management and labour. The latter, in turn, become (formally speaking, at least) spokesmen for what continues to be, under such an organizational model, the priority aim of workers: the reduction of the working week, that is mass working time.

In a traditional industrial setting, the main way to adapt working time to the needs of industry is to resort to overtime, that is hours worked beyond the legal working week. Such time is usually paid at a higher rate. Its use is regulated in different ways in different countries, but generally speaking there are two kinds of regulation. First, the definition of a maximum number of working hours that may not, in principle, be exceeded. And secondly by systems calling for prior authorization: such authorization may be required either from the first hour of overtime or after a certain number of legally or conventionally defined hours. Such regulatory conditions are never very restrictive and recourse to overtime has been the main way to flexibilize working time in all European countries.

This feature is still in place today. The development of non-standard/ flexible work that has developed over the last twenty years is in addition to, not in lieu of, the primary source of flexibility, that is overtime. To understand this, account must be taken of what might be defined as the European style of production and work organization (or better yet, Continental European, since the situation is different in this regard in the United Kingdom). Here the diversity of the various kinds of capitalism has to be emphasized (Crouch and Streeck 1996): they do not all conform perfectly to the single model proposed by standard neo-laissez-faire economic theory. The existence of a stable and skilled (such as in Southern European countries, particularly Italy) or highly skilled (such as in Germany) workforce constitutes the foundation for diversified and high-quality production in continental Europe. Recourse to overtime makes it possible to adjust the volume of this human resource to market demands, without having to resort to further hiring or redundancies. When new needs arise, companies prefer to use their permanent and skilled staff rather than hire new personnel, which entails high costs and uncertain performance.

Working Life

The normal kind of employment (permanent full-time work) has been associated with a normal kind of working life. Taken as a cognitive model, the wage-based relationship that corresponds to that pattern constitutes the definition of normal and standard work, which Ulrich Mückenberger calls the 'SER (Standard Employment Relationship) model'(Mückenberger 1989). Under such a model, employees typically work full-time on a permanent basis for the same concern for their entire career, with promotions as appropriate. This standard can be used as a reference in terms of which more or less all other kinds of work are conceived or structured.

Generally speaking, time as defined by labour law is what might in effect be termed homogeneous time. Substantially, what is involved is the establishment of a stereotype of 'normal time' corresponding to a standard wage-based model. That is to say, there is a set time that defines a standard working day (from 8:00 a.m. to 5:00 p.m.); a standard working week (more or less 40 hours, from Monday to Friday, with the weekend off); a standard working year, with customary, seasonal leave time (Christmas, Easter, and summer holidays). This time also determines the framework for a standard working life, consisting of apprenticeship during youth (not capable of being postponed or repeated during adult life), working years, and finally retirement during old age (beginning at 60 or 65). Consensus based on that model makes it possible to synchronize education, social, and economic time. The formal aspect of that rule lies in its general, standard and *a priori* nature. The rule governing time is not open to question in terms of constraints on individual action or preferences.

Sociological analysis could demonstrate any number of informal practices generated by such formalism (evening work among teachers and executives, weekend work, etc.), as well as the importance of the sectors that have in fact escaped the Fordist model.

The situation is completely different among small and medium-sized enterprises, which today form the majority. A distinction must be drawn between small enterprises with very specialized labour (particularly in certain manufacturing and craft industries) and marginal or semi-marginal enterprises that adopt competitive strategies based on price and are, therefore, interested in maximum use of working time. In small specialized companies, work is barely standardized and workers are often in possession of expertise that allows them a good deal of operational independence and a large amount of control over their own working conditions. Under such circumstances, negotiation of working time often becomes a kind of personal agreement in which the skilled worker sets the price of his or her own professional experience and technical expertise. It is not by chance that, under such circumstances, it is rare to find professionals or skilled workers who prefer regulated working times and production schedules; they prefer, rather, to set their own schedules, especially if that involves some financial advantage, such as piecework or overtime.

The literature on industrial sectors in Italy and, more generally, the 'third Italy' model, together with the large number of micro-manufacturing firms in certain regions of Southern Europe, has revealed that small companies regulate working time and work schedules to meet the challenge inherent in the demand for flexibility largely by combining the elements of the formal regulation of work schedules (legislation, collective agreements, company-wide agreements) with informal solutions.

None the less, such proliferation of informal models has not, for a long time, posed any challenge to the formal and official standard. It is not until many different forms of co-ordination and work that go hand-in-hand with the growth in product and service diversity can no longer be confined to the informal domain—where Fordism had hitherto relegated them—that the crisis hits. Such variety overtakes Fordism's formal standard, questioning it as an ideal, which is exactly what occurred in Western countries after the 1973 economic crisis. Homogeneous time is no longer the central reference for regulating time.

This time norm was based on a reciprocal commitment between employers and employees, a commitment that benefited both (Soskice 1990). Employers obtained in-house trained labour that accepted the Fordist–Keynesian commitment, which, even from the ideological viewpoint, favoured growth; workers, in turn, were afforded the security associated with internal labour markets (union protection, fringe benefits, training, internal promotion, etc.). Such an exchange primarily benefited male labour employed in manufacturing industry. By contrast, women were essentially relegated to a reproductive role and had access to the labour market under less favourable conditions.

Working Time and 'Free Time'

The approach to time in this model of industrial rationalization leads to the consideration of working time, as subordination time, and 'free time', regarded as inactivity, to be diametric opposites. Directive 93/104 of 23 November 1993 reinterprets this opposition in its own way by classifying as a 'rest period' any period during which the worker is not at the employer's disposal.[3] Time measured as the term of performance of the contract is insulated from the contracting party's life time, thereby legally ratifying the economic fiction that work is detachable from the worker. Such a fiction veils everything in economic life that is not directly subject to the logic of exchange.

---

[3] See: *Directive 93/104 concerning certain aspects of the organization of working time*, Art. 2-1 and 2-2.

Reproductive Work
Separating working and free time in this manner ignores, first, reproductive work, that is household work and child rearing, reserved primarily for women (domestic chores, care, and upbringing of children) as well as academic and vocational training (with the exception of apprenticeship). It also ignores time constraints associated with work-related activities, particularly the time needed to get to work from home or free time in fact spent working (as in virtually all creative jobs or jobs involving responsibility, which weigh on the mind long after actual working hours).

The work thus performed during 'free' time is not counted as working time (particularly by major economic indicators). As essential to the survival of society as air or water, it is treated, like these, as something in unlimited supply; it is considered under another conception of time: *Aion*, the eternal and inexhaustible principle of creation, and not *Chronos*, the devourer of energy, which presides over paid work.[4] Just as no provision is made in the accounts for the industrial world's impact on the most essential environmental resources (air, water, land), that world also ignores the actual place that work occupies in a person's time. The actual burden of work should be the sole item relevant to the use of the 'human resource'. What in fact happens is that part of the cost (reproduction, commuting costs, etc.) of the human resource used by employers is borne by wage earners or society as a whole.

On-the-Job Inactivity
Conversely, considering working and rest time as contradictory terms leads, in principle, to ignoring on-the-job inactivity and obliges employers to pay for working time, regardless of how efficiently or inefficiently it is used.

French law, for instance, provides that 'effective work', as defined by Art. L.212-4 of the Labour Code, that is where the wage earner is at the employer's disposal at the workplace in order to be able to undertake work if needed, but without necessarily participating in any task, no matter how minor, must none the less be paid at the same rate as normal working hours.[5]

This favours the employee, but not the employer. Directive 93/104 seeks to reduce the consequences of such situations. Working time is not actually defined therein simply as a 'period during which the worker is . . . at the employer's disposal'; the worker must, in addition, be 'working',

---

[4]   For these two conceptions of time, see Panofsky (1939).

[5]   Soc. 15 Feb. 1995 (Dulac), in: *Droit social*, 1995, 381, obs J. Savatier (nightwatchmen at a retirement home).

'carrying out his activities or duties' (Art. 2-1). But this leaves the door open to classifying the time that an employee must be at the employer's disposal as free time! The appearance in law of such an illusion reveals that time cannot be used as the sole unit of measurement of work and that the boundary between free time and working time is becoming blurred.

Consumption Time

Ultimately one of the major features of the model was to characterize free time as consumption time, which constituted a crucial break with earlier capitalistic treatment of non-work. In the latter case, non-working time was considered simply as recovery time, workforce reproduction time. Fordism tries to subject workers' aspirations to enjoy leisure time to its own constraints: non-working time becomes time to be spent freely, rather than merely as reproduction time. This was a first, an innovation that gave workers 'packages' of free time: they had weekends off or holidays on a regular basis. But this new movement in the history of time cannot be understood without taking account of the new consumption rule prompted by Fordist standard and generic products. Aglietta, contrary to mainstream Marxist theory, draws attention to its effects on global regulation (Aglietta 1976). The consumption of standardized products by the working class became the major activity during the leisure time granted during the New Deal.

According to historian Gary Cross, during the 1930s the objectives of free time were themselves gradually equated with the ability to consume or to dream of a consumer's paradise. Free time lost its status as a goal in itself, a result of productivity but freed from iron-clad economism. Instead, it became the road to a kind of mass consumption that would be able to absorb industrialism's unlimited potential (Cross 1993).

In this way, the distribution of standard goods and services successfully competed with the informal, rural or semi-rural economies around which domestic activity was organized prior to Fordism.

Collective Discipline

Time serves to set a pace to men's and women's work, to set common tempos and schedules. Such schedules and tempos, be they defined by employers or imposed by machines, keep time for workers, much as the conductor or the *basso continuo* does for musicians. This synchronization of workers' lives mechanically breeds two kinds of solidarity.

Working Time and Collective Organization

Standard time as imposed by work leads, first of all, to solidarity among workers subject to the same schedules and tempos: working and organizational solidarity, solidarity in combat. Labour law itself establishes the main forms of solidarity among workers in connection with the collective organization of working time. Working time, understood in the strict sense of time in service, has been used in the negative to define the time of collective independence, whether that concerns the freedom to form trade unions, to be collectively represented in companies or to strike. A universal abstract, 'working time' tends generally to mask the fundamental heterogeneity of work performed and the resulting experience of time. Such identity of legal treatment has also contributed to forging solidarity among workers.

Working Time and Urban Time

The synchronization of workers' lives leads, furthermore, to a solidarity between working time and urban time, the latter (time spent in schooling, commuting, leisure, etc.) being geared to the former. Such solidarity is also not ignored by the law. The organization of working time was devised to leave time—the opposite of working time—for social life, at night, on Sunday, during paid holidays, or for education. The collective disciplines deriving from working time are also reflected in the rules governing commuting time, increasingly longer and more dangerous.

But the reduction in working time favoured by the Fordist model has led especially to the standardization of consumer time. This was indisputably the main innovation of that model. It had to organize a normative context that would allow women to pull themselves away from their kitchens to spend time shopping at fashionable boutiques. Children had to be enticed away from vacant lots and backyards to amusement parks, beaches, and Walt Disney films. The move to mass consumption involves a redefinition of lifestyles. This is why free time is only appreciated to the extent that it lends itself to 'over-determination' thanks to a production apparatus conforming to the rule. But there was an inherent contradiction in that reduction of time devoted to work: by freeing time and simultaneously dashing the hopes that had been placed on it, it provided a space for freedom and diversification in individual and community life choices.

The Fordist consumption regime is new not only because of its content, but more importantly because of the way it works. It is not a formal, a customary, or a contractual rule. It is not imposed by statutory authority, contractual negotiations, community authority, or even tradition. It works rather via systematically organized persuasion. Consumer space is controlled by new powers that impose themselves via marketing and publicity. As in the Taylor-model workshop, the intention is to intensify flows and standardize action. The mere fact that it is positioned in a time considered to be 'leisure time' subjects the operation to other patterns. Psychological suggestion becomes a privileged tool for controlling behaviour: mass mimicry becomes a legitimate avenue. There is an attempt to co-ordinate the actors in the consumer domain, and thereby co-ordinate this domain with the production domain.

Measure of subordination and of collective discipline: from these two standpoints, working time is measurable and divisible, abstract time that can be readily quantified. And it relates to equally abstract work, defined as subordination subject to payment, a prerequisite for collective worker organizations.

The traditional concept of working time arranges the world around two poles. On the one hand, there is the pole of measured time, comprising recognized and paid work, workers, and occupational solidarities; this is male time *par excellence*, to which women must conform if they intend to participate in it on an equal footing.[6] On the other hand, there is unlimited time, female time, a space populated primarily by retired workers, women, and children,[7] their poorly understood and unpaid work, non-occupational solidarities, rest, consumption, etc. This bipolarity no longer describes today's world.

FRAGMENTATION OF WORKING TIME

The new forms of working organization have had a marked impact on the balance of the Fordist model. An analysis of such changes is needed to understand the new concepts of time emerging in labour law.

---

[6] See the earliest provisions allowing women in management positions and positions of responsibility and to work at night: those functions enabled them to participate in male time.

[7] And even men, since they have taken to doing domestic chores!

Changes in Work Organization

Capitalism had, by and large, forced labour to fit into a formal, hierarchical system of time. But that former tendency is showing clear signs of exhaustion, at least in developed countries. New kinds of relationships with time are appearing in the way work is organized on the job as well as in workers' lives. The effect of employment policies on working time contributes even further to these new trends.

Organization of Work in Businesses

This change appears sporadically in the manufacturing sector, where new management methods, coming particularly from Japan, modify time relations. It is even more marked in the developing tertiary sector. In both cases, it is ultimately undermining the model based on homogeneous time.

In the Manufacturing Sector
In mass production, new institutions are reworking the organization of labour. The reference here, of course, is to the different variations of '*ohnism*' (Coriat 1991), which departs from the Taylorian principle of analysing time and motion to rethink the terms of mass production. This 'just in time' model, better adapted to the context of uncertainty that characterizes contemporary economies, has spread more or less throughout all industrialized countries. The characteristic feature of the model is that production patterns are not established *a priori*, but rather are matched to short-term fluctuations in demand. This translates, within companies, to a reduction in stocks and multi-skilling among workers: assembly lines can be quickly altered and reconfigured to favour rapid qualitative and quantitative reprogramming of production. Control, in turn, no longer follows the hierarchical and pyramidal structures characteristic of enterprises: intensification of control goes hand-in-hand with 'flattened' management structures and the deployment of incentive and profit-sharing mechanisms (Coriat 1991).

It is none the less true that this kind of labour organization does not constitute a break from the objectives of Taylorism (intensifying work) or certain of its features (even if it incorporates some restricted diversification, production is still oriented towards standard products, sold with aggressive marketing methods). From this perspective, those who see some neo-Fordism in the model are not misguided (Wood 1993). None the less, this partial change does not leave the principles of the organization of working time unaltered, given that it involves flexibilization of schedules and pace, which depend more on effective demand than on *a priori* programming of supply. In such a context, slavish maintenance of a standard schedule becomes an obstacle to cost rationalization.

In the Tertiary Sector
Service profitability principles are only partially susceptible to the economies of scale characteristic of industrial products. The creation of added value is contingent upon the quality of the interaction that links the service provider and the beneficiary. The expansion of the service society imposes even greater diversification of time regimes: compulsory services which must be provided around the clock and at-home assistance; various kinds of consultancies; new services associated with communication demands (work in the media, financial, and commercial services connected to international networks, in which working times and schedules depend on time zones and financial or commercial exchange business schedules). Tertiarization of cities as well entails a demand for social entertainment (theatre, museums, social services), imposing new scheduling for the enjoyment of certain services that inevitably involve working time restraints.

In Sweden, for instance, the public sector employed 21 per cent of the working population in 1970, 27 per cent in 1980 and 30 per cent in 1990. In the private sector, service activity has grown even faster, employing 39 per cent of the population in 1992. That same year, industry employed no more than 20 per cent of the population.[8]

The tertiary sector is quite obviously the sector where the deconstruction of the formal-hierarchical approach to time is making the greatest progress. It is being replaced by a contractual approach, in which the customer is included as one of the essential components. In many European countries (Great Britain, the Netherlands, France), therefore, there is a movement to extend store and service hours, resulting in a marked impact on their employees' living conditions and entailing the destruction of the last haven of community time that sets the pace in urban life (namely, Sunday rest).

In several countries (France, Germany, Belgium), employees are known to be strongly in favour of a Sunday rest rule despite the campaigns aimed

---

[8] SoU 1996: 145, p. 576.

at encouraging social demand for opening stores on Sunday. For similar reasons, there is strong resistance among employees accustomed to a five-day week to working on Saturday. In contrast, variable schedules (*à la carte* scheduling) were very successful among workers in the 1970s and trade unions were forced to withdraw opposition to the idea. Parental leave is also reasonably popular, as is leave for training, where available. All this leads to a belief that the individualization of lifestyles and behaviours co-exist, for workers, with the desire to continue to lead a normal social life, especially, but not exclusively, as far as family is concerned.

Organization of Working Life

The change in the rules around which work is organized entails the erosion of the employee–employer relationship itself. The archetypal model of 'normal' work time is being questioned.

Such questioning arises from various sources. It may be an outcome of employment policies that favour part-time work or negotiated reductions in working time. Or it may be the consequence of social security policies. The setting of retirement age, for instance, is subject to contradictory measures. On the one hand, employment policies may lead to a cut in the retirement age or to *en masse* early retirement to increase the demand for labour. On the other hand, demographic trends and the lengthening of life expectancy lead to lengthening the amount of time contributions have to be paid to obtain a full retirement pension. On the one hand, labour law favours career breaks and alternating full-time and part-time work and periods of inactivity. On the other, the pension system makes more stringent demands on workers to be eligible for a good pension. All of this leads to individualization of the retirement age and the forms that retirement takes.

Another factor leading to individualization is the sharp rise in non-standard forms of employment, such as fixed-term contracts or temporary work. Holding several jobs and working in the black economy become perfectly reasonable strategies for workers, which leads to the development of an informal, that is illegal, sector, where second jobs prevail among a population subject to casualized working conditions.

Individualization is, finally, the outcome of new ways of managing working time. Surveys confirm the growing individualization of working time and a substantial reduction in the proportion of employees who have the same pattern every day or work the same number of days every week.

In France, the number of employees working a variable number of days per week grew from 11.1 per cent to 14.7 per cent between 1984 and 1991 (Freyssinet 1997). However, the proportion of variable schedules imposed by management demands remained steady (24.7 per cent in 1984 and 24.3 per cent in 1991), while the share of free schedules 'chosen' by employees increased (*à la carte* schedules and free schedules, which rose from 16.1 per cent to 23.1 per cent in the same period). In this regard, the diversification of working time is not primarily the result of new forms of organization open to collective bargaining. This rise in individually determined schedules involves essentially two categories of occupations: executives and professions of an intellectual nature and company administrative and commercial personnel. By contrast, among manual workers and white-collar employees, it is usually the employer who imposes non-standard schedules. Thus, the proportion of shift workers grew from 25.5 per cent in 1982 to 34.1 per cent in 1990. Freyssinet observes that 'the forms that have given rise to the greatest controversy (annual hours, weekend shifts, women's night work) constitute, as a whole, only minor mechanisms for flexibilizing working time. The traditional tools (overtime, partial unemployment) still play the main role' (Freyssinet 1997, p. 192), a comment which should be extended to include part-time work, which has grown substantially since the early 1990s.

In Great Britain, the absence of legal restrictions on the organization of working time has facilitated the diversification of work organization. Only 10 per cent of employees in the United Kingdom work 40 hours a week (and only 40 per cent usually work from 36 to 45 hours a week). In a very few cases, highly unusual models have begun to appear, for instance: working nine days during a two-week period; contracts with an annual number of hours, with a higher number per week during periods of greater activity and a small number the rest of the time; working weeks of from four to ten hours.

The homogeneous time model fostered by labour law thus no longer suits the new circumstances prevailing in the productive world. This explains the pressure building up to flexibilize working time rules, such as annualization of the employment contract or even radical measures such as the abolition of the legal working week. This notion is also challenged by the new way uncertainty is managed, which calls for a high degree of flexibility on the part of both companies and individuals.

Unless account is taken of this change in the production time system, there is a very serious risk that the effects of flexibilization and the allegedly 'necessary' reduction of working time may be misjudged. Indeed, paradoxically, it would appear that whereas we work less, we are none the less overworked. The key to this paradox can be found if account is taken of the fact that the quantitative reduction of working time goes hand-in-hand with a qualitative change. Taylorism segmented tasks and depersonalized work to make employees replaceable. Today, a substantial part of production has been repersonalized as a result of the overall shift in production towards the tertiary sector, calling for more subjective involvement on the part of the employee. A mere quantitative description of working time disregards these profound qualitative changes, which lead to a new and very complex situation where a reduction in time may be accompanied by an intensification of service (or continuing effective or 'hidden' work, such as in the case of executives).[9]

In France, workplace inspectors report a growing tendency among companies to demand a degree of after-hour availability of their employees, with no legal recognition of any kind for such overtime. Generally speaking, deregulation (backed by company-wide 'agreements') of the organization of working time makes it more and more difficult to control and therefore to obtain any practical understanding of actual practices involving after-hours work. Many abuses have been reported in very diverse lines of business.[10]

This is why labour law can no longer govern working time by applying a homogenous rule with apparently automatic effects.

Work Organization and Employment Policies

The existence of high rates of long-term unemployment in most European countries has led to the sharing of working time being seen as a possible tool to solve this problem. The various aspects of such an employment policy have been combined in different ways in different countries.

Encouraging Part-time Work
Comparison of different national codes shows that the encouragement of part-time work may have three major motivations: to facilitate the

[9] Daniel Mothé has rightly pointed out that the 'detaylorization' of work involves an increase in the 'invisible' part of work in the lives of employees. The latter are subject to increasingly stiff competition among themselves, which in the tertiary sector involves acquiring a command of the 'infomation universe'. Such competition takes places essentially after hours. That is to say, effective working time is less and less a reflection of the official duration of working time in post-industrial society (Mothé 1994).

[10] See the case records put together by the workplace inspectors from the Rhône-Alpes Region, '*La ruée vers 'heure des nouveaux temps modernes' CFDT—Voix du Rhône* No. 330 (March 1997).

reconciliation between occupational and personal life, to flexibilize employment and to share employment (Favennec-Héry 1997). At Community level, the social partners have also encouraged part-time work, subjecting it to principles of non-discrimination and encouraging movement between full- and part-time arrangements.[11] Such encouragement of part-time work involves not only labour law, as a review of national legislation shows.

In Germany, the financial incentive to resort to short-time employment ('minor' part-time work), less than fifteen hours per week at a wage of under DM610 (in West Germany) or DM520 (in East Germany), is substantial, since such jobs are not subject to social security contributions. It is estimated that there are between 1.1 and 3.3 million employees in Germany who hold such minor jobs. If the number of people holding such jobs in addition to a main job are included as well, this would account for another 500,000–2,000,000 jobs. On 14 December 1995 (C 444/93), Slg. 4744, the Court of the European Communities ruled that such a regulation is not discriminatory on the grounds of sex, even though it mainly involves women, who are thus excluded from the social security system.

In the United Kingdom, tax law treats husbands and wives as separate units, thereby favouring the model where each spouse has a part-time job. The social security system reinforces such incentives. Workers who earn less than a minimum wage (Lower Earning Limit—currently 64 GBP per week) pay no social security contributions, nor do their employers.

In the Netherlands, a bill under consideration gives workers the virtual right to move into part-time work, a right that they can demand of employers within certain limits established by law. Such a right has already been recognized under more or less mandatory terms in the laws of other European countries.

The very notion of part-time work embraces a wide range of situations which have in common only their divergence from the 'normal' working week. Part-time work is often found to be tolerated rather than chosen, particularly as far as women are concerned, and does not lead to a balanced redistribution of family responsibilities.

In France, in 1996 part-time work employed nearly 3 million people (as compared with under 2 million in 1982), the vast majority of whom were women. This increase is the outcome (difficult to measure) of financial incentives (reduction of contributions) and work-sharing policies. It may be a genuine choice (particularly among public officials), but it is more

---

[11] See: *Directive 97/81 of 18 December 1997 concerning the framework agreement on part-time work.*

often tolerated by the parties concerned, who are unable to find a full-time job. Employees with the lowest level of training and non- or low-skilled jobs are the ones mainly involved. It is centred primarily in the tertiary sector (market and non-market) and affects all age groups, although the brunt of the burden is borne by women over 40 (countering the idea that it would be above all a way of reconciling work and mother-hood) (Maruani and Nicole 1989).

Part-time work began to spread throughout the British economy as early as 25 years ago. In 1980, 21 per cent of all employees (42 per cent of the female labour force) worked part-time. In 1996, 25 per cent of employees worked part-time (44 per cent women). These proportions have not changed significantly in recent years. The overwhelming majority (nine out of ten) of part-time workers hold permanent jobs. Part-time work is highest in the service sector, particularly public services such as health and education, but also in retailing and hotel and catering services. Part-time work rates have fallen in the manufacturing industry over the last twenty years. Women are more willing to accept part-time work; as a result, there are a growing number of families in which the wife is the sole support, whereas the husband is trapped in unemployment.

Part-time work is less common in the Southern countries, but is on the rise there as well. In Spain, for instance, it has followed an upward trend, reaching 7.5 per cent in 1995 (European Commission 1996a); this is the same as the rate in Portugal and higher only than the Italian (6.4 per cent) and Greek (4.8 per cent) figures; part-time work accounted for 2.7 per cent of men's and 16.6 per cent of women's jobs. Between 75 and 80 per cent of part-time workers are women. Among men, part-time work is concentrated in agriculture, the hotel industry, retailing, and education. Part-time work among women is divided between domestic service (a little over 50.5 per cent), business services and recreational, cultural, and sports activities (12 per cent), hotel and personal services (11 per cent), education (9 per cent), and other service businesses. As far as age is concerned, the highest rates are found at the two extremes (over 65 and young adults), where they are both higher among women than men.

In Italy, the very low level of part-time working is also explained by first the greater proportion of self-employment and independent workers (in Italy about 28 per cent of the employed); and second the greater presence of small and very small firms (about 90 per cent of firms in Italy employ less than nine dependent workers). As a consequence, there is a great deal of flexibility on the labour market, since these 'organizational solutions' constitute the functional equivalents of part-time working and other forms of flexible jobs. But we have to stress also that the very low level of part-time working in Italy (as in other Southern European countries) is also due to the large number of informal and black jobs, which provide alternatives to part-time work; and a considerable increase in new forms of atypical jobs (such as contracts for continuous collaboration in Italy), which, in some circumstances, can offer *de facto* alternatives to part-time working. Finally, we should also remember that in European countries where part-time working is widespread, female participation rates are much higher than in Southern Europe. The role of the welfare state as employer (part-time employer for women) also has to be stressed. In fact, there exists a real difference between market part-time work as found in the US and the UK, where women are effectively the 'working poor' in part-time service jobs, and the Northern European models of the welfare state, where female part-time working is largely found in the public sector. For this reason, any growth in part-time working can have different effects depending on whether it is pursued following the neoliberalist model (part-time bad jobs in services) or the 'welfarist model'.

In the Netherlands, where part-time work and new kinds of organiza-tion of the division of work in young families are common, there has been a move in recent generations from the classic model with 'father at work full-time/mother at home' to an intermediate model in which 'father works full-time/mother works part-time'. This favours combining produc-tion and reproduction roles so that both partners often work part-time, usually in the service sector.

In the Dutch model, where part-time work is widespread, it is, contrary to the situation in other countries, primarily voluntary and corresponds to structured models that are sufficiently long-term, stable, and well-paid to guarantee a reasonable standard of living (Van der Heijden 1998). This long-term, flexible model of part-time work, which is accepted as well by young male workers, has produced a steep decline in the unemployment rate and explains the great interest that has arisen in the Dutch model.

Reduction in the Legal Working Week

The idea of reducing unemployment by sharing work is not new and was put forward in the 1930s during the Depression. This may have con-tributed to the development of part-time employment, but it has also led certain countries to reduce the working week or to bring the retirement age forward in order to encourage recruitment.

Germany has led this policy of reducing working time. After a massive strike, the metal-workers' union (IG Metall) had the working week reduced to less than 40 hours, initially to 38.5. In return, the union accepted flexible working time for shifts and the duration of the working

Table 3.2. Trends in part-time work

	Part-time employment per cent of total employment	
	1973	1993
United Kingdom	16.0	23.3
Germany	10.1	15.1
France	5.9	13.7
Italy	6.4	5.4
Ireland	5.1	10.8
Spain	—	6.6
Portugal	7.8	7.4
Greece	—	4.3
Denmark	22.7	23.3
Netherlands	16.6	33.4
Sweden	23.6	24.9
Norway	27.3	27.1

Source: ILO World employment 1996/1997.

week for certain categories of employees. The reduction of working time remains one of the major targets of German trade unions from the perspective of work sharing. They are today willing to accept a proportional decline in pay in exchange for hiring by employers and maintaining employment levels. The most famous of the agreements of this kind *(Bündnis für Arbeit)* was reached with Volkswagen AG. It provides for a reduction in the working week from 35 to 28 hours. Other companies have followed suit. This policy seems to be setting the pace, and flexible working time continues to spread into collective agreements.

In France the Robien Act of 30 May 1996 provides for a 10 per cent reduction in working time to create (or save) 10 per cent of jobs, entitling the employer to a 40 per cent rebate in social security contributions for the first year and 30 per cent for the following six years. Employers are offered an option between this 10/10/40–30 formula and a reinforced 15/15/50–40 formula. This act owes part of its success (as well as the criticism levelled against it) to the fact that employers gain the right to a rebate for seven years whereas, in return, they are only committed to maintain the number of employees for two years. By the end of 1997, 1,142 agreements had been signed, two-thirds of which were intended to create (and one-third to save) jobs. Thirty-seven per cent of the companies involved have reduced the working week while others have linked reductions with the flexibilization of working schedules.[12]

---

[12] Ministère du travail, Premières synthèses 98/01, No 3.

It is essentially on the basis of the results of that act that the Government elected in May 1997 made a commitment to reduce the working week to 35 hours by 1 January 2000 (2002 for companies with less than 20 employees). An act was to be adopted to that effect in 1998. This set out in detail the aid that the State will grant to companies that apply this measure ahead of the deadline and linked the reduction in working time to hiring new employees or safeguarding existing jobs. The implementation of such a reduction is a matter for collective bargaining, which may choose between an effective reduction of the working week and an annual reduction in the form of additional holidays. The employers' association (CNPF) has voiced its firm opposition in principle to such a measure.

In Sweden, the effectiveness of reducing working time in encouraging employment is being discussed. This approach is defended by the leftist parties (Gudrun Schyman) and the ecologists (Birger Schlaug), while the major trade union (LO) defends the idea that reduction of working time should be a long-term objective regardless of employment concerns. The employers' association (SAF: Swedish Employers' Federation), in turn, claims that such a reduction would have a negative impact on the economy and employment.

Recently, the Italian Government presented a proposal for a draft law to reduce the working week to 35 hours, which has prompted a vigorous debate between the social partners. At the moment, the most likely solution is a trade-off between more flexibility (contracted with the trade unions) and less working time, with public funding to encourage firms to agree to such an exchange.

Finally, at Community level, this idea has been backed by a resolution of the European Parliament (1996), endorsing the recommendations of the Rocard report: the idea is to use a sliding scale for social security contributions, which would be greatly reduced for the first 32 hours of the working week and rise sharply above that figure.

Where products and services call for high qualifications, labour—as a production factor—is an essential element in the process of the capitalist creation of value and consequently it risks becoming difficult to redistribute, as suggested by segmented labour market theories. If the prevailing work model is not redefined, therefore, the risk is that measures intended to considerably reduce the working week could ultimately encourage the holding of two jobs (double jobbers). Nevertheless, even if it is not certain that a weekly working time reduction will generate new employment, at the same time, given the large total number of unemployed people, such a possibility cannot be discounted. For the creation of value—useful value—is inseparable from the people who possess the appropriate skills.

But whatever the effects on employment, the measures taken to reduce working time or the length of working life (through early retirement) go hand-in-hand with procedures to diversify their implementation. The French case of a reduction in the legal duration of the working week is a good example. The act imposes a reduction to 35 hours, but since the cut is implemented through collective bargaining, the reduction may take a number of different forms (annualizing working time, deposits in a time-savings account, etc.) and will not be restricted to a weekly time frame. Hence, the implementation of the act will contribute to diversifying working schedules even more.

The Vicissitudes of 'Working Time' in Labour Law

The changes emerging in labour law are a true reflection of the changes observed in the organization of work. Subordinate work leaves room for non-subordinate work, which to date has been classified as a 'free' time activity. Collective disciplines decline in favour of the individualized organization of working time. Thus, a new conception of working time arises, which is both heterogeneous and individualized.

Heterogeneous Time

The idea that working and free time are diametrically opposed was based on a homogeneous notion of working time, understood to be the time spent in subordination. Once that homogeneity is lost, the boundary between free and working time is seen to be permeable, regardless of the vantage point from which it is observed.

Free Time Intrudes its way into Employees' Working Time
On the one hand, there is the entitlement to holidays or other absences which provide employees with free time without affecting the permanent nature of their (subordinate) employment contracts. A number of rights to holidays or leave[13] have arisen in recent years, all sharing the common

---

[13] The list of special holidays becomes longer every year, discouraging any attempt to draw up an inventory. See, for Italy: Giugni *et al.* (1994); for Spain: Sagardoy, Gil Y Gil *et al.* (1995); for France: *Rép. trav. Dalloz*, tôme 1, v '*Congés*' by M.-A. Bousiges; latest update: time off to care for a sick child (Act of 25 July 1994 *C. trav.* Art. L 122-28-8), and leave for international solidarity (Act of 4 Feb. 1995, *C. trav.* Art. L 225-9 s.).

feature that the contract is suspended at the initiative of the employee and the duration, in certain cases—and this varies—is equated with working time. Employees can temporarily interrupt the performance of their contracts to engage in other activities, be they private (care and upbringing of children, sabbaticals, etc.), of public or general interest (political judiciary, administrative, voluntary, etc.), or even professional (collective representation,[14] vocational or union training, founding of a business, participation in trade unions or social institutions, etc.).

In Sweden, parents are entitled to parental leave lasting 450 days; they receive a daily allowance of 75 per cent of their mean wages during the first 365 days and a flat rate thereafter. They are eligible to exercise this right until the child's eighth birthday or the end of its first year of schooling. Parents may, within certain limits, share these rights and use them to work part-time. They are also entitled to leave to care for a sick child up to 60 days per year per child, during which they also receive 75 per cent of their mean wages. That right can be transferred to a third party (a worker's parent, for instance), who receives an allowance based on his or her own income.

In Belgium, the act of 22 January 1985 introduced the so-called 'career break'. If a worker agrees with his employer to suspend his employment contract, or if he requests such a suspension under the provisions of a collective agreement, he qualifies for a (relatively low) interruption allowance paid by the National Employment Office, subject to certain conditions. Such interruption must last for at least six months. A total of five years of such leave may be taken throughout the worker's career. The employer, in return, must recruit one or more fully unemployed worker(s) to replace him.

In the Netherlands, recent legislative proposals allow employees to 'buy back' part of their yearly leave, so they can use it at their total discretion.

The new regulation of maternity leave in Italy dating from February 1998 introduces equal treatment for men and women. Accordingly, fathers will be allowed leave from work to look after children if they so request, if mothers are unable to do this or because the couple choose a more egalitarian division of domestic labour. These equal terms for maternity leave represent a real novelty in Italian family law, as they have not been granted to men until now.

On the other hand, the performance of the employment contact itself is no longer necessarily identified with subordinate working time. Instead of working, employees may, first of all, be called upon by their employers to

---

[14] The 'credit hours' for staff representatives.

take a training course concomitant with or in anticipation of the development of their jobs. Employers may also grant them a good deal of independence in the use of their time in return for the obligation to produce results (management by objective), whereby their situation is likened to that of self-employed workers (the constraints do not disappear, but are internalized).

Conversely, the Shadow of Paid Work is Projected on to Free Time
This phenomenon also comes about in two ways. The first corresponds to an extension in the scope of subordination in employees' private lives. New kinds of teleworking and the potential inherent in networking are well-known examples of such an extension, which reverses nearly all the provisions of labour law (working week, health and safety, child labour, etc.) and inextricably mixes paid working time and free time.

Much the same is true of 'on-call' practices, which fit very poorly with the traditional definition of working time. How to classify time during which employees are not working for their employers but must be prepared to respond to their call if needed? Such time is neither clearly working time nor clearly free time. It is a third kind of time, an on-call time, comparable to the 'on duty' time of certain freelance professionals (doctors, pharmacists, nurses), whose classification and legal regime have yet to be defined in labour law.

The same problem is found, finally, with certain kinds of part-time work. For example, annualized part-time work (also called intermittent work) may lead to workers losing control over the use of their time, as they may be called in by their employers at any time. Here too, the time when the worker is at the employer's disposal is classified as 'free' time. Split-shift working produces similar effects, that is the entire day is devoted to work, although only part of it is paid (Favennec-Héry 1997).

The treatment of certain periods of free time as equivalent to working time is another expression of the same phenomenon, appearing not only as discussed above in connection with employee holidays or leave, but also in activities considered to be socially useful and capable of being performed by non-employees. Three kinds of activities of this nature can be identified, and may possibly be considered to be partially equivalent to actual working time in labour or social security law:

- caring activities (care for dependent persons: children, people with disabilities, elderly people);
- vocational training activities (vocational trainee status) or job hunting (unemployed status); and finally

- volunteer activities of community interest.

Such equivalence also contributes to making the concept of working time even hazier. More and more heterogeneous, working time is also becoming less and less collective.

Individual Time

The duration and management of working time has been at the forefront of the move towards the decentralization of regulations governing working arrangements, which are set out from the top down, from the State to the individual. From act to industry agreement, from industry agreement to company- or plant-wide accord, from collective agreement to individual contract, the regulation of time is infinitely fragmented (see also Chapter 4 on collective organization).

In Spain, the Workers' By-laws of 1980 and especially the revised version dating from 1990 have left the definition of the essential features of working time arrangements to collective bargaining, to the employment contract and even to employers' management power. This has led to the development of any number of flexible forms (annualization, night work, shifts with no break for meals, etc.) which result in working time being defined differently from one sector to another, from one company to another or even from one employee to another in the same company.

In France, a wide variety of deviations from the legal framework have been open to negotiation. Collective agreements may thus increase or decrease the legal amount of annual overtime to which employers may resort without authorization. They may also implement special weekend shifts that bypass the Sunday rest rule. They may organize team work, individualized and variable working hours, and night work. They may replace weekly working time rules with multi-week arrangements (rotating shifts) or with an annually based working time.

In Germany, the collective agreement for the metal-working sector in Rhineland-Westphalia is a benchmark not only typical of that region and sector, but illustrative of a general trend. The collective agreement provides for four areas of action.

- *Total duration of working week*: From 1 October 1995, the total working week is 35 hours per week per full-time employee. Many company-level derogations are possible, however. Companies may reach an agreement with their employees on part-time working. Since 1994, the working week may be reduced to 30 hours for a company's entire staff or certain parts of the company or certain groups of employees under a specific agreement between the management and the works council (*Betriebsrat*), with no need for an individual agreement with the employees concerned. The effect of such company-wide agreements is a reduction in pay proportional to the new working week (as for part-time work). The collective agreement also allows for a lengthening of the working week.

- *Duration of working day and week*: The collective agreement does not further restrict the maximum legal ten-hour working day (without breaks) and 60-hour working week. On the contrary, it extends from six to twelve months the legal period over which an average 8-hour working day must be reached.

- *Shift patterns*: Metal-working companies establish these freely in accordance with company and customer needs. Work may be distributed over six working days (Saturday included, with no need to raise wages). The agreement provides for higher pay for non-standard working hours, but company agreements may derogate from the sums agreed. Work on Sunday and holidays is also permitted in general, but subject to premia of 70 per cent/100 per cent or even 150 per cent for 'highly significant holidays'.

- *Distribution of work over different days of the week during the year*: In addition to the measures discussed above, the agreement allows for each employee's actual working time to be adjusted to the time provided for in their respective employment contracts by giving them days off. The collective agreement does not provide for a maximum readjustment period, thereby permitting a very flexible long-term organization of labour.

The new principle governing working time is self-regulation of time: self-regulation at industry, company or workplace level, by collective labour organizations, and, ultimately, by individuals themselves, now responsible for the organization of their own time providing they commit themselves to their employer's objectives. In the light of this trend, the surrender of their time ceases to be the primary purpose of the obligation of employees, which moves from being means- to being results-based. This is, of course, merely one end of the continuum that the law presents today. Variable working hours, on-call hours, and annual scheduling of working time are the most tangible signs of a change coming about in response to the evolution of technology (teleworking, which shatters working space/time), the increased returns on capital (policy of increasing the service life of equipment) and public demand (demand for permanent availability of public or private services). All of this obviously marks the end for standard time jobs.

Directive 93/104 follows in the same vein, that is individualization of working time. Based on the protection of health and safety at work, its provisions are, with rare exceptions, of an individual nature. And it is presented as a regulation from which it is nearly always possible to derogate by agreement. It specifies that 'on account of the specific characteristics of the activity concerned the duration of working time, (may be) not measured and/or predetermined or (may be) determined by the workers themselves' (Art. 17-1). It leaves the list of 'activities involving the need for continuity of service or production' (Art. 17-2-1) open. It admits that most of its provisions may be disregarded 'via collective agreements or agreements concluded between the two sides of industry' (Art. 17-3). It also allows for (Art. 18-1-b-i) the worker's individual agreement to derogate from the maximum 48-hour working week.

This development has the potential to gradually dismantle all the community time patterns that have governed life on and off the job (night-time rest, Sunday rest, midday break) and bring about the concomitant collapse of solidarities based on such patterns (trade union, family, neighbourhood). Surveys show that some non-standard schedules (weekends, night shifts, etc.) have a strong impact on social life (isolation; disruption of family life) and on the health of the workers concerned. The latter often conceive of their schedules as a temporary situation and would prefer to return as soon as possible to schedules compatible with a 'normal' social life (Meurs and Charpentier 1987).

Laws that continue to consider working time as an objective reference, as a given in the system of working relations, will be rendered wholly ineffective by this move towards individualization and heterogenization of time. Moreover, a laissez-faire policy may endanger the continuity of the most elementary rules for the protection of workers and help to further weaken social bonds. To overcome this dilemma, time must be envisaged not only as working time, as a measure of the exchange of work for pay, but also as a subjective experience, that is to say, as time in workers' lives.

FROM WORKING TIME TO WORKER TIME

Labour law is not immune from the changes in progress. It must undergo a profound change to continue to play a role as a democratic regulator in social and economic change. It is faced with a dual challenge. First, it can no longer be confined to time as a measure of the exchange of work for pay, but must embrace workers' lives as a whole and guarantee the harmony of the various kinds of time making up these lives. But such a broadening of perspective also calls for rethinking the conditions for discussion and negotiation about time. In both respects, the treatment afforded to women will be a move particularly revealing of the change taking place.

Harmony among the Various Kinds of Time: the 'General Principle of Adapting Work to People'

The challenge today is how to make the various aspects of each worker's life mutually compatible, that is to say, primarily paid work, unpaid work, and leisure or rest. This calls for reworking the organization of paid working time in terms of a comprehensive approach to individual time, that is following Directive 93/104 (Art. 13) in implementing 'the general principle of adapting work to people'.[15] The consequences deriving from this principle affect two different spheres: for individuals, they make them masters of their own time; and collectively, they mean the preservation of time devoted to community life.

The Terms of Individual Control over Time

Working Time and Contract Time
This reworking involves, first of all, including the length of the contract in the discussion of working time. Workers' time is not only the time spent rendering their services, it is also the duration of their contract, which may or may not afford them a certain control over their time (this link between duration of contract and working time is perceived rather hazily in Directive 91-383 of 25 June 1991, which authorizes (Art. 5) Member States to prohibit the use of temporary employees for hazardous work).

From this standpoint, that is health and safety, it is commonly agreed[16] that there is a direct connection between insecure employment and work

[15] *OJEC*, No L 307/21 of 13 December 1993. The more restrictive English version uses the phrase 'the general principle of adapting work to the worker'.

[16] Including Directive 91/383 relating to non-standard jobs, in view of the stated purpose. Testimony, surveys and statistics all agree in this regard, see: *Souffrances et précarité au travail. Paroles de médecins du travail*, ouv. coll., Paris, Syros, 1994; *Le dossier noir du travail précaire*, in: *Santé et Travail*, No 8/94.

accidents. The poor understanding of hazards, plus the uncertainty about the future that characterizes casual employment, necessarily reflect back on respect for the law. It is illusory, for instance, to regulate the amount of time that lorry drivers can drive while at the same time deregulating the employment conditions for these same drivers. Community Regulation 3820/85 of 20 December 1985, which requires en route rest times (Art. 7 and 8) and proscribes payment methods that compromise road safety (Art. 10) is doomed to ineffectiveness if the driver's job is so insecure that he is obliged to accept performance levels set by his employer or supervisor. Authorizing fixed-term or 'self-employment' (drivers who rent their vehicles) contracts means accepting that accidents are going to occur. On-the-job safety goes hand-in-hand here with job security, which is the only way to ensure that the worker will be at ease in relation to time.

Non-professional Working Time

This reworking leads, secondly, to the inclusion of non-professional work in the organization of working time. This is what the directive on Young People does, for instance, when it defines a daily working time in which paid working time and school attendance time are considered together.[17] In the same vein, Directive 96/34 of 3 June 1996 on the European framework agreement on parental leave implements certain of the principles that had been previously put forward in Recommendation 92/241 of 31 March 1992 relating to child care.[18] The survey of national law shows the very practical consequences that may be drawn from such principles in terms of training or voluntary activities.

The right to vocational training entails setting time aside for such training under working time regulations. Several of the fundamental objectives of the common vocational training policy established by Decision 62/266 of 2 April 1963 directly concern the issue of working time.[19] The objective pursued by the Community was to 'implement the conditions that make the right to adequate vocational training effective for all'; 'favour, in the

---

[17]   *Directive 94/33 of 22 June 1994*, Art. 8.

[18]   *OJEC* No L123/16 of 8/5/92, p. 199, this new kind of provision should 'enable women and men to reconcile their occupational, family and upbringing responsibilities' (Art. 1); create 'special leave enabling the employed, both men and women, who so desire properly to discharge their occupational, family and upbringing responsibilities' (Art. 4); 'create an environment, structure and organization of work which take into account the needs of all working parents with responsibility for the care and upbringing of children' (Art. 5). See similar guidelines in ILO Recommendation No. 165 regarding equal opportunities and treatment for workers of both sexes with family responsibilities.

[19]   *OJEC* of 20 April 1963, p. 1338.

different stages of occupational life, duly adapted vocational training and, as appropriate, retraining or readaptation'; or 'offer each and every person, depending on his aspirations, aptitudes, knowledge and work experience and with sufficient permanent means, improvement of occupational performance, access to a higher occupational level or preparation for a new activity involving promotion to a higher level'. Such a common policy on vocational training is today explicitly addressed in the Treaty (Art. 127, Maastricht), which enjoins the Community to facilitate the adaptation to industrial change, improve continuing education and favour mobility of trainers and trainees.[20]

In addition to parental leave, Directive 96/34 mentions the right of all workers to 'time off from work on grounds of *force majeure* for urgent family reasons in cases of sickness or accident making the immediate presence of the worker indispensable'.[21]

Working Time and Leisure Time
Leisure time was developed, under the Fordist model, as time for consumption and imposed by soft techniques such as persuasion and advertising. Free time was thus converted into marketable time and its value became a function of purchasing power. In this respect, Claus Offe and Rolf H. Heinze have developed a theory of what they call the 'modernization trap' (Offe and Heinze 1992). Such a trap could be described as the convergence of three lines of evolution: the lengthening of free time; the growing uncertainty regarding the level and continuity of income; and the monetization of free time.

Different factors coincide in such monetization, foremost among which are:

- Changes in family and neighbourhood structures. Thus, for instance, separation and divorce or supporting young people for a long time during their education involve the mobilization of substantial monetary resources.
- The substitution of monetary exchange for non-monetary exchange. This substitution derives directly from the Fordist consumption rule. The tendency is particularly strong today in the service sector, as services are no longer rendered in the context of community solidarity.

[20] Quoted literally in the French text and paraphrased in the English version, because the translator did not have access to the source.
[21] See: clause 3 of the Agreement attached to the Directive.

- The increase in the prices of certain essential welfare services at rates higher than the average inflation figure.
- The general rise in the quantitative and qualitative threshold of what is considered a decent living.

However, for a growing part of the population, income is becoming increasingly precarious. Income levels are subject to change and even continuity is uncertain. This is a direct consequence of the erosion of the Fordist wage-based relationship. But it is also the result of the growing instability of family structures, since separation or solitude can involve greater vulnerability to unstable incomes (Castel 1991). The outcome is a profound alteration of the relationship to time among the most disadvantaged (Leibfried *et al.* 1998).

The outcome of these three tendencies is a decline in the *value* of free time for a substantial part of the population. Deprived of a steady income, they are also deprived of the social and cultural context that would allow them to value the growing *volume* of free time available to them. It is not illogical to consider that, in certain cases, free time is deemed a constraint, due to a lack of monetary resources, whereas working time, supple and flexible, subjectively 'involving', may be seen as a release from a daily routine otherwise bereft of all meaning.

To fail to take such dialectics into account is to founder on the optimistic and disastrous illusion that a reduction in working time is naturally emancipating. Up to now the belief has been that the struggle against inequality involved addressing the question of work; it is now recognized that reducing working time may lead to greater inequalities. The problem posed, by a general reduction in working time, is the status reserved to 'workers with no personal quality'. Indeed, it cannot be otherwise unless free time ceases to be valued in terms of monetary resources. This primarily involves incorporating, in social policy, cultural mechanisms that make a non-market-based valuation of free time accessible to all.

Preservation of Time Devoted to Community Life

Working Time and Time for Private and Family Life

Gender equality implies equal conditions for individual choice of time for paid work, unpaid work (family duties and training for oneself) and leisure time. That is to say, such equality must not be separated from the right to respect for a private and family life, as reflected in the European

Convention on Safeguarding Human Rights and Fundamental Freedoms (Art. 8-1), which has been incorporated into Community law.[22] Sound foundations for the principle of equality will be built not by refusing on principle to consider the specific private situation of employees, but on the contrary, by adapting, in a non-discriminatory manner, legal categories to such specific situations. Only the conjunction of these two principles (equality and respect for private family life) enables the reworking of the regulation of working time in terms of a broader perspective, embracing family obligations, in order to prevent such reworking from becoming a source of new kinds of discrimination.

Time taken out from wage-earning to be spent in training should also be conceived as a normal stage in the worker's career, not as a suspension of his career path. This has very practical consequences from the standpoint of labour law (re-hiring, seniority, remuneration, etc.) and social security (particularly the accumulation of pension rights). This principle of continuity has already been implemented under Directive 96/34 on 3 June 1996 putting the European Agreement on Parental Leave into effect (see clause 2 of the Agreement, §4.s). Another example is the specific prohibition of night work for women, which was a discriminatory way of conserving family time. As this prohibition was declared not to conform to Community law under the Stoeckel judgment,[23] it would be advisable for the issue, in all its breadth, to be taken up again by the Community at that institutional level, on the grounds of the equal rights of men and women to a private and family life. This right obviously entails restrictions on night work by both sexes. Directive 93/104, in fact, addresses night work from the sole standpoint of health and safety.

This question of the reconciliation between family life and the limitations of night work is but one of many aspects of a problem that is crucial to the future of Western societies. In traditional societies, order and stability were largely dependent on a hierarchical division of tasks between men and women. The industrial society arising in the nineteenth century maintained that distribution by instituting a division between masculine, measurable and negotiable time, and feminine time, unlimited and outside the bounds of the market. Our societies, by contrast, claim to be based on the principle of equality between men and women. This is a precious and fragile achievement which poses the question of the organization of time

---

[22] The normative force of the European Convention on the Safeguarding of Human Rights in the Community legal domain was confirmed in the Amsterdam Treaty (amending Art. F.1 of the Treaty on European Union).

[23] *CJEC*, 25 Jul. 1991, Case C-345/89, in: *Droit social*, 1992, 174, obs. M.-A. Moreau.

in radically new terms. It is difficult to imagine measurable and negotiable time invading the entire private sphere, even if some of the tasks performed there might yet be absorbed by marketable time (such as in new kinds of employment or a 'salary' for mothers, that is to say, the general assignment of a 'wage' to domestic chores). The private and family sphere necessarily involves this inestimable time (inestimable in both senses of the word) traditionally allocated to women. It is this time—and not only working time—that must today be conceived in terms of the principles of equality. And this entails establishing rules, for men as well as for women, on compatibility between different sorts of time formerly classified as masculine or feminine and now assigned to specific functions.

Working Time and Urban Time
By encouraging individual control over time, the law contributes to the decline of solidarities that grew out of the collective disciplines inherent in the traditional conception of working time. Such new regulations must not ignore the issue of tempos in collective life, but rather should ensure their existence. Time devoted to social life must not be relegated to merely filling in the intervals between paid work, since such gaps are disappearing. This question involves not only family life, but other kinds of urban socializing (the time for which was defined in terms of collective work-imposed disciplines). The ways public and private services, shops, and all kinds of political, trade union, and communal life operate are affected by the problem of compatibility between different sorts of time. Experiments and surveys have been conducted, particularly in Northern Italy (*tempi della cita*), with the intention of ensuring such compatibility by means of regional harmonization arrangements (time bureaux) that co-operate to adjust the various sorts of time in the cities (Mückenberger 1997, 1995, and 1998*a*).

Conditions for Discussion and Negotiation of Time

Establishment by Law of the Principles of Compatibility among Different Sorts of Time

It is no longer possible to envisage the regulation of working time only from the standpoint of companies or the organization of paid work. Any regulation or deregulation of the organization of working time brings into play the entire story, individual and collective, of human life. Now more than ever, deregulation of working time compromises the interests of society at large.

This rules out the temptation to leave the regulation of working time entirely to regulation by the employer or by collective bargaining as enshrined in current labour law. The decentralization of the source of law, generally desirable in such an area, will not be possible unless supported by general principles of compatibility among different sorts of time that only the law is in a position to establish. Since the interests of society in general are consequently at stake, law is, in a democratic society, the sole legitimate expression of such general interest and the discussion inherent in the legislative function should not be confused with the *negotiation* of specific interests. But restoring that discussion function means that law, on the one hand, establishes certain principles for the organization of time which are not subject to derogation, and on the other outlines the framework for collective bargaining, in which the issue of workers' time may be addressed in all its aspects.

The democratic problem faced under present circumstances is to manage to convert the flexibility of time imposed by the productive world into freedom subject to collective and broadly based management. Collective bargaining is still the necessary vehicle for such a conversion. But it must be profoundly rethought if it is to contribute to compatibility between the different sorts of time in workers' lives. This entails a widening of the scope of negotiation and a concomitant broadening of the circle of negotiators.

Widening the Scope of Negotiation

Such scope must be widened along at least three fronts.

One of the components of the social commitment characteristic of mass production and of its relationship to wages was that management and organizational issues were left to the employer: the deal consisted of exchanging bargaining on pay and working hours for virtually full management freedom for company executives. But negotiating working time arrangements means that bargaining also deals with organizational patterns. It is only under such conditions that the diversity of individual preferences can be addressed.

In Sweden, a recent bill on working time would require employers, within the limits allowed by company requirements, to take account of the personal needs and desires of their workers in respect of working hours.

The reconciliation of company and worker interests would fall under the scope of legislation relating to company co-management. It might also result in case-by-case arrangements with individual employees.

Free time was never an item on the bargaining agenda. It was governed by collective tempos supposedly established *a priori* in accordance with working time. This is no longer true today. Account must be taken of the schedules prevailing in government, schools, leisure time activities, etc. if account is to be taken of the fact that the value of an hour of free time varies depending on the time of day.

Training time was usually disregarded when calculating production time. It is symptomatic in this regard that training has long been low in trade union priorities (Francq 1995). This separation is obsolete today, both from the internal perspective of companies (work involves ongoing development of worker skills) and from the standpoint of workers themselves, required to be more mobile and therefore subject to continuing education. Recent tendencies in collective bargaining in certain European countries seem to indicate a growing awareness of this issue.

Widening the Circle of Negotiators

The widening of the scope of negotiable issues also entails changing the patterns of representation of the interests concerned. The Western European version of the prevailing model was essentially a 'corporatist democratic'[24] model: legitimate representation was reserved to and monopolized by a limited number of organizations, which became powers unto themselves. Preferences were assumed to be determined prior to bargaining thanks to internal representative mechanisms in unions or employers' associations. But the growing complexity of situations, along with the desirable broadening of the scope of negotiations, have rendered such a closed system inadequate. Despite their efforts to reform, unions are still associated with a population consisting primarily of stereotype workers, adult males with a dependent family, thereby leaving non-workers, non-standard workers and women out of the picture. This is a new social and cultural difficulty that has arisen around representation.

It will not be solved only within traditional trade union circles: groups that do not follow the lines of classical Fordist canons should be afforded

---

[24] In the sense of the term as used by Winckler (1976).

direct access to the bargaining table. Furthermore, users, public authorities or interest groups outside the working world strictly speaking must also be present if the logic of widening the scope of negotiation is accepted. Such broadening can only be reasonably expected to be effective if it is regionally based and on a scale whose dimensions are human, as the Italian *tempi dell cita* experience shows.

4

Work and Collective Organization

The far-reaching changes witnessed in the way companies organize work right across the European Union have been prompted by the move away from a production-based economy towards an economy where the services sector rules, by technological progress, and by market globalization. These same changes have a crucial impact on the collective organization of labour relations and on the legal mechanisms governing worker representation, action, and collective bargaining. New groups of workers have joined the labour market and there is now a need to examine employment and labour problems as a whole and not just from the traditional standpoint of the subordinated worker. These factors, together with the way the single market will work once the EMU is in place and the euro becomes the common currency, are creating new frameworks for collective representation. All in all, the social and cultural modifications that have been triggered by these changes require a dynamic response so that collective representation can be brought into line with this transformation, thereby avoiding any discrepancy between the current and future needs of work organization and the industrial model of labour relations on which the collective organization of work has been built.

The collective dimension of labour relations has always been closely related to the ways companies organize work. They in fact determine the structural framework of worker organizations on which the legal machinery for action, representation, and collective bargaining are built. In the pre-industrial organization of work, which was based on a diversity of trades, action and representation were corporatist; in such a model the price of products rather than wages were at the core of collective bargaining. In the industrial model, the craft or trade is no longer at the hub of the organization of work. Industry co-ordinates tasks that become increasingly specialized to meet the needs of mass production. In this new architecture, collective identities no longer turn on the practice of a trade but rather on affiliation with a company or industry (the respective importance of these two levels of collective organization varies depending on the country). This model has not disappeared, but now co-exists with new kinds of organization of work which change the framework of action, representation, and collective bargaining.

As society enters the new millennium, the problems of the collective dimension of labour are crying out for a new approach that takes into account factors involving change and how that change influences the different areas of production and labour relations. The impact of such change is already being felt as it makes a greater mark on the players, the way they are organized and the functions assigned to them, as well as on collective bargaining and worker participation in companies. As far as collective disputes are concerned, the overwhelming impact of unemployment has brought a spectacular decline in strikes in the private sector, although it is practice more than the right to strike that is affected by profound changes in the organization of work (except in Great Britain, where the right to strike has been subject to substantial legal constraints).

As the most dynamic institution for coping with the diversity of types of work organization, the participation of different agents and the progressive overlapping of problems (between educational systems, training and labour skills, between working time and social life or between the environment and the problems of health and safety at work, to list but a few), collective bargaining is the most suitable instrument to assimilate and adapt to change in an ongoing process. What is more, there are indications that agreements become particularly crucial in the face of social contradictions during times of change. Here, collective bargaining proves its worth as a valuable tool that can be used to ensure adaptability, provide security in the face of uncertainty and uphold the principle of equal opportunities by integrating the gender dimension.

The process of European integration, unemployment, the heightened importance of freelance and self-employed workers and the development of sub-contracting practices and stable relationships between companies have already triggered transformations that are visible in the institutions of collective work organization. With the expansion of services, the evolution of technology and the impact of EMU and the single currency, this trend is bound to continue. Collective bargaining must make tackling such realities a priority by enhancing co-ordination between the different agents involved in the production of goods and services and by incorporating the transnational dimension. Moreover, the appearance of new jobs in emerging industries throws up a challenge to the traditional view held of the collective dimension of labour relations.

Information, consultation and worker participation in companies will play a major role in collective labour relations. Community initiatives (some of which have already been approved, with others still pending approval) whose aim is to facilitate such participation in European companies will foster the importance of collective bargaining in the quest for adaptability, in the development of company competitiveness and in the consequences their decisions may bring for employment.

THE DYNAMIC OF COLLECTIVE BARGAINING

Collective bargaining has, in the last two decades, been the area of labour law most affected by legal innovations. Such innovations are of two kinds.

First, the recourse to collective bargaining is generalized. Nowadays it constitutes a mandatory stage in the formulation of law. Its empire extends beyond the realm of the law on paid work into the sphere of legally self-employed workers who are none the less financially dependent on a client firm. It also extends to new functions and objectives, covering more than the distribution of productivity gains corresponding to increases in production and the establishment of working conditions. Wherever collective agreements have a legal base, such changes will involve a transformation in the relationship between the law and collective bargaining.

Secondly, there is a fragmentation of collective bargaining. On the one hand, there is a general move towards decentralization, to agreements reached at the individual firm level; on the other, new bargaining units are appearing at the sub- and transnational levels. In addition to the diversity of forms, this dispersal adds a degree of legal complexity to the question, not to be found in conventional systems. The latter currently have no clear rules on the distribution of competence among the various bargaining levels.

Generalization of the Scope of Collective Bargaining

New Functions

The basic function of collective bargaining consisted of improving the lot of employees.

In France, this function is explicitly laid down in the Workers' Code (Art. L.132-4), which states that: 'Collective work agreements may include provisions more favourable to employees than the laws and regulations in force. They may not derogate from provisions of a public nature in such laws and regulations.' This provision draws a distinction between absolute public order, which is not subject to agreed derogation, and social public order, which defines minimum protection for employees, subject to improvements by agreement.[1] Jurisprudence has inferred, from such provisions, the existence of a fundamental principle in labour law whereby, in the event of conflicting rules, the one more favourable to employees is the one that must be applied.[2] The situation in Spain is very similar, cf. the provisions of article 3.3 of the Workers' By-laws.

The legal architecture enabling bargaining to fulfil this function varies depending on the country: from voluntary application of collective agreements (not subject to enforcement in the United Kingdom) to their direct and compulsory application to employment contracts. The mandatory effect of agreements may also be extended or enlarged, making it possible to extend the benefits of a given agreement to all workers included under, or even outside, its scope. Despite exceptions (particularly significant in Germany), such techniques, which were challenged some years ago, are nowadays generally accepted in the systems of industrial relations that acknowledge and use them.

Such mechanisms were designed to enable collective agreements to comply fully with their function of improving workers' circumstances. But since the early 1970s, many additional functions have been attributed to collective bargaining.

Flexibilization
In the 1970s, the most important change in the functions attributed to collective bargaining was indisputably the appearance, alongside or instead of the traditional function of improving working conditions, of the function of adapting such conditions to the needs of company competitiveness and flexibility. From the legal standpoint, collective bargaining appears, then, as an *alternative* to the application of the law. This alternative exists in so far as the law explicitly authorizes the conclusion of agreements derogating from its provisions (a technique called 'derogatory

---

[1] Conseil d'Etat, opinion of 22 March 1973, in: *Droit Social*, 1973, p. 514.
[2] Conseil d'Etat, 8 July 1994, *RJS* 12/94, No 1386; Soc. 17 July 1996, in: *Droit Social*, 1996, p. 1053; the Constitutional Council decided, in turn, that 'the principle whereby a collective work agreement may contain provisions more favourable to workers than the laws and regulations constitutes a fundamental principle of labour law' (C. consti, 25 July 1989, *Rec.* p. 60, *Droit social*, 1989, p. 627).

accords'). It is also to be found in auxiliary laws, which are only applied in the absence of a common-law collective agreement, or in provision laws, which do not establish a rule to be derogated from, but open up an option whose implementation calls for a collective agreement. The same kind of relationship has developed, moreover, between industry and company-wide agreements, whereby the implementation of framework agreements negotiated at the industry level depends largely on bargaining at the individual company level.

In Italy, such derogatory accords were introduced much later, in the 1980s and subsequently. Social partners are now experimenting with the '*contratti d'area*', that is a sort of collective agreement among trade unions, groups of firms, and the public authorities, to improve production and employment conditions in specific underdeveloped or socially deprived areas, mostly in Southern Italy. Such *contratti d'area* usually guarantee lower labour costs, public spending (as investment or through training policies), private productive investments and fiscal benefits for firms who accept to settle in these areas.

Still under discussion is whether such agreements can reduce minimum contractual wages, although *de facto* wages in these areas are already lower than in other industrialized regions.

The relations between law and collective bargaining are very complex and heterogeneous. Such relations depend on the respective roles that national legal systems attribute to the State and law, on the one hand, and to the social partners and collective bargaining on the other. Such relations may either be defined in terms of equality (conventional systems of organization) or of hierarchy, to ensure that the law prevails over collective bargaining (legal systems involving State intervention).

The general tendency is for the law to be devoid of substantive provisions and to be supplemented by procedural rules designed to guarantee the right to collective bargaining. Depending on the case, collective agreements replace, prolong, develop or implement legislation. In all systems of labour relations, there is a perceptible move towards greater autonomy for the social partners and companies with respect to public authority.

But such a move towards negotiated flexibilization is subject to the general framework of the law to ensure three essential functions:

- the establishment of principles and the overall objectives of social policy;
- the establishment of the necessary conditions to ensure a balance between the parties to negotiations (representativeness; new kinds of representation in small companies);

- encouragement of bargaining to favour its extension to areas reluctant to undertake dialogue. This would be the case with the French legislation on the reduction of the working week to 35 hours.

The role of public authorities is similarly crucial in collective bargaining systems that apply *ex post* extension of collective agreements (such as in France, Holland, and Germany, although infrequent in the latter country). Finally, in most European countries, the State has also intervened in bargaining on wages to curb inflation. It continues to do so, although less directly (except where the State is itself an employer, that is of public sector workers).

Company Management Tool

Since the 1980s, collective bargaining has become, in addition, an essential factor in the organization of work. In the Scandinavian countries, where this trend is particularly noticeable, collective bargaining is instrumental in co-operation in the change and organization of work. New kinds of social dialogue are thus introduced which address not only working conditions, but the organization of work. The object of negotiation is shifting, therefore, from the worker to work.

Certain aspects of the organization of work are naturally and necessarily collective: occupational categories, working hours, organization of very differentiated, specialized and at the same time autonomous jobs. This collective dimension of the organization of work finds in collective bargaining a particularly well adapted management tool. But this leads to new uses of collective bargaining. The uniformity of traditional collectively agreed regulations tends to give way to heterogeneity.

Moreover, collective bargaining becomes, at the company level, a ground for employers to exercise their management power. This is especially true of particularly traumatic decisions, such as dismissals or business restructuring. Selection criteria and the order of dismissals, social plans, compensation and measures for (internal or external) reclassification of dismissed workers have become important issues for collective bargaining.

Implementation of Legal Regulations

Other laws have vested collective agreements with the implementation of their regulatory provisions. Under this device, the legislator imposes a rule or principle, but delegates to the social partners the task of defining the specific ways in which it is to be applied. The law often provides palliative measures where there are no social partners, such as auxiliary decrees or alternative procedures to implement the rights it institutes (for example, electoral agreements). It is a well-known fact that this practice has been widely used in Community law (see, recently, the provisions for the implementation of the directive on the representation of workers in transnational companies) (Lyon-Caen 1997).

Legislative Function

This regulatory function should not be confused with participation—nowadays well delimited—in the formulation of laws, a practice which has flourished since the early 1970s in the framework of 'negotiated laws'. Important as it may be from the sociological standpoint, this legislative function of collective national cross-occupational bargaining was formally enshrined in the Maastricht Social Agreement (Art. 3), whose provisions on that point are reflected in the Amsterdam Treaty (new Art. 118A).

New Objects

The recent changes in collective bargaining affect not only its functions but also its purpose. 'Rich' collective bargaining addressed 'poor' objects. Less generous, today's collective bargaining has a more comprehensive material content. On the one hand, the approach to the traditional objects is new (with, for instance, individualization of wages, and their contingency upon production objectives and employment). On the other, negotiation deals with new issues, previously unknown or disregarded (essentially labour- and social protection-related matters).

Employment policy today plays an important role in collective bargaining, through agreements with differing degrees of legal effectiveness, which contain management commitments to create jobs or maintain existing jobs. Many other objects are now discussed in collective bargaining: worker training and occupational qualifications (initial and ongoing to enable them to adapt to technological change and the uncertainties surrounding the future of their careers); reduction/reorganization (or *modulation*) of working hours; the organization of worker representation at the company or group level; on-the-job health, social protection and supplementary pension plans (including early retirement) and their difficult financial situation; measures to combat discrimination, particularly on the grounds of sex in the context of growing numbers of female workers.

The inclusion of such issues in the scope of collective bargaining entails addressing them in a different manner, making them the object of collective exchange: wage reductions in exchange for hiring; wage and working hour reductions in exchange for temporary hiring or steady employment; adaptation of working schedules to company needs and creation of 'time-saving accounts'; interconnection between guaranteeing the jobs of employees in training and early retirement for older workers; creation of a 'security fund' to facilitate reclassification, etc.

New Subjects: Self-employed Workers

Collective bargaining and agreement techniques tend to extend beyond paid employment, serving to define the collective status of legally self-employed workers who are none the less financially dependent on a business partner. Legislation acknowledging the status of 'para-subordinate' workers (Italy) or 'quasi-employees' (Germany) provides for such workers to benefit from collective bargaining rights. And such bargaining law has, in turn, been a powerful development tool for the collective status of these workers (see Chapter 1). Even beyond such a specific status, there is in certain countries a tendency to resort to collective bargaining to regulate certain aspects of work by legally self-employed workers.

In France, for instance, a collective agreement was concluded in April 1996 between the Federation of Insurance Companies and the unions representing general insurance agents (Barthélémy 1997). Such agents, who provide commercial and consultant services, are bound to insurance companies under commission contracts. They are self-employed, but they are financially dependent upon their principals. This agreement defines the conditions for conclusion, amendment, and termination of commission contracts and contains provisions relating to the remuneration, training, and social protection of general agents.

In the area of health services, French social security laws make broad use of the technique of collective agreements between social security pay-offices and doctors' unions to regulate the working conditions of freelance doctors. These medical agreements address such diverse issues as the service price list, the framework for doctors' incomes, medical training, etc. The importance of such medical agreements has been enhanced by the Juppé reform.

As self-employed workers in Italy are a very large group, their organizations play a crucial role in economic and political national life. In particular, the *Confcommercio* which represents shop-owners, has acquired a growing political relevance, taking over the mantle of the *Coldiretti* (a farmer organization) in the 1950s and 1960s. Finally, some independent workers in the agricultural sector (small farmers and stockbreeders) are organized in 'autonomous' or *de facto* unions.

In Italy, the social partners have entered into negotiations on non-salaried forms of employment (self-employed, quasi-self-employed), with a view to affording appropriate security to workers involved in these new forms of employment. If the negotiations are successful, the government will take into account the outcome of the agreement for the preparation of a bill to be tabled in Parliament on the status of new forms of work.

This all-round enlargement of the scope of collective agreements is indicative of the profound change in the system of law. Agreement between the subjects of the law is tending to become a precondition for the legitimacy of the regulations that govern them. The authority of the law is then contingent not only upon the will of the State, but also on the will of the persons for whom the law is intended. In the same vein, at company level, managerial power will never be legitimate unless backed by the will of the persons who submit to it. The pursuit of conventional legitimacy thus inevitably leads to growth in the influence of collective bargaining. But such growth necessarily involves diversification of the law and practice governing collective bargaining.

The Fragmentation of Collective Bargaining

Until the 1980s, most collective bargaining systems had a centre of gravity, which in continental Europe was, more often than not, national industry-wide bargaining (such as in Germany, France, the Netherlands, Sweden, or Italy), or company-wide bargaining under the British model. In all of these systems, bargaining admittedly took place at various levels, but the consistency among them depended on the identification of a prevalent level of bargaining. This consistency has been lacking since bargaining has become more widespread. The most visible effect of such generalization is the weakening of the national framework in collective bargaining practice. Decentralization of bargaining, on the one hand, shifts the centre towards the company level, and on the other, new bargaining units arise which entail recentralization in ways irrelevant to the national framework.

The Move towards Decentralization: from Industry to Company

The bargaining centre is shifting from the general/national industry level (which continues to prevail in many countries, in terms of the number of workers involved) towards individual firms.

Although the extent varies depending on the country, the company is, for a variety of reasons, a 'sensitive space' for collective bargaining. The steep rise in participatory management and negotiation of the organization of work enhances the importance of company-wide agreements and the role of institutions that represent personnel at that level. At the same time, the tendency to reduce the size of companies and the relative increase in the number of workers employed by such companies pose new problems for rules of representation and collective bargaining designed for large companies. This leads to the enactment of provisions intended to make the right to representation and bargaining effective in small companies. All of this combined puts collective bargaining at the company level in a new light as regards the identity of the negotiators and the issues or objects negotiated and the bargaining procedures. The rapid growth of company-level bargaining raises, moreover, other problems associated with the relationships among the various levels of bargaining.

New Forms of Bargaining

The collective bargaining negotiators at company level are usually union delegations in the company (with bargaining systems monopolized by trade unions). However, bargaining for certain new kinds of company agreements is entrusted to other elected representatives in the firm (works councils or committees); this expansion in the duties of elected institutions to include bargaining may clash with powers vested in unions.

Such company agreements are usually characterized by the informal nature of bargaining procedures. Their functions are many and varied: restructuring, social protection or participation, implementation of auxiliary laws or provisions, or framework agreements concluded at industry level, etc. Certain national legislations require agreements concluded by elected representatives in the firm to be submitted for approval to industry joint committees on which the unions have a seat. Their effectiveness, as atypical collective agreements, varies, but they are generally recognized to have enforceable effect. Such agreements are a powerful tool for rendering company policy more independent, not only with respect to higher-ranking collective by-laws (laws and industry-wide covenants), but also with respect to individual employment contracts.

In small enterprises, the implementation of collective bargaining is hindered by the lack of institutions representing personnel. Formulas for vesting external union representatives with bargaining powers (delegations, area joint committees, etc.) meet with considerable resistance, not to say outright opposition from management, even though they may represent a good combination of many of the advantages of both centralization and decentralization. This solution has none the less been adopted in the field of the prevention of work hazards (especially in construction).

The real change taking place in Italy since 1992 (apart from the brief hiatus of the conservative Berlusconi government) is the creation of a new system of co-ordinated industrial relations. Through such *concertazione*, trade unions are now fully involved in the making of government economic policies, and as a result Italy is on the way to becoming a fully co-ordinated market economy, along the lines of those in Central and Northern Europe.

Another possibility being experimented with today in France consists of authorizing trade unions to issue a bargaining mandate to the employees of a company. A national cross-occupational agreement was concluded on contracting policy on 31 October 1995 (signed by CNPF, CGPME, CFDT, CFTC, and CGC, but rejected by CGT). This agreement, whose terms were reflected in the act of 12 November 1996, opens up two new possibilities for collective bargaining in companies where there are no union representatives. The first is to submit the agreements reached with representatives elected by staff to validation by industry-wide joint committees, which would ensure their subsequent application. The second possibility is to negotiate collective agreements with company employees especially mandated for that purpose by a representative union organization. The implementation of such new possibilities is referred to as industry bargaining.

This act was judged to be constitutional by the Constitutional Council, which refused on that occasion to recognize the existence of a trade union monopoly on bargaining.[3] Trade unions (and doctrine) (Lyon-Caen 1996) disagree strongly in their appraisal of this major innovation. CGT and FO are hostile to what they consider to be a serious derogation from trade union rights and plead for abolition of the threshold number of employees for designating union delegates, whereas the unions signing the agreement see it as a lever for the collective organization of small companies.

In general, efforts are being made in various European countries to ensure a suitable legal bargaining framework in SMEs (small and medium-sized enterprises).

---

[3] C. consti D 96-383, 6 November 1996, in: *Droit social*, 1997, p. 31.

New Problems Associated with Inter-agreement Relationships
The relationship between industry-wide and company-wide collective agreements varies depending on the country. The principles applied to prevent or resolve conflicting provisions differ (the hierarchy of agreements or legal priority of industry-wide agreements over company-wide agreements in Italy and Germany; recourse to the most favourable rule principle in France; application of the agreement adopted on the earlier date in Spain, etc.). Industry-wide agreements, however, often define the scope of agreements at company level. Whatever form it takes, this relationship is governed by relatively clear rules. The results are predictable labour costs, a certain degree of standardization of wages and a framework for competition among the companies in the industry in question.

None the less, the rise in collective bargaining at company level is hardly compatible with the maintenance of strict enforcement of agreements at industry level. Such enforcement, if construed too stringently, may prevent diversification of the right to reach agreements, necessary for the interests of companies, and thereby have a negative impact on employment. But seen from another perspective, the autonomy which company-wide bargaining is allowed should not encourage unfair competition or anti-union practices. Most national legislations have endeavoured to strike a fair balance between these two demands.

Generally speaking, the intention is to safeguard the function fulfilled by industry-wide agreements of standardizing conditions to ensure fair competition. But an analysis of present developments shows, in most countries, a tendency for company-wide agreements to evade industry-wide discipline. These centrifugal forces appear in several ways:

- softening of the compulsory nature of the provisions of industry-wide agreements, which take the form of simple recommendations;
- entitlement to derogation (escape or opt-out clauses) from general rules established by the industry agreement, so it is limited to the definition of minimum guarantees or basic principles.

In Germany, for instance, first in the East and now in the West, so-called escape clauses (*Öffnungsklauseln*) have been introduced in certain collective agreements which enable management to lower wages by a certain percentage, with the works council's consent, if the company is in financial straits. The unions try to reserve the right to veto, but they are under growing pressure to give their consent to such arrangements. This pressure is brought to bear from different sides, partly by management, but partly also by certain political forces that threaten to make such escape clauses mandatory. Under management pressure, such escape clauses are becoming more and more common in industry agreements, while no new balance has been struck between unions and industry agreements, on the one hand, and works councils and company-wide agreements, on the other.

The collective agreement for construction recently concluded in East Germany allows, subject to works council consent, the fixing of wages 10 per cent lower than the minimum wage in the industry. Such a derogation must be justified by the intention to save jobs. The local representatives of the parties to the industry agreement must be informed of the conclusion of such company-wide derogation agreements. The company agreement is valid if the local representatives lodge no written, justified objection within eight days. Such objections are justified only where the purpose of the escape clause, that is to save jobs, is not met. After such objection is lodged, the agreement is not valid until the works council ratifies the decision by at least a three-quarters majority, or two-thirds majority in works councils with only three members.

In Spain, the Workers' By-laws provide that collective agreements reached at levels higher than the individual company must establish 'the terms and procedures for non-application' of their salary schedules to companies falling under their scope of application 'whose financial stability may be damaged as a result of application thereof' (Art. 85.3c and 82.3). These are the so-called 'salary opt-out clauses'. If the collective agreement governing a particular industry does not include such clauses, a company may also opt out of the schedule by agreement between the company itself and the workers' representatives—either union representatives or elected by workers—'when warranted by the company's financial situation'. If no agreement can be reached, the differences are to be settled by an industry-wide collective agreement joint committee, which, if there is no agreement at the company level, is also empowered to establish the new salary terms that will prevail in the company that has opted out of the industry-wide agreement.

The decentralization observed in the relationship between the law and collective agreements (particularly with the development of auxiliary or provision laws) reappears, therefore, in the relationship between industry- and company-wide agreements. In any case, the importance of this move towards decentralization varies depending on the country: in some, indeed, the bargaining system continues to operate essentially at the industry level, even where such industry-wide bargaining deals more often with framework agreements.

In the Netherlands, for instance, empirical observation shows that there is no real decline in industry-wide bargaining, but rather that it is focusing more on framework agreements whose provisions are required for bargaining at the company level. At that level, on the worker side, works councils often bargain on the basis of their own particular criteria, but within the framework of the industry-wide agreement. Large companies such as Philips, Hoogovens, IBM, KPN, Heineken, and others have their own collective work agreements at company level. But that is not the general rule. Other large companies such as ABN-AMRO (banking industry), ING (banking/insurance industry), and large automobile manufacturers (DAT and Scania) work under industry-wide arrangements.

Recentralization: Appearance of New Bargaining Units

Decentralization of collective bargaining towards the company level, considered alone, reveals only part of a much more complex picture. First of all because bargaining at company level often remains within the framework established at industry level (whose content is thus changed). Secondly, because new bargaining levels are emerging, extending beyond the company level without, however, being covered by the national framework. The highest of such new levels is indisputably the group of companies, but account must also be taken of the new regions with boundaries defined by company networks as well as of Union-level bargaining.

Transnational Companies and Groups of Companies
Multinational companies and groups of companies are acquiring growing importance and collective bargaining conducted within such structures will also become more and more important. Admittedly after arduous discussion, Directive 94/45/CE did not attribute bargaining powers to the European works councils to be established in EU-wide companies or groups of companies. None the less, it is hard to avoid thinking that the effective functioning of such institutions for participation (information and consultation) will eventually include bargaining practices. Collective bargaining in corporate groups, regardless of their regional dimensions, admittedly defies the logic of industry-based bargaining, where the companies comprising the group conduct different lines of business. Conducting such negotiation poses serious problems with regard to its relationship to industry-level bargaining.

But collective bargaining in groups of companies is already envisaged in Community law following the establishment of a works council or procedure for information and consultation. This is not a true European-level bargaining process, but transnational bargaining to which the laws of one of the EU member countries apply: the country where such Community companies and groups of companies have their headquarters. None the less, if, once such bargaining is concluded, and the representative institutions created conclude collective agreements applicable to the group as a whole, this will pose the problem of the relationship of such transnational agreements to the national agreements to which the group companies are already subject.

Regional and Networked Companies

The renewal of bargaining on a sub-national regional basis is also reported in certain countries. This tendency is obviously stronger in highly decentralized States. Regional policy makers and social partners pursue social and economic promotion for their regions, including employment policies and industrial relations in the package. This may give rise to collective bargaining involving management and labour. Under its most highly developed form (regional cross-occupational agreements), such bargaining also poses the problem of its relationship to nation-wide agreements (industry or cross-occupational agreements).

Such tendencies may encourage competition among regions. They call, then, for mechanisms intended to prevent dumping, mechanisms such as those specified in Directive 96/71/EC of 16 December 1996 relating to the posting of workers in the framework of provision of services.

But there is another dimension to such new regional bargaining units which may or may not be linked to political and administrative regionalization. This involves contractual links that may arise from networks of companies. The establishment of companies at the regional level (in terms of substructures, employment, and production relations in their territory) is a very important factor in the organization of work, which may give rise to new regional collective bargaining units. The regions whose boundaries are thus drawn may or may not coincide with the ones instituted by public authorities; they may be sub- or transnational.

To the extent that companies establish long-term co-operation for the manufacture of a product or provision of a service and are linked to one another by long-lasting contractual relations (sub-contracts, interim contracts, franchises or awards, etc.), this network is the sole relevant bargaining unit in a certain number of domains. Collective bargaining in such domains is indeed the only way to harmonize certain working conditions and guarantee decision-making by the management in fact responsible for such conditions. The erstwhile classic question of the identification of groups of companies gives way, then, to the even more formidable issue of the identification of networks of companies. Solving this problem will entail determining the relationships and entrepreneurial responsibilities existing between legally independent but financially dependent companies that co-operate regularly in the provision of products and services.

The notion of networks of companies is already envisaged in certain national legislations in the form of a number of mechanisms for territorial representation, agreement, or bargaining. Such is the case with workplace delegates; possible consultation, during negotiation at the company level, with union delegates of third party firms working on the premises or workplace and under the management of the company in question; occupational or cross-occupational joint committees that may act as common collective bargaining bodies for several companies in the same local area or department. At Community level, Directive 92/57 of 24 June 1992 compels all companies working on the same building site or involved in the same civil engineering project to co-ordinate all measures relating to worker health and safety. Such co-ordination entails, most importantly, the possible creation of an inter-company collegiate body whose membership includes employees working on the site, in an advisory capacity, and the extension of certain provisions of labour law to self-employed workers.

The identification of such networks is indeed necessary in order to guarantee respect for certain rights of workers employed by networked companies. It allows for the group of companies concerned to be made jointly responsible and for co-ordination to be imposed among them (regarding pay, on-the-job safety and health and social protection). Such identification is also necessary to strike a balance in the relations among the various companies in the network; it is particularly important to prevent firms in a predominant position from abusing it by evading liability. Bargaining within networks is not restricted to the establishment of relations with paid workers, but may extend to agreements between client firms and their sub-contractors. This may involve a whole chain of sub-contracting down to the level of self-employed workers. Conducting such bargaining will perhaps also encounter the problem of the relationship with industry-wide agreements. But it has arisen in response to a need already identified by companies, as evidenced by a certain number of experiences in this area undertaken at their initiative.

The practice has given rise to other kinds of social consensus within company networks, particularly sub-contracting networks (conclusion of sub-contracting charters, which are not legally binding). Social clauses could also be introduced in the contract by and between the major company and its sub-contractors, guaranteeing that the latter's employees are duly qualified.[4] This kind of initiative might also be implemented through company-wide (but not labour) collective agreements concluded between the main company on the one hand and its sub-contractors (or self-employed workers) as a single group on the other. There are already examples of collective agreements of this nature (see above).

Collective representation and bargaining at the regional level tend, therefore, to develop as readily in the context of networks of financially stable companies as in the framework of cross-occupational bargaining instituted at the provincial or local level. This affords further confirmation of our initial hypothesis about the influence that the organizational structure of public (State, Regions, European Union) or private (companies, groups, networks, etc.) powers has on the framework of collective labour relations.

Bargaining at the Community level
Community bargaining practices—more often a question of social consensus than actual collective bargaining—are indicative of the problems affecting the organization and effective functioning of labour and management at the European level, namely the regulation of their representativeness, the clarification of bargaining procedures and the effectiveness of the agreements reached. One of the foremost manifestations of such Community-level bargaining are the agreements concluded between the CES, UNICE, and CEEP relating to parental leave and part-time work. Limited though they are, such experiences provide substance for cross-occupational Community bargaining, whose development is envisaged in the provisions of the Maastricht Social Agreement as included in the Treaty of Amsterdam.

What is now missing is the essential question of industry-wide European collective bargaining. The issue of the effectiveness of agreements arising from such bargaining and its relationships with the other numerous levels of bargaining must also be addressed.

The idea has been put forward that sectors of general economic interest, as referred to in article 90 of the Treaty of Rome, may be a suitable area for European industry-wide bargaining (Supiot 1996). To the extent that it is accepted that the economic nature of such services implies the right to

---

[4] In 1899, the Millerand decree had already provided that companies tendering for public works must respect the rules on pay and working conditions deriving from local usage in force as verified by joint committees or labour relations magistrates. The purpose of that rule was to make companies bidding for the same works respect the same working regulations; it lies at the root of the development of industry-wide bargaining in France; see Morin (1994 and 1996).

negotiate their delivery, their legal organization should be patterned along the lines of contractual relations. But this does not mean, however, an alignment with common labour law. It has already been acknowledged that imperatives of general interest may be a hindrance to free competition.[5] As far as labour is concerned, serving a general interest involves respect for the professional rules conforming to the demands characteristic of such service. Such rules ensure a balance between the particular constraints that may affect workers in these services and their compensation in terms of employment status. The definition of such professional rules is a matter that would be particularly appropriate for industry-wide bargaining at the European level. This would contribute both to the dynamism of social dialogue and to the assertion of general Community interest that extends beyond the national level, even though, to date, economic services of general interest have paradoxically been referred back to that level.

THE QUESTION OF COLLECTIVE REPRESENTATION

The issue of worker and management representation is one of the most difficult questions posed in labour law. For reasons discussed in the introduction to this chapter, such representation is closely linked to forms of organization and collective bargaining, which in turn depend on the way work is organized. This is a given, common to trade unions and employers' associations alike.

History has also illustrated the variety of forms that such representative organizations can take: purely contractual private agents; political subjects subordinate to or independent of political parties; counter-powers within the company, etc. This evolution has culminated in the dual nature of trade unions, which in addition to their private-law nature perform political and institutional functions.

Further to such general considerations, the most distinguishing feature of the system of collective representation in Europe is its extreme diversity. It is not the intention here to describe this diversity or even to conduct a comparative analysis (European Commission 1996b), but rather to measure the changes and the conservative forces within the system, in order to identify the direction in which it is liable to evolve.

[5] See in this regard: *CJEC* jurisprudence and in particular the Corbeau ruling of 19 May 1993, Case C-320/91, *AJDA*, 1993, 865, note F. Hamon.

Changes in the System of Representation

The forces bringing about the change affecting collective representation today explain the forms that such change has adopted.

The Forces of Change

New Forms of Organization of Work

The representatives defending labour's and management's social and financial interests, their profiles and traditional functions, have been hard hit by the crisis of the Fordist system and its impact on work arrangements and the labour relations established around them.

Today, company changes are producing a wide variety of kinds of firms, which define a similar number of new areas of labour relations (business concentrations and groupings, networks of firms that make use of out-sourcing and the establishment of stable relationships of co-operation, 'dependent' firms, very small firms, and virtual firms). The fragmentation of collective bargaining described above obviously calls the established structures of union representation into question. Whether it involves decentralization of bargaining towards the individual company level, or recentralization via new bargaining units (groups, networks, regions, Europe), taken as a whole the process contributes to weakening industry-wide representation at the national level.

Moreover, the trade unions' homogeneous human and social base—wage-earning, industrial, male workers with a typical open-ended, full-time employment contract—has become fragmented and diversified, as the community of interests represented has splintered. The growing diver-sification of employees and their interests, employment instability, the discontinuity of careers and the expansion of sub-contracting practices, decentralization or delocalization of production are factors that further weaken traditional union representation. The representation function has grown more complex, making it necessary to resort to representativeness techniques.

Unemployment

Mass unemployment has also contributed to the deterioration in the rep-resentation capacity of unions and its declining influence. First of all, the fear of unemployment is a powerful union demobilization factor. The vast numbers of unemployed workers dissuade those who do have a job from actively participating in protest movements.

Moreover, unemployment results in the appearance of new organizations that compete with trade unions and call their representation monopoly into question (non-governmental organizations, associations whose purpose is to defend the disadvantaged and the unemployed, charities, etc.). All unions admittedly claim to represent the interests of the jobless. But as their position in companies is already weak, unions are in fact completely absorbed by the defence of the interests of those who (still) have a job. Hence the appearance, in certain countries such as France in December 1997, of protest action driven by organizations of unemployed workers outside the trade union movement or even openly opposed to it. The question of the recognition of separate representatives for the unemployed has already been posed at the Community level. Hence the report of the Committee of Experts (March 1996), provided for in the Commission's Second Social Action Plan (April 1995), proposed, with a view to promoting the integration of social policies in the Union, the inclusion of explicit recognition in the Treaty of collective actors playing a role in civil society, in particular solidarity institutions that combat exclusion and poverty and which represent the unemployed and excluded.[6] This said, while the unions' contribution to the maintenance of overall social balance and the achievement of social cohesion is still decisive, their appropriate organization and effective functioning are still a priority issue for the European Union as well as for its Member States.

Management's Ideological Initiative
Since the 1980s, in all Member States, management has recovered the ideological initiative, subordinating workers' rights to economic constraints, demanding greater 'flexibility' in labour relations (use of insecure employment, job changes, dismissals), and marginalizing traditional union initiative in the process of the regulation of working conditions. This ideological offensive has forced certain unions to abandon a culture of conflict. Playing on management's field, labour is taking a conciliatory or co-operative approach in its action, in keeping with the preferences of participatory management. Another aspect of management initiative consists of marginalizing the forms of representation instituted by labour law, to the benefit of a management style that favours immediate, direct and ongoing contact with workers.

---

[6] Phrase quoted literally in the French text and paraphrased in the English version, because the translator did not have access to the source.

In short, in post-industrial societies, the transformations taking place in labour and capital as well as in their respective organizations are giving rise to new relations between forces. Such changes have sociological, economic and cultural dimensions that are independent of labour law. These are to be found in all European countries, but under very different forms.

Forms of Change

The Weakening of Trade Unions

The explanation for the weakening of collective representation structures observed in several countries is to be found in the new social and economic context described above. Such weakening leads particularly to a quantitative decline in membership. Whereas this is primarily true of employee trade unions, employers' associations are similarly affected, though to a lesser extent. The incentive to join an employers' association is also small: the fear of strikes or the desire to standardize competitive conditions are no longer important considerations for membership, which remains nevertheless a way of participating in the management of employers' common interests (especially in the field of training) or influencing bargaining on agreements that may be extended to the company in question.

France is one of the countries of Europe with the largest union disaffection rates. In August 1995, the journal *Liaisons sociales* reported that France was the industrialized country with the smallest percentage (9 per cent) of workers who are union members. The same journal also published a survey conducted by CFDT according to which one Frenchman in ten had 'little confidence' or 'no confidence at all' in the three major union confederations (CGT, CFDT, FO). Technological change and the introduction of flexibility in labour relations have contributed to weakening unionism. On 31 December 1989, 50.7 per cent of the companies concerned had union delegates. French unions were originally established in the secondary or manufacturing sector. In recent years, there has been a relatively clear shift in the workforce from the secondary to the tertiary sector, where union influence is weaker and therefore harder to exert. In 1962, the tertiary sector accounted for 45.4 per cent of all jobs, whereas in 1990 it accounted for 65.6 per cent. Trade union involvement is particularly weak in the domain of business services. None the less, the representative union organizations taken together obtain around 65.6 per cent of the votes cast in elections for works councils. But the number of independent representatives elected is growing.

In the United Kingdom, the union membership rate has also dropped (55 per cent in 1980; 39 per cent in 1989; 31 per cent in 1996). This rate is, however, only slightly higher among men than women. It has also declined among manual labourers and in the secondary sector, to the point that the rate is the same for them as for non-manual and service industry workers. The union membership rate continues to be much higher in the public than in the private sector, but the importance of the former has decreased with privatization and compulsory opening to competition (whereby public sector employers are obliged to allow private sector companies to make an offer to acquire the right to deliver specific services). Traditional union strongholds (coal mining, processing industry, and employment in the public sector) have declined and the rise in part-time, temporary, and female work has undermined the traditional union rank and file (male labour with open-ended, full-time contracts). However, that collapse has been mitigated by a growth in union membership among women workers. State support of collective representation has also collapsed, under union law reforms undertaken by conservative governments as part of the policy of deregulation and individualization.

The union membership rate in Sweden has been extremely high since the 1950s, due partly to the centralized bargaining system between the central social partners in the private sector, mainly LO and SAF. Later on, the public sector was included in this centralized bargaining system. The system aimed to include all wage earners and *both* the employers' and employees' organizations aimed to organize all workers and employers and include them in the centralized negotiating system. As a result, the unionization rate is now very high in Sweden. For example, around 90 per cent of the work force in the private sector are organized, and this figure has remained stable over time.

In Germany, membership of employers' associations is tending to fall among SMEs, in a move to evade industry-wide agreements. If a company withdraws from the employers' association, the agreement continues to apply to the existing employment contracts, but management ceases to be bound by new collective agreements. This possibility is used more and more frequently by employers. But the mere threat of disaffiliation forces unions to make more and more concessions. The present problem facing German unions is, therefore, less the loss of their own members than declining membership of employers' associations. It should be added that unions may demand the conclusion of collective agreements directly with employers who are not members of employers' associations, by an adherence agreement or under a specific company-wide agreement. To exert pressure in defence of such demands, they may also strike, but only the employees of the company concerned may be involved. In practice, how-ever, such strikes for concluding company-wide agreements are not called except in large companies with a strong union organization. The SMEs withdrawing from employers' associations or who never join will more than likely be spared union action and be sheltered from collective agree-ments. This works much better when in such cases works councils replace the unions as bargaining agents.

In any case, it should be stressed that the drop in union membership is not a universal phenomenon. It has not occurred in the Netherlands, Sweden, or Italy. In the Netherlands, membership of the large union con-federations did indeed fall in the 1980s, but the proportion of the labour force who are union members, which is currently rising slowly, is around 25 per cent.

Similarly in Italy, increases in unemployment and precarious employ-ment have not had the unsettling effect that they might have had on union membership. The explanation lies mainly in the particular kind of unem-ployment afflicting Italy (typically involving young adults and women in Southern Italy, who live with their families), which helps attenuate the explosive effects that this phenomenon has on society.

Movement towards Union Merger or Splitting

Collective representation is still confronted by the pluralism–unity dilemma. The growing heterogeneity of working situations is obviously a factor that strengthens pluralism and may lead to union differentiation. In contrast, the pursuit of a balance of power between management and labour is an argument for unity. Both movements can be observed in Europe.

In certain countries, there has been a dramatic regrouping of union forces. This is the case with the Netherlands, which has witnessed a sub-stantial merging of organizations, more among management than labour. There are now three employers' confederations in the Netherlands:

- VNO-NCW (major firms in industry, trade and services);
- MKB (small and medium-sized enterprises) and
- LTO Nederland (agriculture and horticulture).

VNO and NCW merged in early March 1995 to form the Netherlands Confederation of Industries and Employers. VNO was itself the outcome, in 1986, of a merger between two other employers' associations. NCW was the Dutch Christian Employers' Federation, formed in 1970 as the result of a merger between Catholic and Protestant organizations. The new confedera-tion for small and medium-sized enterprises, MKB Nederland, was also formed in 1995, from a merger involving the former Dutch Royal Federation of Small Enterprises and the Dutch Christian Federation of Small Enterprises. Also in 1995, LTO Nederland (Dutch Federation of Agricultural and Horticultural Organizations) formed a new confederation from a merger between a Catholic federation of farmers, the Dutch Royal Agriculture Committee and the Christian Federation of Farmers. The newly formed LTO has a membership accounting for around 80 per cent of all Dutch farmers.

As far as labour is concerned, major mergers took place towards the end of the 1970s and early 1980s, the outcome of which was the Dutch Federation of Unions (FNV). Here as well, the merger involved the General Federation of Unions and the Catholic Federation of Unions. The eighteen unions affiliated with FNV have a combined membership of around 1,300,000. In January 1998, five of these eighteen member unions merged to form a new union: FNV Bondgenoten. With this merger, FNV now comprises two large unions, one for the public sector and one for the private sector (food, services, banking, insurance, manufacturing, and transport).

In Belgium, there is no observable institutional merging of trade unions at sectoral or national level, although the 'common front' tactic, which is relatively frequently used, rallies unions around sets of specific demands.

In the United Kingdom, a series of important mergers have led to the creation of much stronger unions. For instance:

- the merger of three public sector unions (NALGO, NUPE, and COHSE) to form UNISON in 1993, today the largest union in Great Britain (current membership: 1,400,000);
- the merger of two primarily manual workers' unions covering most skilled workers in the manufacturing industry (AEU and EETPU) to form the AEEU in 1992 (current membership: 0.8 million);
- the merger of two primarily non-manual workers' unions (ASTMS and TASS) to form MSF in 1988 (current membership: around 0.5 million). MSF is presently considering further mergers with other office employees' unions.

In Spain, since 1987, the two majority unions, UGT and CCOO, have been engaged in a unification process, not at the organizational level, but rather in terms of joint action. The industrial federations comprising these two unions have in turn undergone a series of mergers.

In Germany, too, we see a strong tendency to mergers. IG Chemie (chemistry) and IG Bergbau (mining) have already merged. The small IG Textil und Bekleidung (textile and clothing) has fled into the arms of the strong IG Metall. In the service sector (public and private) a merger of six unions is being discussed.

In other countries, in contrast, the tendency has been to diversify or even split, more in the trade union sphere than among employers' associations. In France, for instance, opposition to the overly 'participatory' line of certain large confederations (CFDT; FEN in national education) has finally resulted in splits (leading most notably to the creation of the SUD union after splitting from CFDT) and therefore led to even greater fragmentation of labour representation in a country already characterized by the weakness of its unions.

In Belgium it should be noted that there is some debate about trade union representation of managers. While traditional unions have made huge efforts to integrate managers and their specific demands in their ranks, autonomous executive unions are emerging, and present separate lists of candidates in labour elections.

Finally, there is a tendency in some countries for employers' associations to favour bargaining with small minority unions to more readily obtain satisfaction when negotiating collective agreements. In Germany, for example, management in the metal-working industry tends to conclude collective agreements with the small Christian metal-working union instead of with the large industry-wide union. This practice breaks with the custom of treating the large unions, members of the German Union of Trade Unions (DGB), as 'unitary' unions, arrangements under which the smaller unions were only given the option of adhering to the agreements negotiated by their large counterparts. If management tries in the future to systematically play off the small unions against the larger ones, a problem will arise with the co-existence of several collective agreements with different unions in one and the same company. It is too early to know whether this tendency will take hold or whether the concessions made by large unions will suffice for management to forgo this practice.

The Rise of Company-wide Representative Institutions

The decentralization of collective bargaining to the company level and the appearance of new company-(group, network)-based bargaining units, obviously enhance the role of worker representation at such levels. The worker representation institutions elected within firms (works councils or co-operation committees) are actually the only forms of collective representation that are in a position to compete with union representation. These works committees or councils have become well-established in dualist systems of representation, the majority in European countries, with a tendency in some cases towards a strengthening of their powers of participation and control (information and consultation) and towards the acquisition of new (bargaining) powers (although in certain countries, such as the Netherlands, their capacity to bind the individual worker by the agreements they enter into is questioned).

The different dualist systems of representation in individual firms establish the relations between these elective representative institutions and the trade unions. Such relations may be based on the separation of each institution's areas of competence or on the presence of unions in the institutions representing company employees (directly ensured by awarding unions seats or indirectly via rules governing the organization of company elections). But this division of roles in collective representation is often belied by actual practice, which tends to favour elective institutions. This trend is also encouraged by legal provisions on information, consultation, and bargaining, which have consistently strengthened the roles of such elective institutions.

The German example is most indicative of such trends. At company level, works councils (*Betriebsrat*) are management's partners. They are elected by all employees regardless of their union affiliation. Works councils are independent of unions but bound to them by the fact that around 75 per cent of the members of works councils are unionized.

Company-wide agreements between employers and works councils are applied like collective agreements, directly and mandatorily to employment contracts. They may also deal with the same items (delivery, content, and termination of employment contract, company issues or organization, joint institutions). The solution to this competitive situation is provided by the act on labour organization in companies (*Betriebs-verfassungsgesetz*). This act specifies, generally speaking, that company-wide agreements are not lawful in areas for which the respective collective agreement contains provisions. But as seen above, collective agreements may contain escape clauses which allow for additional or different provisions in company-wide agreements. Management does all it possibly can to enhance the autonomy of the *Betriebsrat* with respect to unions in the bargaining process. But they meet with the resistance of the latter.

In the establishment of social plans, in contrast, the role of works councils is much more important, because the principle of the priority of industry-wide collective agreements does not apply in that sphere. In companies with a works council, there can be no collective layoffs without a social plan. If the management and the works council are unable to reach agreement, the social plan is established by a joint conciliation body under a neutral chair. To date, such social plans have essentially concerned severance pay. But recently, the tendency has been to develop actual employment plans, which naturally contributes to enhancing the role of the *Betriebsrat vis-à-vis* the unions.

In France, the suite of reforms implemented beginning with the *Auroux acts* have favoured company-wide representation. Works council powers continue to grow. The encouragement of company-wide bargaining enhances the role of the company union delegates and, in their absence, the role of the committees or delegates elected by the staff. As indicated above, the act of 12 November 1996 opens up the possibility of giving a collective bargaining mandate to elected representatives or company members mandated by the union. The agreements thus concluded must subsequently be validated by a joint committee.

The preference for company-wide representation and bargaining has led certain employers to make an even more radical proposal: a collective company-wide contract. Negotiated with the elected representatives or union delegates, such collective contracts could derogate from all the provisions of the workers' code and industry-wide agreements, subject only to the intangible grounds of fundamental social rights. This proposal, put forward by the group *Entreprise et progrès* (Entreprise et Progrès 1995), was echoed in a review recently published under the aegis of the Ministry of Industry (Ministre de l'Industrie 1997).[7]

In view of such developments, the idea that the unions today have, in law or in fact, a monopoly on the collective representation of European workers must be dismissed. In France, the Constitutional Council has decided, with respect to unions, that even though their natural task is to defend worker rights and interests, they do not hold a monopoly over the representation of employees with respect to collective bargaining: 'employees designated by election or holding a mandate ensuring their representativeness may also participate in the collective determination of working conditions, providing that neither the purpose nor the effect of their action is to obstruct the action of representative union organizations'.[8] The Spanish Constitutional Court, reasoning along similar lines, argues that the Spanish Constitution provides for broad acknowledgement of the holders of collective labour rights, without 'any enshrinement of union monopoly', whereby the right to collective bargaining is vested in any sort of labour or management representative. But it adds that 'this does not mean that there is any constitutional imprecision nor is any equivalence drawn among all subjects susceptible of performing union functions'. On the contrary, the Spanish Constitution constitutionalizes the trade union, but not other kinds of representation such as works councils, which are figures created by the legislator (Judgment 118/1983 of 13 December, followed by subsequent judgments).

[7]   See also *Liaisons sociales*, 1997, V, No 47/97.
[8]   C. consti D 96-383, 6 November 1996, *Droit social*, 1997, p. 31.

In the same vein, the importance of Directive 94/45/EC, which recognizes the dual systems of representation (union/elective) in some Member States at Community level, has perhaps not been sufficiently stressed. The core feature of EU social legislative policy is the consolidation of these participatory values in relation to the new forms of organization of work, management demands for flexibility and also worker safety. This is made abundantly clear in the Commission's recent Green Paper on partnership for a new organization of work. The Davignon proposal on worker involvement in European corporations also follows along these lines (European Commission 1997*b*).

Stable Forces within the System of Representation

The changes analysed above are not only taking place with varying degrees of intensity in the different European countries, above all they are acting on strongly conservative social structures. A rigorous analysis of European societies does not predict the immediate disappearance of the Fordist model and its distinctive features, nor that of industrial labour or of the typical worker. On the contrary, the diversity and co-existence of models or systems for organizing production and work are strengths in present-day European societies. These societies, which are in a permanent state of transition, are also witnessing the resurgence and renewal of pre-Fordist forms of labour (piecework, group contracts, home working and telecommuting, assignments of workers, etc.). The change–conservation relationship is therefore essential to a proper understanding of these transformations.

The evolution under way should not, then, be under- or overestimated. Generally speaking, it would be dangerous to conceal the deterioration in unionism caused by time, changes in the organization of work and routine and lack of adaptation. Unions must adapt their organization, that is to say their structures and their action, to the heterogeneity of the working world. But such necessary adaptation should not imply neglect of the forces that tend to conserve the system of collective representation. The stability of union law, the need for union representation and the lack of any alternative to such representation are all factors that make adaptation more likely than a revolution in the forms of collective worker representation.

Stability of Union Law

The various systems of collective worker representation, despite their extreme diversity in European countries, have not, generally speaking, undergone truly fundamental changes in countries where such systems have a legal basis. It is significant that only in Sweden in the 1970s or England in the 1980s, that is two countries where labour law was primarily of a conventional nature, that union law has been subject to major upheavals, with the State regaining control of the organization of the labour market.

In Sweden, Prime Minister Olaf Palme declared that one of the main tasks of the 1970s was to prevent technical developments from causing unreasonable consequences.[9] The changes taking place in stock companies, labour representation on the board of directors and economic democracy, another very important issue, were the subject of discussion. The initiatives taken by Parliament and the Prime Minister marked the beginning of the labour market legislation that was approved in the 1970s and which replaced the Saltsjöbaden convention and co-operation policies that had prevailed in the labour market policy of the three preceding decades. The LO president, Arne Geijer, participated in the parliamentary debate and submitted a motion to Parliament in 1971 in which he proposed an overhaul of labour legislation. That proposal gave rise to the creation of a labour legislation committee and the Government bill of 1976, which culminated in the introduction of the act on the bases for co-determination. A series of other acts on the labour market were adopted during the period from the 1970 parliamentary debates through to the introduction of the act on the bases for co-determination (MBL). The first of the series addressed the issue of labour representation on company boards of directors and led to the act of 1971 on representation on the board of directors. The act on the position of union representatives in companies came into force in 1974. However, this shift from a non-state intervention tradition, with the social partners responsible for establishing a negotiation system, to the state-intervention model introduced in the 1970s did not aim to give the state responsibility for working conditions in companies. The laws introduced were framework laws formulated on the assumption that the social partners were to follow them up with negotiated collective agreements. However, those negotiations between the

---

[9] Phrase quoted literally in the French text and paraphrased in the English version, because the translator did not have access to the source.

social partners did not materialize as expected, due to the harder and more antagonistic relations that appeared between the social partners from the mid-1970s.

Mrs Thatcher's British administration introduced legal changes intended to reduce labour's power relative to that of management. These reforms made solidarity strikes illegal, enabling employers to dismiss strikers on a selective basis (under the previous legislation, during disputes, management was only legally allowed to dismiss all the workers involved or none; they could not selectively fire workers); the definition of the notion of labour dispute, and thereby the due extension of the right to strike, was restricted; union immunity to civil process for losses incurred in the event of illegal strikes was withdrawn; balloting prior to striking was required by law (with a specified time for reflection). Such reforms weakened labour with respect to management (although the requirement to hold a vote prior to strikes could theoretically be considered as a factor tending to reinforce union legitimacy). At the same time, the government marginalized the role of the Trades Union Congress (TUC)—a body engaging in the co-ordination and representation of the union movement nation-wide—and of the unions in general by reducing the consultation of such bodies and their participation in quasi-governmental organizations, while continuing to allow employers' associations to participate. The main formal expression of social consensus was the National Economic Development Council (NEDC), whose membership included labour, management, and government. The NEDC's main role was to produce national and sectoral economic development plans. Throughout the 1980s, the NEDC was marginalized (funding was reduced and its proposals largely ignored) and finally dissolved. Conversely, management participation in quasi-autonomous non-governmental organizations was encouraged, particularly in the Training and Enterprise Councils (local, quasi-autonomous non-governmental training bodies), whose boards of directors had to have a minimum level of management representation. Union representation on such bodies was much less significant and not compulsory.

In other countries, the union role in the organization of the labour market has not been questioned and new laws have even extended certain of their prerogatives. This relative preservation of the systems of collective representation does not mean that new forms of work and employment, characterized by the decline in the manufacturing industry and the rise of services, the impact of information technology, the spread of temporary and insecure work (particularly among young adults), subsidized jobs, self-employment, and unemployment, have had no effect on the social partners in their essential function of representing social and economic interests or in their traditional behaviour and methods.

But such changes, while considerable and calling for structural and functional adaptations, do not imply the existence of an actual crisis for the social partners themselves, their representative role, or their instruments for collective action, in particular collective bargaining systems. Only the British system constitutes an exception to this rule, in which the 'Conservative revolution' of the 1980s and 1990s clearly strove to move towards total individualization of labour relations and the eradication of traditional union representation and its replacement by a more conciliatory, less confrontational approach, backed by greater involvement of union members in decision making within the union.

In pluralist union systems, the fragmentation and diversification of the community of social and economic interests represented has led to greater use of representativeness techniques to provide unions with a legal basis for their capacity to represent their constituencies. Such techniques serve to identify the partners, measure their representative capacity, ensure the legitimacy of the most representative organizations and guarantee the application of their decisions to all workers (members and non-members). Such techniques not only ensure their legitimacy in the sphere of collective bargaining, but also lay the grounds for their participation in public institutions with responsibilities in economic and social affairs as well, such as in the institutions managing social security systems or arrangements.

Legal presumptions of representativeness continue to meet with objections because they afford weakly supported unions a formal legitimacy and a series of legal powers to which they would not be entitled on the grounds of their membership base alone. None the less, in dualist systems, where elections are held for representative institutions within companies, the popularity of such unions among workers is readily gauged. Besides, presumptions of representativeness generally go hand-in-hand with (legal or jurisprudential) corrective measures intended to guarantee pluralism through the operation of the principles of majority and proportional representation.

However, not all European models are equally successful in reconciling the demands for balanced representation between employers and employees with the imperatives of labour or management pluralism.

The Need for Representative Unions

It has often been noted that management interests are poorly served by an excessive weakening of union representation; companies that have long-term success in the market are rarely those that have based their strategy on the destruction of all their workers' collective representation. This explains certain management initiatives intended to counter deunioniza-tion.

In France, new collective agreements are aimed at encouraging union action in companies. Known as union rights, or Axa accords (the first com-pany to sign one of this type), they provide for management subsidies for union activity and endeavour to improve staff career opportunities and training. These agreements show a common determination on the part of certain management and labour leaders to counter deunionization and strengthen union representation in companies. Despite the strong criti-cism levelled against this kind of agreement (Adam 1990), they constitute part of the strategies of certain unions[10] and have been endorsed at cross-occupational level by the Agreement of 31 October 1995 on contractual policy, which encourages their general application. This framework agree-ment calls for bargaining on 'affirmative action' to counter union discrim-ination at company level.

The present role of management organizations and unions does not dif-fer essentially from their historical role. Employers' associations and trade unions contribute, now as in the past, to maintaining the major social bal-ances and ensuring consensus and social cohesion, with greater or lesser management powers depending on the country. The composition of soci-eties is nowadays more complex and the interests of their members more fragmented and heterogeneous than those formerly grouped in the opposing camps of capital and labour. The stability of social order, now more than ever, hinges on the capacity of labour and management organ-izations to express this diversity while contributing to the general interest.

States, in turn, require the assistance of the social partners to ensure social cohesion. They depend on them especially for the formulation and implementation of employment policies and law. The acknowledgement of the increasing importance, in most European countries, of collective agreements as sources of labour law and collective bargaining, as a way of preventing and governing disputes, adds to the need for institutions rep-resenting management and labour.

---

[10] See: the 1991 article by N. Notat, Secretary-General of the CFDT in *Droit Social.*

Similarly, the evolution of Community law, which stresses social dialogue and collective bargaining as the preferred way of building a social Europe, makes the existence of strong and representative union organizations indispensable. The question of representativeness must, then, be posed at this level. The EC Treaty (Art. 118B) refers to 'management and labour' but does not define them. The issue of cross-occupational or sectoral bargaining has not been broached to date except in a Commission communication (14 December 1993 on the implementation of the protocol on social policy), which carries no legal weight. CES membership does not include all the unions recognized as representative at national level (for example, the CGT, still the most representative union in France, is not a member); on the management side, small and medium-sized enterprises would like to voice their own opinions.

In its Communication of 1993 on the implementation of the Social Protocol, the Commission included a list of twenty-eight organizations of social partners who may be validly consulted at Community level, a list based on the criteria of representativeness defined in that communication. As regards representativeness, this is examined in accordance with the criteria of the 1993 Communication and confirmed after examination by the Council.

According to the Commission, the representativeness of the signatories to an agreement is determined in the light of the nature and purpose of the subject-matter of that agreement, while the list established in the Communication serves to limit the number of social partners who may be validly consulted by the Commission and who may be potential participants in negotiations. Moreover, the number of participants in itself is not the decisive element for determining representativeness; other factors must be taken into account such as the negotiating mandate at national and international level, or the dual affiliation of certain national organizations to European organizations.

The Commission has recently been led to define its position in the response to an appeal for the annulment of the first directive (on parental leave) adopted to implement the first agreement reached by the social partners under the Agreement on Social Policy. The issue is therefore important because it questions the Agreement on Social Policy. This position is the outcome of an analysis of the system established by the Agreement on Social Policy. This system distinguishes three major stages: the consultation of the social partners, the possible negotiation among the social partners and the implementation of the agreement concluded with the social partners. Consultation has two phases and permits the social partners to express their views; it is compulsory where the Commission is contemplating decisions on social matters. Negotiations must take place with due respect for the freedom of the social partners. The third stage (implementation of the agreement) implies control by the Commission of the legality of the decision and of due respect for the principles of subsidiarity and proportionality, along with examination of the representativeness of the parties signing the agreement. The possibility that the Commission may not ask the Council to implement the agreement is not ruled out.

The European Union cannot reasonably avoid a genuine debate on representativeness. The self-recognition mechanism can only work in systems of industrial relations where collective agreements are acknowledged to have no legal force (as in Great Britain). But this is not the case in the EU, which, on the contrary, allots collective agreements a privileged status amongst the sources of law. Moreover, because bargaining has such normative effects, the European Commission is now the guarantor of the balanced representation of the parties to such bargaining.[11] Insofar as the social partners are involved in the discussion or negotiation of lawfully enforceable provisions, representativeness is a question of general interest and one which public authorities cannot ignore. This obviously implies that the European Union should be vested with competence in the field of trade union law to the extent required to ensure due operation of the system of consultation and dialogue set out in the Maastricht Agreement on Social Policy. But in any case, such representativeness should be in keeping with the principle of concordance broadly recognized in national law: that is to say, it should be assessed against the backdrop of the level of representation concerned. This means that it does not suffice for an organization to be deemed representative at the national level for it to be vested, *ipso jure*, with Europe-wide representation.

The Lack of Alternatives to Union Representation

Mass unemployment and the appearance of new forms of organization of work and employment obviously undermine the traditional bases of unionism and industry. And there are advocates of the idea that unions are institutions fallen into disuse, doomed to be replaced by new forms of collective representation better suited to expressing the diversity of

---

[11] See: Art. 3 of the Agreement on Social Policy, as reflected in Art. 118 A of the Treaty of Amsterdam.

interests in the working world (non-governmental organizations, feminist and ecological movements, unions of unemployed, voluntary organizations, charities, consumer organizations, co-operatives, etc.). But the facts do not confirm that such organizations are actually in a position to compete with trade unions in the representation of collective interests and the organization of solidarity based on labour.

In Italy, 'para-unions' or organizations for the unemployed, in contrast with the 'institutionalized' union movement, as represented by the CGIL, CISL, and UIL, are practically non-existent. The 'organized unemployed' in Naples are mentioned from time to time, but they are, in fact, hardly more than a handful of individuals well connected to the local or even neighbourhood solidarity networks and assistance/non-official work networks. We should, however, recall that Italy has very powerful independent unions, especially in specific sectors—like railways, airlines or education—which are able to mobilize their entire industries in specific or even corporatist struggles.

In France, the appearance of '*co-ordinations*' during the strike movements in the late 1980s (particularly in the public sector) may have been considered by some authors to represent emerging alternative forms of representation, more inclined to defend the (often corporatist) demands of their members than to fit into an overall labour strategy. But such initiatives had very little future and the December 1995 strikes showed a return to the fore of the large confederations in dispute management. Opposition to the overly 'participatory' line of certain large confederations (CFDT; FEN in national education) has ultimately resulted in union division (leading most notably to the creation of the SUD union after splitting from CFDT) and therefore to even greater fragmentation of union representation, though not to the appearance of alternatives to such representation. The unemployed movements in the winter of 1997/98 have re-opened discussion of the difficulty encountered by unions in representing the interests of the unemployed. But the associations of unemployed today seem to be no more in a position to be a lasting force able to challenge union representation than the *co-ordinations* were in the 1980s. Such associations play more of a 'goading' role, obliging the unions to include the defence of the jobless in their strategy.

Certain unions have endeavoured to broaden their scope and extend their representation to atypical forms of recruitment, to the self-employed—although, in certain countries, self-employed workers join employers' associations—and to the unemployed. Social reality is certainly rich and complex and accommodates other organizations engaged in defending interests, which are not, however, involved in labour relations and are less representative, in terms of membership, than trade unions and employers' associations. In other words, these other organizations and associations play no role in obtaining a consensus between labour and management, even though they have increased the pressure brought to bear on the political activity of the State (enabling the latter to favour dialogue with these new interlocutors). Trade unions and employers' associations continue to occupy a key place in the formulation of labour regulations and to contribute to social consensus in the broadest sense of the term.

The management association movement, in turn, continues to play a decisive role in the representation and management of employers' common interests. The appearance and development of new relations between companies and small companies leads, certainly, to some exodus from or desertion of employers' associations. But to date no organizational formulas (management clubs or reflection or opinion trusts, no matter how influential, Chambers, etc.) have appeared in any country as a true alternative to employers' organizations. Management unions, like labour unions, moreover, are strengthened by labour law, which vests certain of their decisions with regulatory force *vis-à-vis* non-member companies (particularly, techniques for extending and enlarging on collective agreements) and attributes to them a wide variety of representative functions in the public sphere.

In short, current changes in collective relations illustrate both the continuity and stability of collective subjects and the need to adapt their structures and activities to new demands, diverse occupational situations, and unemployment.

Prospects for Evolution in the System of Collective Representation

In concluding this analysis, the idea that a true revolution in forms of collective representation is possible or desirable must be dismissed. In contrast, two models for adapting the systems of collective representation emerge in view of the new forms of organization of work. The first, which prevails in France or Germany, is a shift of representative power towards employee-elected appointees in companies; the second, which prevails in the Netherlands (and may also develop in the United Kingdom), is the merging or regrouping of labour and management forces. Such regrouping allows for centralized bargaining of agreements on security/flexibility, which are then fine-tuned at company level. But neither of these models can actually work alone. Regrouped union forces need officials in companies to implement the guidelines laid down at the highest level. And conversely, representation at the company level should be able to rely on co-ordination bodies at higher levels for support. It seems, then, that each representation system has to combine the various aspects of the two models, in varying degrees. The British system has for a long time relied on union officials drawn from among the workers in a company, negotiating with management at company level, but able to draw on the resources of the wider union regionally and nationally for information, training, representation in more complex negotiations or disputes, and legal advice.

An attempt may be made to chart the possible directions of the evolution of the system of collective representation on the basis of such established facts. Such reflection turns, first and foremost, on the representative organizations themselves; a number of them have, moreover, already given a great deal of thought to the adaptation of their organizational structure and their activities to new social and economic circumstances.[12] The contribution made by 'experts' to this reflection is necessarily limited since they lack both legitimacy and the necessary practical experience. The most they can do is suggest possible evolution scenarios, to pose questions whose answers elude them. Such questions, which derive directly from the changes observed in collective bargaining, can be essentially summarized as follows: represent whom? represent why? represent how?

Represent Whom? The Subjects of Representation

The reply to this first question is essentially the same as at the dawn of industrial society. Trade unions or worker appointees are in charge of representing labour interests, whereas the employers' associations are in charge of representing management interests.

On the basis of this reminder, certain ideas occasionally suggested for the future of unionism can be ruled out straight away. First of all, the idea that the interests of both parties will spontaneously converge, making it possible to forgo collective representation law and rely on the law governing individual labour relations; the dynamism of collective bargaining stands as evidence to the contrary. Secondly, there is the notion that trade

---

[12]   See for instance Centrale de l'industrie du métal de Belgique-FGTB (1997).

unions should cease to represent labour interests *per se*, and turn themselves into agencies offering their members commercial services or defending their interests as tenants, citizens, or consumers. Admittedly, certain aspects of collective bargaining (for instance, on working hours, see Chapter 3) should be extended to represent interests other than those of labour and management; but that need does not mean confusing such interests with those of employers or employees.

The real options, therefore, lie elsewhere. They result from the diversification of employment and companies, diversification that makes the identification of 'labour interests' or 'management interests' much more complex. In this context, the real question is whether or not trade unions will be able to continue to represent the interests of all workers and employers' associations those of all management.

On the labour side, change may take two directions. First, it may focus on the hard core of the working world, that is the representation of the interests of the most highly skilled workers in the highest performing companies. Several signs of change in this regard may be observed; most trade unions seem to have real difficulties in their attempt to represent the specific interests of people with insecure jobs, women, young adults or the unemployed or those of employees of sub-contractor companies or quasi-self-employed workers. A parallel might be drawn, then, between companies focusing on their core business and unionism focusing on its main workers, who constitute the stable core of workers in such companies. The rise of company-level representative institutions is a step in this direction, as is the decentralization of collective bargaining to the individual company level. The second possible development would be, conversely, for unions to embrace the diversification of employment arrangements and include workers who are presently more or less excluded from collective action into mainstream collective representation.

On the management side, the question posed is whether or not the rise of dependent companies, essentially in the context of sub-contracts or the provision of services, will call for specific forms of representation. As pointed out above, there are already cases of collective agreements between client companies and sub-contractors. An increase in the number of such arrangements would obviously be a move towards new forms of diversification of management representation.

Represent Why? The Functions of Representation

This second question ties in directly with the change observed in the domain of collective bargaining. Such bargaining is no longer restricted to the definition of the terms of the exchange of labour for wages, but now also contributes, through varied and complex procedures, to the definition and implementation of law. Trade unions and employers' organizations are, therefore, vested with a mission of general interest, which in some ways contradicts their primary task of defending the particular interests of labour or management. Here as well, several scenarios may be envisaged. Certain trade unions or employers' organizations may wish to return to the mere defence of their members' interests and refer the question of reconciling such interests with those of society at large to policy makers; others, on the contrary, may be tempted to position themselves on broader political ground and claim the pre-eminence of collective bargaining over political discussion in all matters related, closely or otherwise, to labour or social protection issues. Between these two attitudes, there is a narrow path that would consist of arguing that trade unions and management organizations should, simultaneously, defend the particular interests of their principals and seek to reconcile such particular interests with those of society at large.

A similar question arises with respect to employee representation at company level, whether it be union or elected representation. The rise of company-level collective bargaining leads labour representatives to participate in the definition of the company's interests at any given time, and probably to influence certain management choices. Such choices may affect workers outside the company or affect secure workers and employees with insecure jobs differently. For instance, a company may seek to negotiate an agreement increasing overtime instead of hiring new staff, or to negotiate a social plan that saves jobs in the company to the detriment of employment in sub-contractor firms, or even decide to relocate the business, creating jobs in one place by eliminating them in another. In all these cases, the question posed is whether or not the function of collective labour representation is to represent the interests of workers in general or only those employed by the company where the bargaining takes place, or even those of permanent workers in such a company to the detriment of those who hold insecure jobs. One of the historical functions of European trade unions has been to prevent competition among companies in a given industry from leading to lower pay (this is the primary justification for industry-wide bargaining). Where that function has been best fulfilled (in Germany, for instance), it has had the beneficial effect of directing competition among companies towards questions of quality and competitiveness and away from the impoverishment of workers. But the industry-wide framework for that unifying function entrusted to unions has been weakened by new kinds of company organization and particularly by subcontracting, which is not subject to industry-wide agreement discipline. Companies can, therefore, play one industry against another to reduce labour costs.

In such a context, the option open to the unions is either to transform into company-level unionism or to continue to extend their scope beyond the company level in the exercise of their representative mission. But choosing the second avenue leads to another question: union organization and operation.

Represent How? Organization of Representation

Due to the imitative effect stressed at the beginning of this chapter, union organization was copied from management. The move from trade unionism to industry-wide unionism represented an important turning point in the history of unionism, which followed the lines of Fordist organization, that is based on lines of business or industries, whose boundaries, moreover, differed substantially from one European country to the next. In Europe, trade unions, like employers' organizations, were primarily organized on the lines of functional industries, where the essential features of collective bargaining developed. This marginalized not only craft-based unions, but regional forms of representation as well (the 'employment services') that played an important role in early unionism. It was therefore the industry federation which constituted and continues to constitute the backbone of unionism, in which cross-occupational groupings take the form of union federations (confederations).

Despite such similarity, there is a huge organizational difference between labour and management representation. On the management side, the true power is at the bottom, held by member companies which, in possession of the real economic power, regard collective representation along the lines of the mandate model in civil law: the representative is thus actually a proxy unable to exceed the bounds of the power with which he is vested. On the labour side, the 'bottom' has no power of its own or decision-making autonomy economically speaking, except in the form of 'wildcat strikes', whose lawfulness is not, moreover, always recognized everywhere. It is the representative, then, more than the principals, who actually holds the power in the organization.

The industry is still the main organizational framework for collective representation. But this framework is threatened by the splintering of collective bargaining observed elsewhere. First, decentralization from the industry to the individual company shifts the centre of gravity of collective representation towards the latter: employee-elected institutions or company union delegates gain, obviously, in autonomy *vis-à-vis* industry-wide federations. Secondly, the emergence of new bargaining units, whether at regional, group, network, or even Community level, inherently calls into question the role of industry-wide federations in union organization.

The present situation is one in which, by sub-contracting or forming subsidiaries, companies may evade industry-wide frameworks and diversify their opponents and their collective agreements in one way or another, obviously favouring the formulas involving the least demanding terms. Trade unions, by contrast, continue to be bound to the industry framework and cannot embrace capital's new organizational structures. The functional industry is, therefore, like an iron cage in which labour representation is locked, but whose door is open for management. In order to open the door for unions as well, the development of relevant bargaining units at the group, network, company, or regional level must be encouraged. The conclusion, on an experimental basis and taking all due legal precautions, of agreements at such different levels, allowing them to derogate from industry agreements, is one possible avenue. This would obviously favour a kind of organization of representation that would extend beyond affiliation to either an industry or a company. The sole alternative to such a development seems to be the gradual impoverishment of industry-wide union representation to the exclusive benefit of representative institutions in companies, be they union or otherwise.

Such a development would not mean the disappearance but rather the transformation of the role of centralized union authorities. Instead of acting as decision centres, they would be responsible for co-ordinating demands, action and bargaining conducted in companies or emerging bargaining units (network, group, region).

Our study confirms the necessity of this development. Although national and European organizations representing the interests of workers and employers remain indispensable, agreements between these organizations will not be sufficient to ensure an appropriate balance between management and labour interests. It is also necessary to have European law deal with the issue of company-level employee representation on two different levels: first, by formulating general conditions for companies in

the Member State and secondly by further directives for companies operating across borders. The Directive on European Works Councils as well as
the national laws implementing this directive prove that the idea of a
European social dialogue can be transferred from central to company
level. This directive has also helped to solve problems concerning
employee involvement in the European Company, so long in the making.
We welcome this development, because it allows for a combination of the
European idea, the idea of a social dialogue at the company level, and the
need to take account of national considerations.

5

Work and Public Authorities: The Role of the State

INTRODUCTION

In Western tradition, there is no durable social order without laws and institutions with which society can identify. The invention of the State in the Middle Ages and then of the Welfare State one century ago have given the West an institutional horizon to which to refer. It is that horizon that is lacking today, and it is too early to know whether we are witnessing a transition to a new kind of State or if the latter is destined to give way to other references on which social bonds are based.

With the nation-state model prevailing (at least nominally) throughout the world, such States provided the setting to build what might be called the citizens' social State. The foundations for all three mainstays of that structure—labour law, social security, and public services—are national institutions. It is obvious, though, that the State's fundamental role in this regard is being questioned today by the dual forces of internationalization and regionalization. This weakened capacity of national institutions to ensure a decent standard of living for their peoples is evidenced by the host of new pockets of unemployed or working poor. And it is accompanied by rising poverty, violence and despair, visible everywhere and especially in the very heart of the market economy, that is large urban centres in the wealthiest countries.

The 'social question' is thus making a comeback under new patterns that have yet to be legally formulated, because 'social' is a theoretically flimsy notion, which serves no purpose except as a fallacious antonym to 'economic'. Any contract, particularly any employment contract, is, indivisibly, an economic and a social bond. And contracts have no legal meaning except with reference to the State as guarantor of their legality and binding force.

The law and the State are not disconnected from economic forces or social life. They affect and are affected by them. Laws that do not take account of economic and social circumstances are unenforceable. Conversely, in today's world, the State provides a legal framework without which no economic or social order could exist. In all countries, the inter-actions between the State, the economy, and society are complex and reflect history and cultural traditions as well as traditional political div-isions. The legitimacy of the State rests on different grounds from one country to the next, grounds which determine the different economic and social expectations arising around it. This cultural and historical diversity renders developing a single European framework for regulating the labour market particularly difficult. The scope of the institutional framework for the labour market should be based on the dynamic of the interaction between State, economy and society and take account of the diversity of legal cultures.

There is universal acceptance in Europe that the modern State has some fundamental responsibilities from which it derives its basic legitimacy. These are: the promotion of law and order, personal safety and the safe-guarding of goods, the protection of property, the support of individual and collective freedom, and the maintenance of an appropriate economic and monetary framework. It is also widely (but not perhaps universally) accepted that the State has a responsibility to promote social cohesion, and to ensure the welfare of its people. However, these individual and group aspirations have become more diverse, which has presented new challenges to governments and also produced some rethinking about what is the appropriate role for the State.

Some mention must be made of the contrast often seen between two broad ways of viewing the role of the State: the authority-based or mini-mum State (*l'État-Gendarme* in French) and the protective or provider State (*l'État-Providence*). All European Union Member States in practice display elements of both, which do not necessarily conflict with one another, and strive to guarantee their citizens both freedom and security. Thus, in most countries, the State derives its authority from its ability to protect the weak-est members of society. Part of today's problems arise from the waning of State authority due to its failure to afford such protection.

The way freedom and security are reconciled varies widely from one country to the next (Bercusson *et al.* 1992). Great Britain is where the social State has proved to be most worthy of the name, in the sense that, in the Beveridge tradition, the State was directly involved in the delivery of many fundamental social rights (and this is still true today in the field of health care), whereas the other public groupings developed what might be called 'municipal socialism'. In the area of labour law, however, the prevailing system was what Otto Kahn Freund characterized as 'voluntarist' and 'abstentionist', that is based on collective bargaining without any direct legal enforcement. The alliance between Government and management over the last twenty years has entailed an undermining of the collective bargaining system and more generally a questioning of the social State model.

In Germany on the other hand, after the collapse in 1945, the State has played only a minor role in the market-based economic and social system built on a co-operative ideal known as *Mitbestimmung*. The major labour market responsibilities are entrusted to organized trades and, until very recently, the State's attempts to impose its own solutions have been doomed to failure. German economists have also theorized about this market-based social economy (a theory called 'ordoliberalism', which analyses economic relations in the light of local institutional orders and the global order in which they take place). The importance of the State's role in this 'Rhineland model' should not, however, be underestimated. Many laws regulate the labour market: for example, layoffs (*Kündigungs-schutzgesetz*), maintenance of pay in the event of illness (*Entgeltfort-zahlungsgesetz*), job creation (*Beschäftigungsförderungsgesetz*), or the organization of work in companies (*Betriebsverfassungsgesetz*). Although there is no State-wide minimum wage, such regulation has an indirect effect on pay. Since the most important working conditions are regulated by law, trade unions are free to concentrate all their efforts on wage increases and the reduction of working hours. Furthermore, wage levels are kept high by the level and duration of unemployment benefits.

The French model is different from both. Theories on the role of the State were thoroughly overhauled at the beginning of this century by Council of State jurisprudence and the work of legal writers such as Duguit or Hauriou, who reversed the concept of the minimum State. Whereas the latter is held as a power which individuals must serve, the social State, in contrast, is conceived to be a force at the service of individuals (and hence the predominant place reserved to public service in that design). In the sphere of labour relations, the State intervenes to impose social law and order, which re-establishes the balance between the parties to employment contracts or collective agreements. In such a design, the State appears first and foremost as the guarantor of respect for the principle of equality among its citizens.

The point at issue in the political and legal debate is not the nineteenth-century concern over the choice between intervention and laissez-faire, but rather the State's ability to continue to ensure social cohesion in today's world. Broaching that question entails understanding the changes affecting the role of the State today before embarking on projections as to how that role is likely to evolve in the years to come.

THE CHANGING ROLE OF THE STATE

The Factors of Change

We do not undertake here an exhaustive analysis of the factors involved in the changing role of the State in Europe. Only two will be addressed, in view of their relevance to labour law and social security.

Individualization

What all EU countries appear to have in common at the present time is the general retreat of the State at national level. The speed at which this retreat is taking place varies depending on the country, but there are no exceptions to the general shift of responsibilities from the State to the individual, the enterprise or mutual organizations. Part of this movement has been due to the re-emergence of the idea that individuals have responsibilities as well as rights.

Part of the reason for this shift has been an increasing desire on the part of citizens to take greater control over their own lives. Some of the most important social developments of the last generation, such as the rise of the women's movement, have been based on the ideals of freedom of choice and opportunity for all. Moreover, the aspirations and expectations of citizens and consumers have diversified considerably. This has been aided by changes in production technology, which have made small batch production and frequent changes in specifications much more feasible.

The days when you could have any colour car as long as it was black are long gone. The motorist of today is expected to choose not only the engine size of his car, but the colour, the colour of the seats, whether or not it has air conditioning or a sun roof, the type of brakes, and the exact model of hi-fi system. The car will then probably be built to order by the factory and delivered within three weeks. Taking the same approach as they do as consumers, citizens are no longer satisfied with a State and public services that do not take account of their individual needs and aspirations.

More generally, there has been increasing recognition that the ability of the State to control events, as opposed to influencing them, is more limited than the founders of the post-war States believed. Thus, until the 1970s, States believed that they had both the ability and the responsibility to support demand in the economy. The view now is that since the State cannot stabilize domestic markets, it should aim to ensure that the economy has the ability to respond to structural or circumstantial changes (by ensuring, for instance, access to education and training and promoting competition).

In the labour field, most people would agree that it should also act to prevent discrimination, and promote health and safety at work. Going beyond that, the debate about the role of the State is more open (see below).

European Integration

The European Union is witnessing two major trends that should bring about radical changes. On the one hand, the advance towards Economic and Monetary Union (EMU), the central pillar of the Maastricht Treaty, and on the other the enlargement planned by the third phase of EMU. These two trends should be kept under control as part of a pre-enlargement strategy to ensure that enlargement does not lead to the compartmentalization of Europe. The control of these developments, the management of the unpredictable, the maintenance of the dynamics of integration also call for true institutional reform to be tackled at Union level.[1]

Regarding the operation of labour markets, the Treaty of Amsterdam has paved the way for new actions that have already been politically translated into the *Guidelines on Employment*, adopted by the Council meeting in Luxembourg on 15 December 1997.

This new strategy for employment rests on four pillars, namely:

- *Employability*, which accords priority to investment in human resources, the improvement of skills and vocational qualifications in the struggle against unemployment, particularly among young people. Quantified targets have been set, equivalent to the criteria of economic convergence.

---

[1] On the impact of European integration on national labour law, see the survey of the German experience by Hanau (1997).

- *The enterprise culture*, centred on the need to foster the spirit of initiative and the creation of business undertakings by appropriate social, fiscal, and administrative measures.
- *Adaptability*, which involves adjusting the institutional and legal framework to the organization of work and new forms of employment. The social partners at national or Community levels are invited to play a major role in the establishment of such a framework and to participate actively in its implementation. The European Commission has often stressed that this approach represents a break with the old debate on regulation/deregulation, insofar as it seeks to reconcile flexibility and security of labour. This is a global approach designed for the long term.
- *Equal opportunities*, which should be embodied in each of the above-mentioned pillars. The correction of inequalities, particularly the reduction in women's unemployment rate relative to men's, is not only a question of social justice; it also addresses an economic need, bearing in mind the anticipated fall in the active population in the coming years, which should favour the entry of a growing number of women into the labour markets.

All the Member States have implemented these guidelines in National Action Plans for Employment, which they submitted to the European Commission on 15 April 1998, and of which certain elements have been included in this book. In May 1998, the Commission issued a communication containing a preliminary assessment of the results. A programme of social convergence has already been set up: economic integration and social integration are linked by the Treaty of Amsterdam.

The transition to EMU, which represents the crowning achievement of the single market, is a powerful vehicle for integration. It is a major step, some even see it as the prelude to political integration, a leap in the direction of political Union. The single currency certainly commits the future of Europe and the future of its citizens. The latter must be in a position to understand the potential and consequences of this fundamental choice in favour of the euro: this transparency is necessary in order to foster a direct relationship between the European Union and ordinary citizens, to dispel the mixture of fear and enthusiasm currently felt by public opinion. This involves the risk that citizens, workers in particular, may begin to feel that the European Union is little more than an economic and monetary machine, governed by capitalist logic intent upon destroying national schemes for social cohesion. Social issues, particularly employment and social rights, should occupy a central place in the Union.

Of the outstanding issues, those concerning the social consequences of the single currency and particularly employment are priorities today. There is no consensus among economists about the impact of monetary union in this regard. On the one hand, the implementation of the euro may provide for a stable environment in which macro-economic shocks can be handled more appropriately and speculation of the kind affecting the Asian currencies during the crisis in late 1997 can be avoided. Such a stable economic environment would enable healthier growth, allowing investment development to focus on new productive capacities and thus encourage the creation of jobs. On the other hand, however, the single currency involves the risk of greater competition on the basis of lower labour and tax costs. That risk is all the greater because the price transparency as a result of the single currency will facilitate comparison. Such practices may lead to a questioning of social cohesion and undermine the dynamic of European integration. This risk arises in particular from the fact that after monetary union Member States will no longer be able to use devaluation as a way of making necessary adjustments. Moreover, their workers are neither as mobile as in the United States nor is the Community budget at all the same as a single nation's Federal budget. There is some danger, then, that flexibility, particularly on wages, will become the only adjustment factor. In this context, where collective bargaining has an important role to play, trade unions may be placed under a good deal of pressure.

In view of such questions and uncertainties, the group believes that the European Commission should undertake a study without delay to evaluate the social impact of the single currency on collective agreements, particularly on wage bargaining.

The euro should also bring about an acceleration in movements of capital within the single market, the first signs of which are now visible. In the capital markets, a traditionally Anglo-Saxon shareholder culture is beginning to take root on a European scale. Companies are becoming more and more sensitive to the needs of shareholders and increasing interest is being accorded to the financial participation of workers in firms. By eliminating the risks of investment within the Union, the transition to the single currency favours transnational investments and the acceleration of capital movements, which will no longer depend on the disparities between monetary policies but will be concerned exclusively with the search for efficiency within the euro zone. It is likely that pension and insurance funds will increasingly make use of the new possibilities which the single market affords them to invest in the capital of foreign companies, as American pension funds already do. These developments, which are already observable, need to be studied more thoroughly insofar as they are likely to give rise to company takeovers and may have an impact on employment.

The creation of the euro should ultimately facilitate the recognition of a legal status for Europe-wide companies, organizations that are essential to the effective operation of a pan-European market. Given such legal standing, companies established in more than one Member State will be able to conduct their business throughout the Community as a single European firm governed by a single body of rules under the supervision of a single head office, with no need to set up a complex network of subsidiaries subject to different national laws. Europe-wide companies will encourage further restructuring, whose possible consequences for employment need to be anticipated. More generally, Europe-wide company status cannot ignore the situation of workers. For this reason, the proposal for their regulation goes hand-in-hand with the proposal for a directive on organizing worker information, consultation and/or participation in European companies and acknowledgement of their place and role in such companies. All kinds of cross-border restructuring (mergers, joint ventures, takeovers, company groups) that may affect employment call for a legal framework to take account of workers' interests. This implies that laws governing collective labour relations must be swiftly adapted to capital's new geographic structures.

This discussion of European companies illustrates how social, economic and monetary aspects are closely related and need to be treated as a whole. Any economic decision made at European level should be contingent upon preliminary proceedings intended to limit the social consequences of that decision. This is all the more necessary since the Member States taken individually are still themselves unable to provide national solutions to problems arising from decisions taken at European level with a transnational impact. It is inconceivable, for instance, to liberalize services in a particular sector without prior analysis of the impact of that decision on employment or workers' rights in the Union and without an associated and suitable social policy, wherever warranted. The European level is often the most appropriate place to solve questions requiring transnational social treatment, such as the directives on European Work Councils, Posting of Workers, the draft directives on Transnational Mergers (10th directive) or the creation of a legal status for Europe-wide companies.

Certain economic decisions made at Community level may have social consequences in only one Member State; this is the case, for instance, with Commission decisions on State subsidies. The Group feels that the social partners should be more directly involved in the procedures leading to such decisions where they may have an impact on employment. The rationale for hearing workers' representatives in the Court of Justice of the European Communities if they challenge a Commission decision relating to competition should be the subject of an in-depth review.

The tasks incumbent upon Community institutions must be defined within the bounds imposed by the principle of subsidiarity. This leads to the general issue of subsidiarity. Although the traditional way of viewing subsidiarity is within a pyramidal, hierarchical system, the emergence of the Community level should not be analysed in this way, because the sovereignty of Member States is not, in principle, subject to the authority of the EU. Subsidiarity calls for the distribution of sources of law at the most appropriate level. That is to say, it involves a constant discussion of which level is the most appropriate. Wherever such a level is not the Union, subsidiarity involves the diversification and differentiation of legal rules. This is equally true of *'vertical'* subsidiarity (between the Union and its Member States) and *'horizontal'* subsidiarity, between the law and collective agreements (Bercusson 1996). This means, in practice, that collective bargaining becomes a legal power. In certain cases, the results will be better, but in others they will inevitably be worse. No consensus has yet been reached on this issue and there is a dearth of analysis on the risks inherent in this kind of transfer of responsibilities towards the private sector.

The key question in the employment field is whether in future the social partners are likely to be able to take over the role which the State has traditionally occupied in many countries in the field of labour market regulation. How far is the State necessary as an intermediary between the social partners, or between companies and the market?

Protection of Social Rights

Universal Social Rights

Equality among Citizens
One of the widely accepted functions of the State is to enforce the principle of equality among citizens and, most particularly, to combat discrimination at work. In France, Italy, and Spain, there is a general legal prohibition against discrimination on a wide range of grounds. In France, for example, this includes place of origin, lifestyle, political opinions, and family situation. In Spain, it includes 'opinion or any other personal or social condition

or circumstance'. Further, all EU countries have legislation that make it unlawful to discriminate against women (and generally against men as well). These laws extend to discrimination on the grounds of marital status, except in the UK, where discrimination is prohibited against married people but not against those who are single, widowed, or divorced. In general, gender discrimination laws have been transposed from Article 119 of the Treaty of Rome, and are therefore reasonably uniform.

In Belgium, the act of 4 August 1978, which transposes the European directive of 9 February 1976, guarantees equal treatment for men and women with respect to access to employment and training, working conditions and dismissal. It should be noted that the act entitles anyone unfairly treated to institute proceedings, including workers' representative organizations. Moreover, it is important to note that it attributes injunction powers to the judge: the judge may enjoin the employer to put an end to such a discriminatory situation under penalty of penal sanctions.

There is specific legislation preventing discrimination on grounds of race or ethnic origin in Sweden, the Netherlands, the UK, and Germany. Legislation covering other forms of discrimination is rarer. Sweden, the Netherlands, and Germany cover religion. Germany and France cover age (the latter in advertisements). Sweden, Germany, France, Spain, and the UK cover disability.

In most countries, there remains a gap between the legal prohibition of discrimination and actual outcomes for traditionally disadvantaged groups. Legal proof of discrimination tends to be difficult.

Access to Public Services

Ensuring all citizens have equal access to a certain number of what are considered to be essential services enhances individuals' rights, while making them more universal. While found under different formulas in the various countries (Moreau 1996; Centre Européen des Entreprises à Participation publique 1995; Cartelier *et al.* 1996), it is in France that public service theory has been most fully developed. Its connections with employment are as strong as they are misunderstood: the nature of the labour market varies depending on whether vocational training, for instance, is considered primarily to be a matter covered by public service, that is the State, as in France, or a matter for private enterprise, as in Germany, or the market, as in the UK. Considering vocational training to be a right or otherwise is tantamount to promoting or otherwise the principle of equal opportunities on the labour market (it all depends on the specific content attached to the acknowledgement of such a right). Similarly, whether or not energy, health care, transportation, or child care

are considered as collective benefits or otherwise has a profound impact on the shape of the labour market and the lot of workers.

The content of the very concept of public service differs from one country to the next. Thus, for instance, access to the health care system is regarded as a public service in the United Kingdom or Italy, but as social insurance in France or Germany. There is, indeed, no such thing as a natural public service, since service can barely be conceived if it is not provided by funding that is subject to market logic. Public service is always an institutional construct that rests on the choice of which services are to be permanently and equally accessible to all. Such choices may depend on technical considerations (territorial registration of technical networks, for instance, but the argument is equally valid for motorways, railways, or electric power lines) or economic factors (reduction of transaction costs; prohibition of *de facto* monopolies), but it is always ultimately a choice of values that identify the State and contribute to the definition of citizenship. Such choices inevitably entail offsetting the costs involved in the universality, continuity and equality of the service rendered and thus restricting competition. They also entail redistributive effects, which ought to be assessed to obtain an accurate view of their social significance. But where such choices lack universal support, they will obviously be vulnerable to the opening up of an international marketplace.

It may be expected that the notion of 'service of general economic interest' set out in article 90 of the Treaty of Rome would provide the basis for defining what a general Community interest might be, which would, in turn, contribute to consolidating the European Union. But an organic (deriving from the legal nature of the service provider) rather than a material (deriving from the nature of the service rendered) criterion has prevailed in the definition of such services, while article 90 has become a basis for national renderings of general interest, rather than providing an opportunity for dynamic reflection on the notion of European general interest.

There have also been differences in approach to the provision of welfare services: direct provision by the State (*Etat gérant*) or services provided by private or mutual bodies, subject to the rules set by the State to guarantee all citizens equal access to such services (*Etat garant*). In France, Germany, and Belgium, there is a long tradition of the State setting standards for, supporting, and guaranteeing a welfare system based on mutual organizations, joint institutions in which the social partners are involved or which are subject to locally based democratic controls.

In France, many public services are not managed directly by the State and its officials, but by public companies whose staff are in an intermediate situation: parties to private law employment contracts, their collective by-laws are none the less defined by governmental regulations (hence the name *entreprises à statut*) rather than by collective agreements.

In all European countries, there is a shift on the part of the State away from organizing economic services of general interest. Beginning in the UK, this movement has gradually reached the Continent, where it has taken on diverse forms. The general tendency has been to exclude services of general economic interest from the public sector and entrust autonomous legal entities, which may be public or private, with their management. The purpose everywhere has been to design legal structures adapted to the opening to competition and therefore to internationalization and decentralization, as well as to the establishment of contractual relationships with users, today more often considered to be customers.

In the case of postal services, for instance, a recent survey shows that, of fifteen companies in the countries studied, seven were still considered to have public administration status in 1990, whereas none were so considered in 1996. Other examples of public sector autonomous bodies include: the switch in 1988 of Sweden's *Statens Jarnvagar* (railways) or the Italian *Ferrovie dello Stato* (in 1986), and the German postal services (1994) to public sector companies. In the case of transfer to private entities, privatization may involve legal status only (commercial company whose sole shareholder is the State: for example, the creation in 1994 of the *Deutsche Bundesbahn AG*, a stock company wholly owned by the State in Germany, or the *Vatenfall* in Sweden in the electricity industry, in 1992) or be economic in nature (privatization of capital: for instance, in Great Britain, the electricity industry since 1990, telecommunications since 1984). An extreme case is the split of British railways in 1994 into twenty-five Train Operating Units headed by the British Railways Board. Decentralization dates from quite some time ago in certain sectors, such as electricity in Germany, which is related to the federal nature of State structures.

But this movement has not resulted in total privatization anywhere, which would mean, purely and simply, bringing services of general interest into line with commercial law. Even where such reforms have been carried out most strictly, such as in Great Britain, the State has never withdrawn from the scene altogether and continues to be the ultimate guarantor of the provision of services of general interest (Deakin 1998). This is the reason for the establishment of regulatory authorities in charge of overseeing such provision. Cases in point are, for instance, the *Eisenbahnbundesamt* in the recent reform of German railways or the British rail regulator, or the *Svenska Kraftnät* established following the reform of the electricity industry in Sweden or Great Britain's Office of the Electricity Regulator in this same industry.

The prevailing trend has been towards greater autonomy rather than privatization: services of general economic interest win their independence from public powers but remain separate from services provided by private powers. Such a trend is not unlike the outsourcing practised by private sector companies. However, there are several models of outsourcing, depending on whether the sub-contractor is considered as a partner bound to the principal by a long-term co-operation agreement or as a completely independent and liable supplier. The development of outsourcing for State services has not yet settled down into either of these patterns. However, certain negative experiences with privatization reveal the risks of an approach based exclusively on customer/supplier dynamics.

One of the most noteworthy aspects of this trend from the legal standpoint is the establishment of contractual relations between the State, public service providers, and the beneficiaries of such services. The move is from a regulatory and hierarchical system to a contractual and egalitarian one, with all the concomitant effects such evolution brings, especially in terms of diversification and heterogenization of legal situations.

This leads some authors to consider the State as an equal party to contracts, with no more rights than the other parties to the contract in question. This analysis is acceptable as long as the State acts in defence of its own interests as a legal person (to administer its own estate, for instance). By contrast, when it acts in representation of general interests, it may not be placed on exactly the same level as the private interests with which it negotiates, unless it disappears as a State. This is the core difficulty in contracting public services: having to maintain a hierarchy between public and private interests in a legal framework that treats all interests equally. In this perspective, the establishment of contractual relationships should be conceived as a means for defining the general interest rather than as merely a means of accommodating the general to private interests.

Fundamental Social Rights

The Treaty of Amsterdam, due to come into force in 1999, improves the existing provisions relating to fundamental rights. Among the improvements, mention should be made of the new article L, which gives jurisdiction to the Court of Justice in cases of violation of fundamental rights, within the framework of the first pillar; article 13 on the prohibition of discrimination, the Community-wide regulation of a certain number of questions previously included in the third pillar (immigration, visas, rights of asylum, refugees' rights), the enlargement of Community competence regarding equality of opportunities between men and women (Art. 14). It is also worth noting the reference to the *Social Charter* of the Council of

Europe and to the *Community Charter of Fundamental Social Rights of Workers*, the principles of which are to guide Community social policy (Art. 136), as well as the inclusion of a new Chapter on employment and the incorporation of the Social Protocol in the Treaty. Finally, reinforcement of equality of treatment and pursuit of a high level of employment are also among the principal objectives of the European Union.

The group has noted the creation by the Commission of a High Level Group of Experts charged with examining the situation of fundamental social rights under the new Treaty of Amsterdam and tabling recommendations for action at Community level. In this context, and since the new Group of Experts on fundamental social rights was due to submit its final report in December 1998, the Group feels that there is no need to undertake an exhaustive analysis of fundamental social rights issues at Community level in the present report.

None the less, our Group feels that, in this context, progress needs to be made in several areas, namely:

- Reinforcement of the right to free movement (including the free movement of workers) and the extension of that right to non-Community nationals legally established in the European Union. Special attention should be given to the situation of non-Community workers. Essentially, fundamental rights are not based on nationality. Furthermore, social rights associated with work are not based on nationality, but on legally performed work. The many problems arising around the issue of non-Community workers could not be studied at any length by the Group, so a specific, in-depth review of this issue is recommended.[2]
- Resolution of the contradiction between the social partners' right to conclude collective agreements at Community level (Art. 139) and the prohibition of legislation on matters relating to trade union rights under article 137(6).[3]
- The need to establish, by appropriate means, a European framework for information and consultation in companies operating on the single market.

---

[2] A review might be carried out on the basis of the (1997) report by the High Level Group on free movement of people chaired by Mme Simone Veil and the interesting initiatives envisaged or already implemented by the Commission in this regard. Generally speaking, there is little worker mobility within the Union, and the European Commission has recently adopted an action plan (Commission Communication of 12.11.1997 COM (97)586) to improve perspectives and encourage the free movement of workers.

[3] See in this regard the discussion in Chapter 4 on the problems of trade union representativeness at Community level.

- The need for recognition in the Treaty of the role assigned to non-governmental organizations in the formulation and implementation of Community social policy.
- The pursuit of action taken at Community level to combat discrimination, especially on grounds of race.
- The implementation of the fundamental principle of adapting work to the worker, particularly in the context of working time.[4]

In this context of fundamental social rights, the Group has studied the potential of the notion of European social citizenship. The ambiguities in the concept 'citizenship' should be stressed, as the meaning of the term varies depending on national legal cultures.

In the United Kingdom, citizenship would seem first to refer to the individual's rights with respect to the community, which may encroach upon his autonomy (State, trade unions, monopolist companies, Europe, etc.); which means, for instance, that the citizen should not be bound to a given service provider but must be able to exercise his right to choose. Today, such an approach tends to confound citizens' rights with consumers' rights. The strength of this approach, however, is that it is not linked to a given State or nation; it claims to be as universal as the market to which it relates.

In France, on the contrary, citizenship refers first to equal participation in public affairs. The definition is primarily political, with very little economic or social content. It is closely related to the Republic and the concept that one may have of it. To the extent that the Republic is acknowledged to have public service missions, citizenship leads to the demand for equal and effective provision of such services to all, and to refraining from challenging the monopoly thus exercised by the State or public companies.

In Germany, there are reasons to believe that the success of the notion of social citizenship among certain authors is not unrelated to the community culture that characterizes that country. Citizenship tends to be translated as community membership, rather than in terms of an egalitarian concept of the Republic or the defence of individual rights as opposed to group forces.

The meaning of citizenship depends necessarily, therefore, on the definition of State in each country, which differs even today. The difficulties to which this may lead in defining true European citizenship are readily imagined, with each country tending to extend its own notion to the Community as a whole. In this context, the notion of social citizenship

---

[4] See Chapter 4.

does not seem to be immediately operational at the Community level. This should not, however, mask the actual legal potential of the concept. Social citizenship is the individual equivalent to social cohesion. It entails recognizing each person's equal capacity to take full and active part in the social and economic life of his or her respective community, a capacity based on rights guaranteed by the State. And it reflects individual participation in the life of institutions, including, as appropriate, participation in decision making. At the Community level, the specific social content is still limited (equal treatment in comparison to nationals),[5] but it may become a melting pot for a common concept of European Union social responsibilities.

Social Security

In all the countries of the Union, social security systems are ultimately covered by the State. But there are important differences in whether the State itself handles social security (as a public service) or limits its role to establishing a regulatory framework for a social security system managed by the social partners.

In the UK, the role of the State as direct provider of the key elements of the social State is nearly as well-developed as it is in Scandinavia. The Beveridge tradition has meant that health care, social insurance, social protection, and care services are all currently still direct State responsibilities, although in recent years there has been a move to sub-contracting care services for the elderly in particular. The British National Health Service has become Europe's largest employer.

In the field of social security, the French and Belgian position has been to attempt to combine the Beveridge model with a 'social democracy' ideal. Instead of it being the State that directly administers social security, this mission has been entrusted to the representatives of the insured. The roots of the concept lie in particular in historical traditions and the vitality of the Proudhonian, mutualist, or Catholic Socialist experience, which mistrusts State intervention in social matters. Even more characteristically, the unemployment insurance system has never been in the hands of the State, but rather is based on a cross-occupational collective

---

[5] It should none the less be stressed that labour law directives adopted at the Community level (Working Time, Protection of Young People at Work, Part-Time Work, Parental Leave, Worker Transfers, etc.) are applied independently of whether the workers involved are Community nationals or otherwise.

agreement; the State only intervenes subsidiarily, in the event of failure of the conventional system. Similarly, characteristically, the Juppé social security reform (1995) upholds that autonomous tradition, attempting merely to reconcile it with budgetary discipline. Such reconciliation is no longer sought through authoritarian action (under principles of legal protection), but rather by conventional techniques.

Social insurance systems are often based on the Fordist model of working life, that is in which workers were male, were employees, worked full-time, and supported families. In that model, not all of them reached retirement age, but those who did had a life expectancy of only a few years (typically three to five years after retirement). The amount paid in retirement pensions was very small compared to the income of employed workers.

Those who did not work as employees fell into three groups: the wealthy, who could be expected to take care of themselves; dependants of workers, who would be covered by the worker's insurance, and the farmers and small business and professional classes (shopkeepers, lawyers, doctors, etc.), who were regarded as people who had responsibility for themselves, and who were not subject to the decisions of employers. In insurance terms, they involved in any case a higher risk of fraud in that they could make themselves unemployed or regard themselves as sick, or make their own choices about when they retired. This is one of the reasons that early social insurance schemes excluded them from their scope of application.

Today, however, the relationship between social insurance and employment is substantially less direct. Patterns of work have become more diverse. With the development of women's employment and retirement pensions, fewer adults are wholly dependent on other adults. Unemployment has become structural and more long-term, and is concentrated among particular groups in the population: the young, the over-50s, immigrants, and the unskilled. Many of these groups have not fully established their rights under social insurance rules, because they become unemployed soon after their entry into the labour market, or suffer repeated unemployment which does not allow them to develop sufficient credits. Another essential factor of imbalance in social insurance systems is that life expectancy after retirement has gone up from three to five years to twenty-five to thirty years. This means that pension schemes are confronted with payment levels that were never envisaged when they were first established.

The composition of the self-employed has also changed. No longer is self-employment mainly the preserve of the traditional professionals and the small business proprietor. Many skilled manual workers (such as plumbers or carpenters) are self-employed. The same is true of people who have relatively scarce skills and can therefore free themselves from dependency on a single employer (systems analysts or industrial designers for example). In addition, there is the emergence of the new self-employed over the last twenty years: shoe repair people, sandwich delivery services, shirt ironing services, etc. These people have little or no financial capital tied up in their businesses, so unlike the traditional self-employed, they have no business to sell to finance their retirement. They are selling their labour in the same way that employees do. The only difference is that they sell it to a variety of different employers. These people too need the standard social insurance protection, and they do not always get it. In Italy, for example, the self-employed enjoy very few social insurance rights.

The different branches of social security are evolving along different patterns in Europe today. On the one hand, family allowances and health coverage acquire universality and are thereby no longer associated with employment. The move in the retirement pension system, on the other hand, is in the opposite direction, with increased reliance on contribution funding reinforcing the link with employment. The former fills in certain gaps in the social protection afforded 'non-standard' employees. The latter, however, lowers the likelihood that such 'non-standard' employees will be able to benefit from a full pension.

The desire to adapt the social protection system to new kinds of employment has led to the development of social minima that act as safety nets for people with such jobs. This is the case, for instance, with State pension allowances in the Netherlands, Income Support in the UK or the minimum old age benefit in France. In Germany and Spain, there is increasing reliance on a system of complementary benefit, that is not based on contributions. In Belgium, there is a process of reform under way which it is attempting to shift some of the costs from employer contributions to general taxation. In Sweden, the unemployment insurance system is independent and run by the trade unions.

The recent evolution of the Spanish social security system is characterized by

- reinforcement of contribution funding, restricting access to contribution-funded benefits;
- the relative growth of benefits with universal coverage, with a concomitant shift to an 'assistance'-type system;
- the separation of the sources of financing for contributory benefits (social security charges) and non-contributory assistance (State contributions), an operation to which the unions have given their consent but

which poses essential questions with respect to the future of the system and its financial viability.

In contrast, compulsory social security tends to play a lesser role among people with good jobs, who are encouraged to insure certain social risks on the private market. In the Netherlands, for example, health insurance is divided between private insurance for those whose incomes are above a certain threshold and compulsory insurance for employees and system beneficiaries with incomes below a certain sum. In Netherlands and Sweden, employers take responsibility for income security based on 80 per cent of an average income for a worker. In Sweden, employers take responsibility for this payment for the first two weeks of sick leave, but after this period sick leave is paid by the state insurance system (*Försäkringskassan*). In the UK, employers are only responsible for the first six weeks.

In the UK, a majority of the current working generation will derive their main income after retirement from their secondary pensions, not from their State pension. The shift towards secondary pensions is also taking place in France and Germany and in Spain. The pension issue is a matter of concern in all European countries. Governments are changing the terms of State pension schemes, so that the basis on which people have made decisions in planning for their retirement will no longer exist. These changes relate both to the age at which pensions are paid (many are being raised) and to the rate at which they are paid relative to earnings.

There have been some recent suggestions in the UK that State pensions should be subject to an income test, although there have been no formal proposals to this effect. Relations with private provision institutions (either through invested savings schemes or through employer pensions) are based on a contract rather than on the discretion of the State, which may change with changes of government. People may expect legal guarantees to be sounder in such cases. But scandals such as the Maxwell affair may ruin that trust if the State fails to establish a legal framework to protect the interests of those taking out retirement plans.

If these tendencies become more widespread, a new kind of social law will make its appearance, instituting minimum solidarity between two distinctly different categories of workers, on the basis of their respective status: on the one hand, workers in a position of strength, whose social protection will be increasingly based on private insurance; and on the other the weak, whose status will be independent of their contracts. The essential characteristic of such a law covering the weak is that their social protection is not linked to their employment contract but rather results from minimum solidarity measures, organized essentially at the national level (hence the present expansion of minimum social coverage). The employment contract would be gradually emptied of its protective content, to become a 'bare contract', while social protection would no longer be geared to the employment contract but would derive, rather, from minimum social guarantees financed by the State (Supiot 1995*b*).

Subjecting family allowances to income tests, a measure recently adopted in France, is a good example of such evolution. The centre of gravity of social security shifts: it is no longer a matter of compensating everyone for the costs of having children, but exclusively of bolstering the incomes of the poorest families. The logic behind the British family credit[6] is similar, since payment of that benefit, reserved to self-employed workers or employees with at least one dependent child, is subject to income levels. The difference is that the family credit is also subject to minimum employment conditions and plays a role in workfare, to supplement low pay.

While there is no change in vocabulary (solidarity is still the term used), the State's role changes radically. Instead of basing solidarity on the possibility of *risk*, where everyone is expected to give (contributions) and receive (benefits), it reverts to public charity, that is solidarity based on *need*, where the better off give but receive nothing in return whereas the poor receive but are not expected to give. The Welfare State, where everyone's link with the social security system is bilateral (everyone is both debtor and creditor of everyone else's security) gives way to an assistance State, where the bond is unilateral (some citizens are social security debtors while others are system creditors). This shift, which is already visible in the course charted for health insurance in the Netherlands, family allowances in France or the retirement system in the United Kingdom, is the result of the desire to constrain social spending, concentrating such spending on the most disadvantaged, while the middle and upper classes are referred to savings or private insurance for protection against risks. The danger of such a trend is, obviously, that it leads to the institution of a dual society, where the notion of social citizenship will no longer have the same meaning for all.

---

[6] Now replaced by the Working Families Tax Credit, which is more generous and is paid through the tax system, but which is based on the same underlying principles.

Organization of the Labour Market

There are important differences in the way the social State has developed in the various European countries. In the United Kingdom and the Nordic countries particularly, the question of the regulation of working relations has not been considered to come under the direct responsibility of the State, whereas in most other countries, it has been regarded as a primary function.

Diversity of Conceptions of the Role of the State

No two European countries view the State's role in labour relations in the same way. None the less, three overall models of intervention can be distinguished.

In the 'Continental' model, the State acts as protector of the weaker party in labour relations. The purpose of its intervention is to mitigate the inequality between the parties to the employment contract by vesting workers or their representatives with minimum rights from which employment contracts or collective agreements cannot derogate.

The Spanish constitution of 1978 defines the Spanish State as a 'Social and democratic State subject to the rule of law' (Art. 1). According to the Constitutional Court (Rulings 3, 8, 14, 63 and 75/1983 of 25 January, 18 and 28 February, 20 July and 3 August, among many others), that expression means that the State guarantees respect for the principle of social equality and the correction of inequalities. 'The legislator, when regulating labour relations, must necessarily consider categories and not particular individuals and, aware of the social and economic inequality of workers with respect to employers, attempt to reduce it by establishing adequate measures to ensure equality. The specific nature of labour law derives therefrom, whereby, through the application of indeterminate rules that are indisputably bound to the principles of freedom and equality of the parties on which contract law is based, it provides a way to compensate and equalize by, partially at least, correcting essential inequalities' (Ruling 3/1983, legal grounds, 3). This doctrine is echoed in Ruling 14/1983, also referred to above, legal grounds, 3.

In France, given the background of weak collective bargaining, which has led to the risk of unequal relationships between employer and employee, the State acts to underpin those relationships and to set limits to the terms to which the parties to the employment contract can agree. Such intervention is warranted by the fact that employees effectively give up some of their civil rights when they enter into an employment contract. Furthermore, because of the weakness of collective bargaining in many parts of the economy, the law seeks to establish a standard 'social public order'.

In Belgium and the Netherlands, civil society is strongly self-organized. The State is not perceived as an *external* force as it is in France, but works alongside social groups, acting in partnership with them rather than directing them. In Belgium in particular, trade unions are closely linked to political, cultural and social associations around which Belgian society is organized, and express themselves politically through parties that often head government coalitions. This means that there is a close connection between labour market institutions and other political and cultural institutions.

In Germany labour law has its origins in the Bismarckian social State, but it is now mainly part of the wider legal framework. The post-war philosophy of ensuring checks and balances and the development of consensus has led to the prime importance given in labour law to collective agreements. The concept of the social market economy is important in making the connection between the economic sphere and the social State.

In Italy, the picture is mixed. There is a tradition of a minimum State, leading to little regulation in many areas, but with strong and detailed regulations in others. The social State is not very well developed except in the field of pensions, where it is unusually generous, but only for employees. The self-employed remain excluded. There remain many sectors where collective bargaining is undeveloped, and where enforcement of regulations is not strong, alongside Fordist industries and the public sector, both with strong collective bargaining and observance of regulations.

In the British model, on the other hand, the State only intervenes to place industrial relations outside the scope of common law and to thereby guarantee the possibility of making autonomous arrangements for such relations, primarily based on collective agreements which have no legal force. This so-called 'voluntarist and abstentionist' system has none the less evolved enormously in the last forty years, first of all with the enactment of Continental-type laws under Labour administrations, and then under Thatcherist policies of weakening union power and the individualization of labour relations and finally under the impact of Community law, which requires the transposition of certain European directives into law. None the less, there is a persistent tendency to consider that social protection should be wholly separate from labour law, where voluntarist tradition with minimum State intervention continues to prevail. The Scandinavian model also differs from the others. As in the Continental model, the State acknowledges its responsibility to establish a general framework for organizing the labour market. Specifically, it establishes a legal framework for collective agreements. But, in contrast, as in the British model, it tends to refer the question of individual labour relations to the social partners. The Nordic philosophy is that the State should take responsibility for labour market policy and unemployment insurance, but what happens at the workplace is a matter for employers and employees to determine.

More generally, however, there are examples of developments in the social State being reflected in labour market regulations. For example, there has been a shift away from State monopoly in the provision of employment placement services, with the development of private placement agencies. This has happened in Germany, the Netherlands and Sweden. In Italy, job placement services remain a State monopoly, but the service places less than 5 per cent of new recruits.

These tendencies reflect both the wider changes in the role of the State, but also the shift towards a demand for greater freedom of choice in all aspects of life.

The State and Collective Bargaining

Collective bargaining has already been addressed in Chapter 4 on the collective organization of work. The discussion here will be limited to certain observations on the State's role in this regard. The shift in the centre of gravity of labour law from the legal realm to collective bargaining is a feature common to all European countries. This has two general consequences. First, there is growing recognition that collective agreements freely entered into by both parties may be more beneficial than a regulatory framework. The traditions in Germany and Sweden in particular allot a primary role to collective bargaining and limit the degree of State intervention in the terms of these agreements. But more generally, it is increasingly common for regulations (at both EU and national level) to contain derogations for collective agreements. This means that the State transfers certain responsibilities hitherto acknowledged to be its own to the social partners.

The State's role is also evident in the technique of extending collective agreements, a practice which is quite widespread in Europe (for example, in Belgium, the Netherlands, Germany, and France). In Spain, extension of another kind is legally possible, but is not used, since collective agreements are generally effective *ex lege*. Generally, one of the parties (sometimes both or all) to the agreement has to request its extension. In the Netherlands, extension can only take place if the majority of the workers in the industry are already covered by the agreement. The State seeks to avoid undercutting or social dumping. If all those in an industry are bound by the same agreement, then it is not possible for one company to take market share from another based on their inferior treatment of their workers. They have to be more innovative or more productive to achieve that.

In the UK and Sweden, there is no extension of collective bargaining to those who are not party to it. Collective agreements are valid only in those workplaces where the employer was directly involved in the agreement, either on an individual company basis, or as part of an employers' association. In Sweden, most workplaces are covered by national collective bargaining arrangements, but in some companies there are supplementary local agreements. In the UK, most bargaining is at company level.

In Belgium, there was a long history of national collective bargaining covering a wider range of issues than employer–employee relationships. In effect, the State endorsed and implemented the decisions reached by the social partners. However, the budgetary crisis in the early 1980s meant that the State for the first time imposed limits on negotiators, and in practice this resulted in the State taking and imposing key decisions in a way which had not happened before.

More generally, there are some concerns that the institutions of collective bargaining are not necessarily as well developed in all countries as they need to be in order to deliver the increasing weight of responsibility placed on them. There are clear differences between countries in how well-established collective bargaining is in different sectors. There is also debate about the status of collective bargaining agreements which are in effect regulations. In particular, if they are regulations, are they subject to cancellation or amendment by the courts or by legislative process?

The State and Collective Representation

Institutions for Representative Rights

Collective rights have traditionally been important in the field of labour law, which has tended to provide protection to all workers, or to groups of workers. In Italy and Belgium, this remains firmly the case. However, in France and Germany there is growing emphasis on the rights of workers as individuals. In France, individual freedoms and trade union pluralism have contributed to the general weakness of both trade unions and collective bargaining. In Germany, the deregulation of labour law has been concentrated in the sphere of collective rights, thus changing the balance between the individual and the collective. This has had the effect of strengthening works councils at the expense of trade unions.

In the UK and in Spain, in contrast, the shift has been in the other direction. The traditional emphasis has been on individual rights, but increasingly the law is defining collective rights. In the Netherlands, the legal framework contains a mixture of individual and collective rights. In Sweden, rights are given to the individual, but the enforcement of those rights is difficult unless it is done collectively. But the individual does not have the right to remove himself from a collective agreement which covers him, which provides a balance in the other direction. The overall pattern is convergence, with most systems now based on a mixture of individual and collective rights.

As regards the legal treatment of trade unions, there is no clear single trend. In some countries (for example the Netherlands and Sweden), they are treated the same way as other voluntary associations. In others (for example Italy, Spain, and Germany), unions meeting specified criteria (national unions in the case of Italy) have special privileges. In Belgium, trade unions, in contrast to employers' organizations, refused to apply for legal personality under the terms established in the act of 1898 on professional associations. This refusal is justified on several grounds: the list of members must be public knowledge; civil liability suits may be brought against the association; there is an obligation to submit yearly financial statements to a ratification committee, and so on. For similar reasons, the unions refused to become not-for-profit organizations (act of 1921). None the less, despite the fact that they have no legal personality or the associated rights, workers' representative organizations are recognized by the legislator to have some specific capacities to take legal action and to sue in civil actions. Legal doctrine readily refers in such cases to 'restricted legal personality'. In the UK, trade unions have both special privileges and special obligations.

Institutions for Consultation with the Social Partners
In some countries, institutions reconciling and advising the social partners play a major political role. This is perhaps at its most developed in Belgium. The *Conseil National du Travail* (National Labour Council) formulates 'all expert opinions or proposals regarding general problems of a social nature involving employers and workers' (Act of 29 May 1952). These recommendations are addressed to the ministers or Parliament on the Council's own initiative or at its behest. In practice, such recommendations play an extremely important role. Certain laws provide that no executive measures can be taken without hearing the Council; certain (exceptional) executive measures cannot be taken without its consent (Act of 16 March 1971) or its unanimous consent (Act on Employment Contracts of 3 July 1978). In certain fields, the government may act only upon the proposal of the Council. The Council, in short, may express its opinion on conflicts regarding competence arising between joint committees. The social partners also participate in the Central Council for the Economy.

In the Netherlands, the long tradition of consensus building is reflected in the National Social and Economic Council, which is the main national advisory body, and the Labour Foundation, a private institution in which the major federations of trade unions and employers work together. The Foundation discusses issues of major economic importance with the government. For example, it concluded a landmark agreement in April 1996 on flexibility and security. It also produces guidance for collective labour negotiations. Similar institutions exist in Sweden.

In Spain, there is a national Economic and Social Council, with similar bodies at the autonomous regional level as part of the wider social dialogue. In Italy, the National Council for Economy and Work is an institution for the consultation and involvement of the social partners in social and economic issues. Its real influence and importance is limited, however. The same may be said of France's Economic and Social Council.

In the UK, the only national consultative body, the National Economic Development Council, was abolished by the Conservative administration, and there is no sign of any desire on the part of the Labour administration to revive it. However, the social partners continue to be actively involved in the Health and Safety Commission, which is responsible for all matters relating to health and safety at work. In Sweden there is a National Board for Occupational Safety and Health, on which the social partners participate.

Institutions for the Resolution of Collective Disputes

This is an area in which, generally speaking, the development of Fordism has meant a shift away from the use of the courts towards systems of collective reconciliation and arbitration conducted by the social partners. This tendency is the outcome of the growing emphasis on collaboration and co-operation in labour relations, which has led to the avoidance of legal action; it must none the less be noted that there is a trend in Europe today to question such avoidance of the courts. Recourse to the judiciary is found in collective disputes (in Belgium particularly) and the judge is seen as the final guarantor of compliance with labour law in contexts where the position of workers' representatives is gradually weakening (in France especially). Certain legislative innovations (for instance, the French law on collective dismissal, the Aubry Act) tend to enhance potential judicial control of the collective bargaining process within companies. This tendency can be seen, moreover, as an expression of a general evolution of the judge's role in Western societies, which in the long run may entail a profound change in the regulatory model.

In Spain, regional and nation-wide cross-occupational agreements have gradually assumed conciliation, mediation and arbitration responsibilities through the creation of joint committees and voluntary arbitration bodies and procedures. Increasingly State regulations recognize the out-of-court settlement of labour disputes, although the constitutional right to use the courts still exists for individual and collective disputes, although this right may be voluntarily restricted or waived in the terms indicated.

In the UK, there is a State agency (ACAS) charged with responsibility for conciliation between the parties to industrial disputes with a view to their resolution. Since collective agreements are not legally binding, disputes have to be resolved either by conciliation or by private arbitration. In Belgium, the law places reconciliation bodies at the disposal of the social partners (essentially the joint committees); specialized public officials, under the aegis of the Ministry of Employment and Labour, play the role of 'social conciliators'. In Italy too, there are institutions for local dispute resolution, but with ultimate recourse to the courts. There are institutions at the local and regional levels for resolving disputes, although the parties concerned always have the right to take their disputes to court. In Sweden, the Labour Court exists to settle legal disputes and access to it is restricted to the parties to collective bargaining. Also being examined is the possibility of establishing an arbitration commission to deal with pay disputes.

In Germany the system of labour courts deals only with the resolution of disputes between employers and employees, and not collective disputes. There are no State institutions for conciliation. In the Netherlands, private sector disputes may be resolved through the courts, while public sector disputes are resolved by conciliation and (exceptionally) arbitration. In France, courts of law are competent in collective suits (for example, concerning the interpretation of collective agreements), but not in the resolution of collective disputes (conflict of interests). The latter fall under the scope of optional conciliation, mediation, and arbitration procedures, which are in practice barely used; the labour administration often plays an unofficial role in the resolution of disputes.

The State as Employer

One of the areas of greatest change in all European countries in recent years has been the change in the relationship between the State and those who work for it. Generally speaking, in Europe, public officials had no formal contract of employment and their legal situation was unilaterally decided by the State. In return, they enjoyed job security and favourable conditions, particularly with respect to retirement. Their wages were none the less lower than in the private sector in exchange for these privileges. Public sector organizations were large and hierarchical and left little room for individual initiative or responsibility. Often, public servants had no right to strike and rarely had collective bargaining rights. This model corresponded to a public service ideal, which implied loyalty and availability on the part of officials. Practice was more or less removed from that ideal, depending on the country and the administration involved.

Similarly, the scope of the application of that model has varied substantially from one country to the next: a given activity may fall under the competence of public service in certain countries and labour law in others. Frequently, as in the Netherlands and France, the public service includes employees of regional and municipal governments. In France, it includes the postal service, hospitals, and public education. In Spain, some of these groups are State employees, and others are not. In Germany, it also traditionally included State industries, including the railways. The general tendency in Europe has been to bring certain sectors formerly regarded as public services within the scope of labour law. It is now rare for employees of State enterprises to be treated as State employees, and where they are, this category of workers is being phased out. The definition of what constitutes a State employee has been progressively narrowed in many countries to focus on central government functions, or restricted by the introduction or expansion of State employment on a temporary basis, as seen in the Netherlands, Spain, and Belgium. In certain countries such as Italy, recent reforms have made all State officials, in principle, subject to labour law, although maintaining certain derogatory provisions (for instance, as regards the establishment of remuneration levels or codes of ethics).

The privatization of certain public services has contributed to such narrowing of the scope of public officialdom. In some instances (for example in telecommunications), the standard model has been the transfer of State functions to a new private company. There has also been a shift towards business units, either within public authorities, so that one part of the organization contracts with another part, or via contracts with private or voluntary providers. Sometimes this has led to State employees becoming employees of the new contractors (in line with the Transfer of Undertakings Directive). In others, it has led employees to seek recognition that they are taking real personal responsibility and real risks, and that therefore they should be treated more like private sector employees, particularly in terms of pay.

However, it is important to note that the shift towards treating public sector service providers as business units has meant that the State has broken the terms of that implicit contract based on mutual trust. There has been a move away from public and political accountability towards business efficiency. However, it is not yet clear whether this move has produced better services. There are risks that the shift to a contract-based culture, even between different parts of the public service, may in certain cases lead, on the contrary, to a failure to deliver common public service objectives (continuity, equal access at the lowest cost).

There is growing concern that a new class of disadvantaged State employees is developing. In the case of Italy and Sweden, for example, this is because State workers have lost their privileges but because of budgetary pressures have seen no resulting compensation by way of higher pay. This impoverishment of the public service is also an outcome of employment policies that have brought about increasing numbers of special contracts for the unemployed in government, universities, local groups, or hospitals, that is 'minor' and poorly paid jobs, subject to precarious conditions of employment. There has been growing casualization of some State services, particularly hospitals. But in most countries, there are a growing number of people who are working in State institutions on special employment or training schemes. These people, who work alongside State workers, often have neither State employee nor private employee rights.

Increasingly, those who continue to fall under the definition of State employees are likely to be treated as though they are part of the wider public sector. In Italy, Sweden, and the UK, for example, all State employees now have standard employment contracts which allow for dismissal. In Italy, the previous situation where State employees could retire after fifteen years' service for women or nineteen for men has been reformed, and by 2008 the normal working life for State employees will be forty years. In the Netherlands, special arrangements for State employees are progressively being dismantled as part of a process of normalizing labour relations in the public sector.

This turbulence in the employment relationship of State employees reflects the changes in the way in which public services are provided, but most countries are still going through a learning process which has not yet settled down into new stable patterns of proven effectiveness.

It is difficult to ascertain the respective advantages and drawbacks of public service and labour law to ensure the public the best possible service. The question, indeed, cannot be answered simply. If, for instance, research institute employees are State employees with tenure, they may be less likely to develop new ideas than if they were confronted with new people and new ideas every few years. By contrast, experts subject to market pressures and the fear of dismissal may avoid undertaking risky work when the outcome is not assured. Another example is in the transport industry: if highly protective by-laws enable officials to strike readily, the demand for continued service is not met and the legitimacy of these by-laws declines in the eyes of the public. In contrast, if privatization forces the workers in this industry into precarious forms of employment, for which they are poorly trained and poorly paid, transport safety may be at stake. This is why contrasting labour law with public service in abstract terms leads to a false debate. The real problem, in both cases, is to define the occupational statutes of public officials, a collection of indivisible rights and responsibilities. In their pathological forms, however, both public service and labour law may ultimately dissociate rights and responsibilities: public service may vest certain workers with specific rights while demanding no responsibilities in return and labour law may burden workers with specific responsibilities but fail to offset them with the rights that enable them to assume such responsibilities.

EVOLUTION OF THE ROLE OF THE STATE: PROJECTIONS

The Legacy of the Welfare State

Essentially, we are the heirs of the Welfare State, born of the industrial revolution. Set against both the *gendarme* (or minimum) State, conceived to be a mere arbiter, but taking no direct part, in social relations, and the Leviathan State, which attempts to assimilate all of society, the Welfare State becomes actively involved in social issues over which it admits it has no monopoly. But the visible strain under which it is labouring serves as a reminder of the current validity of the two fundamental questions that led to its birth.

The first is an outcome of the fact that in a society whose material survival is based on commercial exchange, rights and lifestyles are being *individualized* at the same time as its members become more and more *interdependent*. This paradox, identified early on by Durkheim, is growing deeper and deeper before our very eyes. Individualization is apparent in the slackening ties in all aspects of collective life, from the family to the trade union or the company (which tends to be thought of today as a mere network of contracts), whereas interdependence is the result of increasing specialization, enhanced by technological development and internationalization of trade. How can such individualization and interdependence be reconciled?

The second question has arisen with the institution of the labour market, where labour is treated as a marketable asset. However, such assets do not exist unless educated and trained throughout a human lifetime. Indivisible as human capital is from people, it hinges entirely on people's education, life, and reproduction. This bond is reinforced by technical progress, which heightens the demand for skilled labour, the kind of exclusively human work that no machine can perform, because the performance of any skilled work, even if hired for a specified time, entails vocational training acquired over the long term. How can the discontinuous nature of the paid labour market be reconciled with the continuous nature of human life?

Confronted by the totalitarian experiences that marked the twentieth century, the Welfare State was the democratic answer to those two questions; by reconciling freedom and security, it afforded the old royal States a new-found legitimacy. Its two sides, while often treated separately, are structurally related.

The first is the notion of public service, under which the State no longer stands as a power superior to civil society, but rather becomes its servant, the creator of a social bond that ensures continual and equal access to essential services (education, transportation, communication, power, hospitals, and more generally all kinds of services that are necessarily associated with territorial continuity). Under such an approach, public service enhances the rights of individuals while making them universal. Although found under many different forms and in all countries, it is in France that public service developments have been most notable.

The second side of the Welfare State was the notion of employment, understood from the individual standpoint. Employment describes not only an object of exchange, but also an occupational status, that is to say, a system of rules imposed above and beyond the will of the parties to the relations so governed. Employment as a status necessarily associated with an employment contract is a German invention. Systematized by German legal writers beginning in the late nineteenth century, it spread throughout Europe, taking root under different forms in different countries. In all European nations, the State has played an instrumental role in the development of employment (by directly protecting labour relations, such as in the Latin model, guaranteeing collective independence in industrial relations, such as in the British model, by providing a legal framework for a social market economy such as in the Rhineland model or by formulating conventional labour law, such as in the Nordic model, etc.). Under all these various systems, employment contracts have been made subject to statutes to protect workers against the risks of loss of earning power. Employment, in that sense, is the child of both labour law and social security. Through social security, employment enrols its holder in a system of financial solidarity to meet such risks.

Over time, protection against some of these risks has shifted to the other side of the Welfare State, with the risks being assumed by public services. This is especially true in the case of the invention, British on this occasion, of the national health service, which affords universal social protection against the risk of disease. Adopted in a number of European countries (Nordic countries, Italy) and implemented in others at the cost of distorting occupational systems, such national health protection illustrates the dynamic of how certain rights deriving from employment have gradually come to be considered citizens' rights.

The Welfare State, which made it possible to master the dual phenomenon of individualization and social interdependence, has at the same time fuelled the development of these two phenomena. Inclusion in broad and anonymous universal systems frees individuals from their family or economic environment: wives with a job or the elderly with retirement pensions are not dependent on their husbands or their children. From being an answer to the above issues, the Welfare State has gradually become part of the problem.

The State and 'Globalization'

Instrumentalization of the State

In modern societies, the State is the long-term guarantor. Both neoliberal and neo-corporatist analyses tend to misunderstand the unique place occupied by the State, as both see the State as an instrument rather than as a guarantor of social and economic relations.

Under the traditional conception, the State is entrusted with manifesting and implementing the general interest. The law that articulates such general interest is enforced among groups and individuals and establishes the limits within which they may make their own rules (that is define their own contractual law). Two levels of written law are thus distinguished and posited in a very hierarchical fashion: one level represents the general will, as expressed via laws and regulations; and the other represents the will of parties, of private persons, as expressed in contracts. The first level is the realm of public law; it is the sphere of things fixed and unilateral. The second level is reserved to private law; it is the sphere of things negotiated and bilateral.

The Welfare State brought these two levels closer into line. The expression of general will no longer appears as an *a priori* fact imposed on individuals, but as the result of the consideration of the diversity of private interests. Acknowledging the limits of its own capability (which is what distinguishes it from the totalitarian State), the Welfare State seeks to express the diversity of interests running across society either by involving the representatives of such interests in the formulation of laws and regulations, or by vesting them with the task of defining the general interest. Such evolution, which may be thought of as 'neo-corporatist', leads to the merging of negotiation and deliberation, and the vesting of agreements with a kind of legitimacy that is at least equal to that afforded to the law. In neo-corporatism, the general interest shifts away from the notion of 'otherness' and must compromise with the various specific interests, while the latter, on the other hand, gain access to legislative or regulatory functions.

Neoliberal renewal and deregulation theories also result in the questioning of the hierarchy of interests underlying the classical theory of the State. As a point of departure, such theories consider law as one of several forms of regulation, which must respect (or better, express) the dictates of supply and demand, as set out in standard economics. Economic globalization leads to attributing to such dictates a universal value on which to build a business empire, imposed on all nation-states, which merely express local solidarities, tolerated only to the extent that they do not obstruct the free movement of goods and capital. From this perspective, the true general interest lies in universal respect for the laws of supply and demand, whereas States embody only specific national interests; such interests must bow to the higher demands of free trade.

Such theories have a substantial impact in today's world. This is demonstrated, first, by the establishment of multinational institutions based on the partial relinquishment of State sovereignty, of which the European Union is the most highly developed example. But such multinational entities are today themselves subject to the same kind of constraints that they bring to bear on their Member States: particularly, the regional interests they represent must bow to the imperatives of worldwide institutions, established by international conventions (such as the World Trade Organization).

Neo-corporatism and neoliberalism have, in practice, joined forces to strip the State of certain of its sovereign attributes, to shift the hierarchy of public and private interests and blur the distinction between deliberated law and negotiated agreement. In each of these ideologies, the State is perceived to be the tool of a level of rationality that extends beyond it: namely society or the economy. The tendency is to regard it as just another of several actors, not in a position to lay claim to special treatment under common law.

The State as Long-term Guarantor

The visible weakening of the State in modern day Europe is fraught with injustice, risks, and uncertainties. Injustice, because it is unacceptable for broad sectors of the population in rich societies to be consigned to poverty or social annihilation. This opinion, expressed long ago by Beveridge, is equally valid today; the development of a kind of social Darwinism, insidiously leading to the belief that the victims of the 'economic war' deserve their lot, that they have made no contribution to society and that the only concern should be to keep them entertained and prevent them from starving or freezing, is simply intolerable.

Risks, because if, under the pressure of corporatism or world-wide markets, States prove to be incapable of ensuring their citizens have a decent living and no other institution rises to take their place, what may be expected is the speedy unravelling of the social fabric, which will rapidly lead to aggressive (nationalist, regionalist, fundamentalist, racist, or xenophobic) hubs of identity, of which today's world is rife with examples.

Uncertainties, finally, because the issue is to know if, and how, States will be able to reassert their role as long-term guarantors. First, it is not at all certain that the State, which is not an eternal or a universal legal category, but rather a relatively recent product of Western history, is still going to be capable of a metamorphosis of the sort that gave rise to the Welfare State. A hypothesis has been put forward, backed by a rigorous historical analysis, to the effect that our societies are heading towards unknown forms of re-feudalization (Legendre 1997). Judging by the present European legal framework, States no longer hold a monopoly over the definition of the general interest; they must take account, on the one hand, of Community authority and, on the other, of the social partners, which regard themselves, for different reasons, as being entitled to establish law.

A prospective reflection on the reassessment of the State's role could be addressed from two standpoints, one procedural and the other substantial.

Procedural Approach

A procedural approach is inevitable once it is admitted, on the one hand, that the State continues to be the long-term guarantor of the general interest and, on the other, that in complex societies it does not have the means, on its own, to define what that general interest comprises. That dilemma arises each and every time non-quantifiable common goods must be safeguarded, goods which by definition fall outside the price-based co-ordination imposed by markets. Such is the case, for instance, with nature, education, or health, the potential for creativity among the unemployed, in short, the non-marketable aspects of individual and collective well-being. Purely administrative and regulatory techniques have long found it difficult, and sometimes impossible, to conserve such non-marketable assets. Neo-corporatist solutions, which consist of making the definition of the common good an object of negotiation with intermediary groups, lead to deadlock, because the general interest cannot be the product of trade-offs between representatives of specific interests. The most powerful and best organized groups tend to impose their own notion of the common good, that is make their own interests prevail.

The shortcomings of neo-corporatist arrangements as described above shed light on something which, prematurely, has been called the retreat of the State. This movement is, in fact, ambivalent. Wherever the State withdraws from bargaining with intermediaries, renounces its role as the co-manager of social affairs, in some cases at least it is to reassert and better fulfil its mission as guarantor of the general interest. The various tentative efforts to reorganize public services illustrate such an attempt to reach beyond the neo-corporatist model. The State has rarely confined itself to surrendering the management of a particular service to private powers. It has also established a legal framework intended to guarantee respect for the general interest in the provision of such services and created *ad hoc* institutions (so-called regulatory agencies) reputed to be independent of both the State and the service providers.

This also entails a re-evaluation of the State's role and a reassertion of the prevalence of law over agreements. It is the law that establishes the system's key objectives. But its prevalence is at the expense of the State's withdrawal, to a certain extent, from the implementation of such objectives, because implementation falls entirely within the terms of the agreements. Agreements are no longer merely a way of governing the relations between parties, or as an alternative form of regulation, but now constitute a legal tool for joining parties in the pursuit of public service objectives established by law. In this task of meeting the general interest through intermediary individuals and groups, the expertise provided by independent agencies constitutes an objective standard, a common language for the State and private parties. Such a common language is in fact indispensable once the State, on the one hand, asserts its role as guarantor of the general interest (breaking away from neo-corporatist practice) while on the other hand admitting its inability to satisfy such general interest alone.

The new feature of this emerging model, which is also its weak point, is the role assigned to expertise. These 'regulatory' agencies (Ethics Committees, High Councils, Independent Authorities, etc.) run two risks which have not in practice been fully eliminated. The first is that the science underlying expert opinion can never be anything else but the reworking of one ideology or another; the second is the danger that such agencies will become a forum for trade-offs among the lobbies indirectly represented by the experts comprising their membership.

Substantial Approach
States, and the European Union as well, cannot confine themselves to organizing rules of procedure to allow the involvement of intermediary individuals and groups in the definition and implementation of the

general interests with which they are entrusted. It is also incumbent upon them to establish the underlying principles that should guide such definitions and guarantee individuals and groups their fundamental social rights.

This was the premise behind the adoption of the Community Charter of the Fundamental Social Rights of Workers. More recently, the Treaty of Amsterdam has reaffirmed the fundamental rights guaranteed by the European Convention for the Protection of Human Rights and Fundamental Freedoms, and resulting from the Member States' common constitutional traditions, as general principles of Community law. This represents a decisive step towards the constitutionalization of fundamental social rights at EU level. The need for such constitutionalization has been discussed before in several papers (for example, Rodríguez-Piñero and Casas 1996), and it was not felt useful for our group to address this point in the context of the present book.

On the other hand, it was felt that the notion of European citizenship included in the Maastricht Treaty could be a useful framework for implementation, at the individual level, of the social rights proclaimed. In terms of article 8E of the EC Treaty itself, citizenship in the European Union is an evolutionary notion, which can be extended to include new rights (or duties) that reach beyond the restrictive provisions adopted at Maastricht.[7] There is no guarantee that it will ever be possible to develop its political side very far, due to the pressure brought to bear by the reassertion of national sovereignties (European Commission 1997c). Its social, or better social and economic, aspect (generalization of free movement and residence, initially granted to workers alone), however, is very much in the mainstream of Community dynamics. It constitutes a fertile ground for developing Union citizenship in terms of social citizenship.

Like political citizenship, social citizenship can be defined as equality of rights and responsibilities; what distinguishes them is merely the nature of the rights and responsibilities: political in one case and social and economic in the other.

Equal access to high quality services of general interest (not conceived in terms of universal minima) would be certainly involved in a definition of social citizenship. The determination of such services is a matter for political deliberation, but must definitely include health and safety, education and training, and essential goods (air, energy). The legal status (private or public) of the service providers is immaterial provided they are subject to a common legal framework that guarantees the quality of the

---

[7] Articles 8A (freedom of movement), 8B (voting rights and eligibility for local and European elections), 8C (right to diplomatic protection) and 8D (right of petition).

services rendered and equal access to them for all citizens. Such demands for service continuity, equality, and quality warrant certain limitations to free competition under article 90 of the Treaty, as interpreted by the Court of Justice.[8]

Acknowledgement of occupational freedom would also form part of social citizenship; this should be understood to mean not only formal freedom, but also the opportunity open to every citizen to be able to make a living from a job that best expresses their own aspirations and talent. Such a guarantee should not be confused with the right to a job, which concerns work as an employee only, but should embrace all sorts—dependent and independent, marketable and non-marketable, public or private—of activities undertaken in the service of others. This also would include a specific approach to the freedom of enterprise. This specific, occupational-freedom approach would entail, in particular, the right to life-long learning (as provided for in the guidelines for employment adopted in Luxembourg in November 1997). As far as work in the employ of others is concerned, occupational freedom would also include specific rights within companies, in particular the rights to participation and representation. Indeed, as a general principle, stressed in many references in the present report, it is not advisable to separate the acknowledgement of rights from that of responsibilities: social citizenship would imply responsibilities that could be assumed only if rights were publicly guaranteed.

There are, none the less, reasons to question whether the notion of social citizenship provides a sufficient framework for developing a social model equally respectful of freedom, equality, and solidarity. Such a notion in fact excludes non-citizens (that is non-EU nationals) from the social circle it defines itself and thereby contradicts the universal nature of the values it enshrines. Basing free movement, for instance, on European citizenship, rather than on status as worker, would lead to denying free movement to foreign workers living legally in one of the member countries on a permanent basis. The circle of labour-related human rights and that of citizenship do not necessarily coincide, and making human rights at the workplace subject to citizenship could lead to excluding non-Community workers from such rights, despite the fact that the number of such workers, already substantial, can only continue to grow given the respective demographic and economic prospects of European countries and their neighbours to the South or the East. This is why the proposed reflection on European social citizenship must necessarily address the affirmation and deepening of fundamental social rights at the Community level.

[8] *CJEC*, 19 May 1993, Case C-320/91 (Corbeau).

6

Changes in Work, Women's Work and the Future of Labour Law: The Gender Dimension

The important changes taking place in labour relations, and the even more important changes forecast for the decade to come, have—or may have—substantial consequences for women's work—consequences as important as those resulting from industrialization in the past.

One of the most prominent structural changes affecting European labour markets is the increasing number of women who have entered the market over the last three decades, particularly in the Scandinavian countries and the United Kingdom. In view of this, there has been a tendency, in discussions on employment and growing joblessness in European societies, to place some degree of responsibility for the severe unemployment situation on that rise in female activity and employment rates. This, in turn, has gradually led to changes in the traditional approaches, after overcoming some initial resistance, and the introduction of a new focus in both the organization and (more challengingly) the practice of labour relations, with a view to working towards greater gender equality.

The need to respond to changes in labour markets and employment through adequate labour regulation is also bound up with the issue of women's work, particularly from the point of view of the development of labour legislation in the course of the evolution of European social policy. The need for such a response is also confirmed by events such as the recent adoption of the Amsterdam Treaty and Council Directives 97/80/EC and 97/81/EC, both of 15 December 1997, the former relating to the burden of proof in cases of discrimination based on sex and the latter to the Framework Agreement on part-time work reached by UNICE, CEEP, and CES, as well as the many European Commission community action programmes for equal opportunities for men and women.

Furthermore, the proposals and guidelines arising from the expert group's work have been formulated to take account of the gender issue and, therefore, of the impact of such proposals on the European goal of equal opportunities, in line with the premises contained in article 3 of the Treaty of Amsterdam and European Parliament recommendations.[1]

EVOLUTION OF WOMEN'S WORK IN EUROPE: REPRODUCTIVE WORK AND MARKET WORK

Any analysis of women's labour relations and the regulation of such relations needs to be set against the backdrop of an historical review.

Birth and Consolidation of Industrial Societies: Male Productive and Female Reproductive Work

It is a generally accepted fact that industrial society, in which women and children were initially recruited to the productive labour market in large numbers, in the absence of any kind of legal regulations and usually under very harsh conditions, engineered a profound change in the organization of the productive world, and the resulting social model turned on a gender-based distribution of work. Men were assigned the so-called 'productive' tasks in the public and the public–private business domains, which were performed under wage-based labour relations and increasingly regulated employment conditions, subject in turn to developing labour law and collective bargaining between the social partners. Women, meanwhile, were to engage in so-called 'reproductive' tasks, performed in the private, family sphere and governed by civil law, largely unregulated and under conditions in which women's and children's rights were barely recognized.

Scholarly analyses of the dynamics involved in the transition of predominantly agricultural societies to industrial societies (Polanyi 1944, Offe 1984) show that after an initial stage of reaction to the new production conditions, non-property-owning men began to organize around political associations and in trade unions to obtain recognition of their civil and political

---

[1] Resolution A4-0251/97 of 16.9.1997 relating to the Commission's Paper on *Integrating equal opportunities for men and women in overall Community policy and action* (COM (96)67 final).

rights and demand labour and social rights. T. H. Marshall's thesis (Marshall 1950) of the gradual constitution, development, and expansion of rights provides some very clear insight into these issues.

The process of inclusion and recognition of rights was not the same for men and women. The consolidation of this model entailed the withdrawal (or expulsion) of most women from the labour market and their confinement to the private sphere, as part of a gradual change in family models, from the extended family characteristic of farming societies to the nuclear family, the model prevailing in industrial societies.

Notwithstanding that social order, women did continue to have a substantial role to play in certain branches of industrial activity, such as textiles or food, generally as low-skilled labour and in low-paying jobs. During the war periods, women temporarily took many of the jobs left vacant by men. This did not mean, however, that they were relieved of their family responsibilities. Moreover, women had always been employed in domestic work, although this traditionally female activity was always poorly and belatedly regulated and difficult to subject to legal control.

Legislative logic during this period as a whole, as far as women's work was concerned, was paternalistic and protectionist, largely focusing on their reproductive role (including, for example, measures to protect women against unhealthy or strenuous jobs, prohibition of night work, etc.), as reflected in the earliest ILO Conventions.

Labour law, from the outset, had a clear gender (masculine) bias and much of the doctrine of that body of law was developed assuming that the central figure in a contractual relationship involving subordinate work—the employment contract—was a skilled male full-time industrial worker hired, as time went on, under open-ended terms, and with a family to support. Notwithstanding national diversity, labour law throughout Europe was built around the male worker model. Subsequent recognition of the formal equality between men and women before the law was more a consequence of an extension of existing doctrine to women than of the consideration of the specific characteristics of each gender within the framework of the social division of work; moreover, since these arrangements remained largely unquestioned, no real legal innovations were introduced. This is what some texts refer to as the 'egalitarian' perspective of law which, with some modern retouching intended to eliminate inequalities, still prevails in the most recent provisions (articles 6A, 2 and 3 of the EC Treaty, amended by the Amsterdam Treaty).

The appearance and development of Welfare States (with national variations, but in all cases based on active State intervention in the regulation of labour relations) during the Fordist period opened up new work opportunities for women, primarily in public education and health services. In the former, they were hired to teach the primary grades, a task associated with their role as mothers; and in the latter, to take subordinate positions in support of higher-ranking professional and, in general, 'masculinized' activities. At the same time, the growth of administrative tasks in both the public and private sectors offered opportunities for women, although largely at lower occupational levels.

The fact that women entered formal education later than men and often with a curricular slant that in itself led to a narrowing of occupational choices, had an important impact on the ways women could participate in the world of work.

Women joined a highly masculinized working world, in terms of the definition of rights and the participation in collective bargaining of the social partners, as well as in terms of the daily organization of the work to be done. Regardless of whether or not it was in fact true, women's activities tended to be conceived socially as additional to what was understood to be their major role: family and reproduction. Consequently, their earnings were perceived to be complementary to those of male heads of families.

From the 1960s onwards, women in Europe began to enter secondary and higher levels of formal education. This enabled them to acquire higher qualifications and some diversity in their employment, as well as the tools to analyse the social relations in which they were immersed, affording them a growing capacity to question those relations and assert their rights.

Productive and Technological Change and Gradual and Growing Incorporation of Female Labour in European Labour Markets

The 1970s were a decade of new social phenomena of various kinds, perhaps the most prominent of which were: the beginning of a change in production, with the tertiary sector growing in importance compared with the (primarily male) industrial sector and the appearance of new activities, as yet unregulated; the growing heterogeneity of family structures (single-parent families, unmarried mothers, single men and women, blended families resulting from separation and remarriage, etc.), indicative of a further transformation, perhaps equivalent to the change from the extended to the nuclear family; higher education for women and consequently their increased presence on the labour market, particularly in services, since traditionally employment rates in these sectors are more closely related to women's training and qualifications than men's; an important change in domestic management, as a result of the development of public services to assume some of the tasks previously relegated to families (nursery schools, expanded education, hospitals) and the private distribution of goods and services that replace other tasks, along with the development of household appliance technology, permitting (at least potentially) new ways to organize time; the appearance of women's movements varying in form and degree of radicalism, which began to question different aspects of the prevailing social division of work and the conditions under which women access the labour market.

As a result of this series of factors, women with higher qualifications than previously began to join the labour market *en masse*, often in the emerging tertiary sector, while at the same time labour regulations and legislation (flexibility processes or policies) started to undergo increasing change as a result of alterations in production and technology. This undoubtedly has provided new work opportunities for women who are also faced with a growing need to supplement the family income or to ensure they had a source of income of their own in view of changing family structures. The public sector is becoming feminized to some extent, with greater occupational diversity among women, and there is increased female participation in the private sector, particularly in the service sector, with a tendency in the latter for that participation to concentrate around specific kinds of activities and jobs.

However, the changes in the social model on which the division of work is based are not as profound: in addition to participating in the labour market, women continue to be primarily responsible for society's reproductive tasks. This phenomenon, known as the 'dual day', divided between working and 'non-working' time—even though the latter, devoted to reproductive tasks, constitutes an additional burden, and results in unequal competition between men and women on the labour market, despite the acknowledgement of their formal equality under the law. This situation runs alongside the inroads made by women into what have traditionally been considered to be men's social terrain and working time.

Women's ability to hold jobs despite this double burden has depended, to some degree, on the existence and development of public social services, and the introduction of certain legal provisions that tend to remove some obstacles affecting women's careers (for example, maternity and nursing leave, leave to care for family members who are ill, etc., some of which are granted equally to men and women).

The 1970s were also the period when 'affirmative action' (a concept originally referring to the integration of the black minority in the United

States) made its appearance, as a way of establishing measures to correct ongoing *de facto* structural inequalities rooted in the past. In the case of women, affirmative action measures attempt to mitigate or compensate for unequal opportunities to join and take an active part in the labour market which arise from the traditional model for the division of labour, which continues to carry considerable weight in social awareness and regulations at large.

Nowadays, women's greater participation in the labour market takes place in a context of further production and technological change that generates new kinds of (post-Fordist) labour organization with a diversity of co-existing production models and some clearly emerging trends, particularly the variety of employment terms, recourse to (real and fraudulent) self-employment, sub-contracting, and outsourced labour. This gives rise to new and very diverse arrangements in working relations and thus to the 'flexibilization' of employment relations. Women are provided job opportunities just as pressure builds up against regulating and/or deregulating working conditions, in a context that parallels the situation prevailing early on in nineteenth-century industrial society.

WOMEN AND FUTURE TRENDS IN LABOUR LAW

Changes in the Employment Contract, Non-standard Employment Terms, and Self-employment among Women

The new kinds of employment relations (part-time contracts, temporary contracts and temporary employment agencies, work from home and teleworking) particularly affect women. The way gender difference affects new 'non-standard' employment conditions and work organization must be taken into account in order to assess their impact and determine the actual level of protection afforded to women's work by labour and social security law.

At the same time, however, flexibilization of the labour market opens up new employment opportunities for women, who show initially greater adaptability to less favourable conditions ('new vein' or 'secondary labour market' jobs), although often under deteriorating labour, economic, and social circumstances.

All of the above implies—or may imply in many cases—that whereas a larger number of women are entering the labour market, they face greater obstacles to accessing rights and social benefits established and regulated by a labour law conceived for an industrial society and a standard employment contract.

Flexibilization policies, with growing demands on employees in terms of initiative and independence, competition, skills and adaptiveness, as well as availability, place women at yet another crossroads: either they forgo their careers (withdrawing from the labour market altogether or accepting lower positions with limited promotion opportunities or temporary and casual employment conditions) or their family responsibilities. Declining marriage and birth rates, delayed marriages, later age at first birth and broken homes, are not unrelated to this decision presented, perceived, and experienced in many cases as an option between two mutually exclusive alternatives. If flexibilization translates into greater demands on employee availability, it may entail a greater burden for women, which is in turn incompatible with reproductive tasks unless a greater, more equal share of such tasks is assumed by men and society as a whole via public services.

Moreover, a more equitable distribution of family responsibilities, given the growing demands on employee involvement and availability, may become impossible for both women and men, other than at the price of greater subordination and casualized employment, and consequently greater personal insecurity for both. In the light of this, it may legitimately be wondered whether the new social and legal system on which the world of production turns, and which does not question the validity of the old social model for the division of labour, will also be built along strongly biased gender lines, discriminating against women from the standpoint of economic independence and professional careers; and against men with respect to the development of bonds of affection and family relations.

A model whereby men and women would share working time and keep enough free time for both without forfeiting social rights is an extremely interesting approach in this regard. If part-time work is not afforded protection in the form of recognition and preservation of labour and social rights; if it means the loss of all potential for professional development and reinforces the bonds of economic dependence; if it has an adverse effect on pay levels and access to social security benefits with the concomitant strengthening of the bonds of financial dependence, women will have succeeded in entering the labour market but will continue to be in a position of inequality and social disadvantage.

It may be particularly detrimental to women to restrict the scope of application of labour law and its main guarantees to the field of subordinate employment and the traditional contractual form of such employment, namely the employment contract, without taking account of work performed for others which is channelled through other kinds of legal or contractual relations: known as independent, autonomous, or self-employment or similar. The continued identification of labour law with the regulation of the prototype of labour relations associated with the industrial model that gave rise to such relations—which, moreover, was never fully representative even of all dependent or subordinate work—limits the protection afforded to a smaller and smaller core of workers and leads to even greater segmentation of the labour market.

Under such circumstances, labour law may act as a mechanism for exclusion rather than for promoting adaptability to change, integration, and social advancement.

Similarly, according to recent Eurostat data, whereas women still constitute a minority among both the active and the employed population—the activity rate for women is around 45 per cent in the EU as a whole, compared with 66.2 per cent for men, although distribution by country is uneven—a larger proportion of women than men are affected by unemployment, except in the United Kingdom, Sweden, and Ireland. In the case of Spain, where the female activity rate is a mere 35.4 per cent (compared with the male rate of 61.9 per cent), the 62 per cent net increase in women's participation in the working world over the period between 1976 and 1996, it is no exaggeration to state that virtually three-quarters of new female recruits have joined the ranks of unemployed women. Similarly, young women find it more difficult than young men to secure their first job, among other reasons due to the (statistically unfounded) belief that they are less productive, have higher absence rates and cost their employers more due to the impact of their family responsibilities—that is the reproductive role they are expected to assume—on their work.

Where women's status in private enterprise is concerned, Spain is proving to be a very typical case: there is no correlation between the educational achievements of women in recent decades and their access to jobs or their position in job hierarchies.

State employment and Community structural policies should explicitly address the gender dimension and provide for specific equal opportunities measures to take account of the social and economic factors particularly affecting women, in accordance with the Employment Guidelines adopted by the Luxembourg Council in December 1997.

Employment Discontinuity and Continuity of Employment Status among Women: the Need for Affirmative Action; the Persistence of Discrimination in Pay

Women are particularly prone to employment instability, due to the problems surrounding career interruption. Sometimes women workers are dismissed on specific pregnancy- and maternity-related grounds (although nominally for other reasons), or are pressured into returning to work before they are legally required to do so, and/or find it difficult to return to work under the same conditions as before taking their leave of absence.

Labour law should always respect equal rights between men and women, taking account of their individual characteristics, life cycle, and reproductive tasks, so that careers do not suffer because of interruptions due to maternity, adoption of children, child rearing, and care for relatives, with the consequential impact on access to benefits which are contingent upon payments into the social protection system. The main problem lies in the pursuit and identification of mechanisms to make this discontinuity and instability in women's careers compatible with their return to the labour market and the maintenance of their employment status, characterized by entitlement to employment rights and social protection; in other words, to make work and family life compatible, reconciling diversity and continuity in the career cycle.

Moreover, certain kinds of work have been traditionally associated with women, as a public extension of the non-marketable activities performed in the domestic sphere: tasks relating to health care and care for the ill, nursery and primary school teaching, domestic service, cleaning, cooking, etc. This has produced occupational segregation based on gender stereotypes that hinder women's occupational diversification and their integration in non-traditional jobs, except in de-regulated or unregulated contexts (the underground economy), and this is at the root of indirect and hard-to-prove discrimination in pay. Most home work and teleworking, which often involve low-paid activities requiring little skill, are performed by women.

In this regard, State intervention—not only via labour and employment legislation, but through political and public action in general—and collective bargaining seem to be essential to enforce the prohibition of discrimination and to ensure greater equality of opportunities between men and women in their access to employment and career development. Examples would include affirmative action measures such as incentives to hire young women in permanent jobs; the implementation of networks of nursery and primary schools with flexible schedules in keeping with labour market demands; support for building and maintaining women's careers; access to life-long learning and new technologies; incentives for the actual take-up of parental rights by both men and women (as called for in Council Directive 96/34/EC of 3 June 1996 relating to the Framework Agreement on parental leave concluded by UNICE, CEEP and CES), and the introduction of preferential treatment in hiring or promoting women in professions in which they are under-represented ('quota or priority systems').

Given women's traditional inequality in the working world, a policy of affirmative action measures has been developed, with the encouragement of the Commission of the European Communities, in an attempt to counter unfair situations and eliminate *de facto* structural inequalities, with such measures receiving priority or preferential treatment in order to achieve truly equal opportunities for men and women.

None the less, the legitimacy and suitability of legislative polices designed to promote affirmative action, together with the scope of such action and their impact not only on opportunities but on results, is currently under debate. The Kalanke Judgment of 17 October 1995 delivered by the Court of Justice of the European Communities[2] is a significant example of developments in this debate, along with the reactions and criticism levelled at the interpretation and application of Community Law—Art. 2.4 of Directive 76/207/EEC—in the ruling. The Kalanke interpretation was subsequently partially revised by the Marshall Judgment of 11 November 1997,[3] according to which the establishment of preferential promotion for women if equally qualified,[4] is compatible with Directive 76/207/EEC, providing such preference is neither absolute nor unconditional (Rodríguez-Piñero 1997).

Equality of opportunity, a principle of Community law, is now laid down in the Amsterdam Treaty (Art. 119.4 ECT). It is, however, still weakly formulated and considered as an exception to the general rule, in which the intention is merely to ensure that Member State legislation on affirmative action conforms to Community law; it imposes no binding objectives on Member States nor does it require Community institutions themselves to adopt measures favouring the implementation of such action, despite the provisions of the new Art. 6A in the EC Treaty, which vests the Council with the power to 'take appropriate action to combat discrimination based on sex . . .'. The purpose of equal opportunities is to ensure 'full

[2] Case C-450/93.   [3] Case C-409/95.
[4] Phrase quoted literally in the Spanish text and paraphrased in the English version, because the translator did not have access to the source.

equality in practice between men and women in working life' and to that end, according to the new wording of Art. 119.4 of the ECT, 'the principle of equal treatment shall not prevent any Member State from maintaining or adopting measures providing for specific advantages in order to make it easier for the under-represented sex to pursue a vocational activity or to prevent or compensate for disadvantages in professional careers'.

Discrimination in pay and remuneration on grounds of sex persists despite the acknowledgement, more than twenty years ago, of the principle that men and women performing the same work or, in the new version of the Amsterdam Treaty, 'work of equal value' should be remunerated equally (Art. 119.1 ECT and Directives 75/117/EEC and 72/107/EEC). A recent Eurostat report (Eurostat 1997a) shows that in this regard the gap between men's and women's pay is larger among the highly skilled, older age groups, and professionals with university training. The average female wage at the normal hourly rate is 84 per cent of the male wage in Sweden, 73 per cent in France and Spain, and 64 per cent in the United Kingdom. On average, according to Eurostat figures, the difference in pay between men and women with a comparable level of education and holding the same job in the same industry or business sector in 1995 was 13 per cent in Sweden, 22 per cent in Spain, and nearly 25 per cent in the United Kingdom.

The Issue of Women's 'Working Time'

It is generally agreed that the relatively stable and homogeneous paradigm for working time (the working week as a reference, collective time, etc.) is also growing weaker, particularly under the combined effect of the development of the service sector, the introduction of new technologies (that is in information and communications), competition of more and more open markets, changes in worker behaviour with respect to time and new consumer demands. The primary purpose of breaking away from or flexibilizing this model is to adapt it to business needs. But the flexibilization of working time also serves other interests. The value of heterogeneity and, where appropriate, of individualization is rising, to the detriment of the former standardization or formal homogeneity of working schedules.

Traditional, scientifically standard Taylorist/Fordist working time—which, none the less, allowed for both informal practices and derogation from rigid standardization to accommodate business specifics—was well adapted to men, but excluded women from the labour market or placed them at a disadvantage. Working time was established around a wholly male reference point, defined in opposition to female reproductive time. The prohibition of night work for women is a particularly eloquent expression of this male approach to working time.

One of the issues addressed in the current treatment of working time is the intersection between the two contradictory lines discussed above in connection with labour law: the regulation of employment conditions for the new kinds of working arrangements, the defence of the continuity of women workers' employment status, and the compatibility of such continuity with possible work and employment discontinuity, all of which has a substantial impact on women's potential and their capabilities in their active working lives.

The demands for flexible adaptation of working time—the working time relevant to labour law—can, if shared with male workers, enhance women's working potential by allowing them greater leeway with respect to their individual preferences and their ability to control their own working conditions, but may at the same time clash with family responsibilities—with their other working time, their reproductive time, which is not considered by labour law. Women's employment and promotion potential will continue to be adversely affected by such situations while the traditional social model of the division of work—under which they are expected to assume the brunt of the burden of family responsibilities—persists. Under such social conditions, permission for women to work at night, granted under the Stoeckel Judgment of 25 July 1991,[5] the flexibilization and irregularity of working schedules (weekends, for instance) coupled with the stepping up of the pace of work as demanded by the market and the need to fully exploit capital goods, may aggravate such negative consequences. Moreover, no profound change towards sharing family responsibilities seems possible unless a similar change in all the necessary services is also forthcoming.

The new non-uniform arrangement of working time has a decisive impact on the organization of social life as a whole (school system, transport, leisure), raising crucial questions of different kinds and scope. How can working, family, and personal time be organized within the context of growing demands on workers' time in terms of availability for paid work? Moreover, the crisis affecting the traditional nuclear family and the emergence of heterogeneous forms of family organization are issues that should be taken into account in labour law and the regulation of social insurance, in view of their significance in terms of a break with former models of social organization.

[5] Case C-345/89.

Policy and practice with respect to the reduction and organization of working time in different countries are very highly dependent on each country's legal and cultural traditions. In the Netherlands and the Scandinavian countries, part-time work fits into a pattern of cultural choice to allow for a better balance between professional and family activities and offers, for that reason, an appropriate contractual form for female employment. However, according to surveys conducted by Eurostat in the EU Member States as a whole (where 32 per cent of women work part-time compared with 5 per cent of men), a high percentage of women currently working part-time state that this is not a matter of choice, but rather a result of labour market demand under present circumstances and that, if they could, they would work full-time. Furthermore, part-time work contributes to broadening the gap between men's and women's pay, since the hourly wage for part-time work is lower than for full-time work (85 per cent in Sweden, 71 per cent in France, 69 per cent in Spain, and 60 per cent in the UK). Nor has it led so far to a balanced redistribution of family responsibilities (Eurostat 1997*b* and 1997*c*).

In Spain, although part-time work has recently seen a sharp upward trend as a result of legislative policy intended to flexibilize and facilitate this kind of employment, it is not nearly as common as in other EU countries, and is more likely to involve women (67 per cent) than men. Even among the latter, however, growth in part-time work has been substantial in the last two years, particularly among young men, since such employment—albeit casual or temporary—has job creation incentives attached, that is lower wage rates and social security contributions. According to the figures published by the Spanish Economic and Social Council in its 1996 report *El trabajo a tiempo parcial* (part-time work), part-time work among men is most common in agriculture, the hotel/restaurant trade, retailing, and education. Female part-time work is concentrated around domestic service (a little over 50 per cent), business services, and recreational, cultural, and sports activities (12 per cent), hotel/restaurant trade and personal services (11 per cent), education (9 per cent), and other services. As for the average time worked under part-time contracts, the average working day for women in 1995 came to 43 per cent of the hours worked by women with full-time jobs, whereas the proportion for men was 46 per cent.

Leaving aside the solution of voluntary part-time work—for which, as indicated above, appropriate regulations are required to ensure the labour and social security rights of workers employed under these terms together with a more equitable distribution of their application between men and women—the growing demands in terms of adaptation and flexibilization of working time may lead to discriminatory results, since it puts people with children or those who have other relatives in their care at a disadvantage. This is a particularly serious problem for women, who, in most cases, are the ones who care for children and other relatives, although as indicated above, a growing number of men are also affected by such demands. Workers' increased autonomy and ability to control their own working lives, along with a growing range of choices as a result of the development of the consumer society and the impact of new technologies, may again place women in a marginal situation unless the necessary changes are made in other areas of social life.

Collective Representation and Women's Participation in Trade Unions, Employers' Associations, and Collective Bargaining

The growing participation of women in the labour market does not correspond to their membership of trade unions and employers' associations or participation in collective bargaining, which ties in, on the one hand, with the problem of gender representativeness and legitimacy of the social partners and, on the other, with women's effective exercise of their collective rights as tools for participating in working and social life.

The origin and development of trade unions and employers' organizations associated with the Fordist (industrial and masculine) production model seems to hinder addressing and accepting the profound changes in production, women's growing participation in the labour market, and taking into account the gender dimension of their actions. This produces defensive positions that associate women with the causes of unemployment and casualization of the labour market. It also leads to difficulties in accepting the specific work-related demands of women as opposed to assuming them to be included in general bargaining—despite the fact that this is the institution that best adapts to changes in the world of work. Similarly, an imbalance occurs between the proportion of women in the working world and female presence in collective bargaining and decision-making bodies in such representative organizations.

Moreover, the very history of trade unions, their organization and culture may limit more active membership on the part of women. Where due account is not taken of the persistence of the old model for the social division of labour and no serious effort is made to change the distribution of family responsibilities in terms of gender, union representation activities will themselves constitute an extra burden for women, to be added to the time devoted to work and other occupations, making it extremely difficult if not impossible for them to participate in such activities.

In European countries, women's membership of trade unions is, generally speaking, proportional to their presence in the active population, although it is particularly high in countries such as Finland and Denmark and low in France, Greece, and the Netherlands. However, even in countries where women's union membership is high, they are severely underrepresented in executive bodies (Kravaritou 1997).

None the less, due to the convergence of a series of complex social causes, including factors relating to the development of women's and similar movements, women have been participating in society in new ways that may enable them to acquire a more relevant role in different decision-making domains. One of the needs facing trade unions and employers' organizations is to incorporate both the structure and representative action of such social movements.

As far as employers' organizations are concerned, although there are unquestionable differences among European countries, it may be generally asserted that the logical consequence of the limited number of businesswomen, and the greater *de facto* difficulties they face in holding top-level positions, is a similarly small number of women in the decision-making positions of such organizations and on collective bargaining bodies. While at such levels the burden of traditional roles may be lighter (among other reasons because greater affluence provides more ready access to services to support reproductive activities), the unequal presence of men and women is yet another indication of the complexity of the problem; the traditional model for the social division of labour and the associated gender stereotypes seem not to have been broken at this level, either. The situation of women who work with their husbands in the latter's business constitutes a good example of this.

Trade unions and employers' organizations must extend their representative capacity to embrace new subjects, new realities, and new needs, particularly those arising from the gender issue.

Role of Public Authorities and Social Partners in Combating Discrimination and Implementing the Principle of Equality of Opportunity

The struggle against discrimination and the furtherance of equal job opportunities by including the gender dimension in public action and policy and, where appropriate, unequal, preferential treatment for women in order to actually achieve such equality should, inescapably, be one of the elements considered in the construction of European social citizenship—or the constitutionalization of social rights at the Community level, insofar as they are tools to enable full and active participation in community life, tools that are closely related to the right of access to employment and social protection and that continue along the lines drawn—albeit hesitantly—in the Amsterdam Treaty. The principle of substantial equality must be enforced by public authorities, who are furthermore bound to adopt the necessary measures to do so in their policies.

Encouragement of legislation which recognizes women workers' specific needs for protection and promotion should continue to be developed and expanded in the future for as long as gender continues to be a source of prejudice and discriminatory consequences, as the European Commission acknowledges in its recent report on the follow-up to the Paper *Integrating equal opportunities between men and women in overall Community policies and action*: despite the many activities to promote equality between men and women, more often than not they comprise isolated measures with no essential impact on overall gender equality.[6] Despite the difficulties considered above, collective bargaining has an instrumental role to play in correcting such situations. Affirmative action, as *ultima ratio*, is a necessary tool if the formal equality endorsed in legal texts is to be converted into actual and substantial equality, a concept which is not wholly foreign to such texts, albeit under different formulations with varying scope and on occasion somewhat modestly worded, as in the new version of Art. 119.4 of the ECT, amended by the Amsterdam Treaty.

---

[6] COM (1998)122 final, Brussels, 4.3.1998, p. 3. Phrase quoted literally in the Spanish text and paraphrased in the English version, because the translator did not have access to the source.

Labour Law and Economic Performance

The uncertainty which surrounds the economic context of market, production, and work, brought about by swiftly evolving market situations, the changeability and diversity of demand, and continued innovation in processes and products is undeniably the new dimension, with many implications. This should not, however, lead us to the conclusion that European economies are about to swing from the Fordist model of mass production, based on the management of foreseeable risk, towards a model defined by uncertainty. We are entering an era of diversity which affects products, services, work, methods of co-ordination, and efficient production models (a diversity made possible by the accelerated development and application of information technologies) (Salais and Storper 1997). Globally speaking, this implies that we should think of the development of collective economic frameworks in terms of co-ordination, rather than of strict regulation. Surveys conducted in Europe show that a substantial proportion of workers feel that they are enjoying increasing professional quality and autonomy in their work, which gives them a feeling of greater control over what they do.[1] We must therefore seek to manage such pluralism in the most efficient way possible. All of this can be subsumed under the term 'flexibility'[2]—an umbrella word commonly being used to sum up the changes taking place in the world of work. But first and foremost, we must put flexibility into its wider European economic con-

---

[1] See Beretta (1995): 45.4 per cent of Italian, 47.2 per cent of Dutch, 40 per cent of British and Irish, 33.4 per cent of Austrian, and 28 per cent of German workers consider that they are in full control of their work.

[2] Or '*souplesse*', the French translation of the term used in the paper presenting the Presidency's conclusions on the outcome of the Special European Council Meeting on Employment held in Luxembourg (20–21 November 1997)—Note SI(97)100 of 21 November 1997.

text. For the point is not to return to the (outdated) principles which constituted the basis of the interventionist centralized state in the post-war
period, but to determine both what flexibility is and what it is not, in
terms of economic efficiency and its capacity to sustain a new model of
economic development. In this regard, there is a clear framework for
economic analysis, which, although obvious, always merits restating
explicitly. The creation of jobs with reasonable or high added value and
the wealth they in turn create is the way to alleviate the tax and social burden resulting from unemployment and its social repercussions (poverty,
dependence, health disorders, etc.). First, the creation of jobs will reduce
social costs and the volume of passive social spending needed to defray
such costs; and secondly, the expenses involved will be financed by a
larger number of taxpayers.

Flexibility is defined in this chapter to be the pursuit of a collectively
efficient response to economic uncertainties and risks. This, however,
involves breaking out of a vicious circle. If such a response is found, a flexible economy is in a position to create jobs and wealth, and to procure the
means for greater security than a rigid economy. But to find that response,
it is necessary to provide people with greater security in the crucial problem of developing their human capital. It is a matter, therefore, of breaking the circle, of setting in motion a 'virtuous' process. We know from the
history of our productive organizations and markets, that there exist,
roughly speaking, three possible responses to events. Either adjustment is
left to those who offer their labour on the market, for them to adapt what
they have to offer or make precautionary savings. Or responsibility is
passed to the State (otherwise called the community), which bears the
social and financial cost of errors in adjustment to events made by private
actors—an example is public compensation for unemployment. Or
responsibility is shared between partners in the work relationship (companies, employees, communities), and they agree on a redistribution of
responsibilities which is equitable and efficient—these two requirements,
moreover, being connected. This third response—fair and efficient distribution of responsibilities—seems to be the only one responsive to economic uncertainties and risks, that is to say the growing number of events
taking place on the market, in labour and production organizations or at
the core of economic relations, events which are impossible to foresee and
which must be addressed with initiative, autonomy of decision and action,
skill, and the effective deployment of people's capabilities.

PUTTING FLEXIBILITY IN ITS EUROPEAN ECONOMIC CONTEXT

The flexibility debate carries with it ideas that need to be addressed initially (in the next section) before moving on to examine how and in what form flexibility is required by the economic development of Europe (in the subsequent section).

Combating the Flexibility Ideology

Among the false conceptions of flexibility, there is first the scarcely concealed hope of those who identify flexibility with gaining all the benefits of social and economic co-ordination without having to pay anything in exchange. Work performed for nothing and social security exclusively financed by its beneficiaries would be the ultimate outcome of these hopes. They are not as fanciful as one may think, when one observes, in the most vulnerable sectors of the population and the labour market in Europe, the emergence of underpaid and insecure jobs, the refusal of social security due to failure to satisfy the criteria for granting it, the gradual exclusion of entire regions and social groups from standards of life considered to be normal elsewhere; and when one observes, in certain countries, the proportion of wage and social contributions paid from the State budget or social funds in the name of promoting employment. Such a concept of flexibility does not permit the development of the social dialogue in Europe. Its only perspective is a continued fall in pay and social guarantees. And as for employment, it simply generates illusions.

Nevertheless, it turns up repeatedly in certain conceptions of globalization and the position occupied by the European economy. One can distinguish three concepts of globalization: the economic war of all against all; mobility without cost; the enlargement of the area of activity of each company to cover the entire world. Only the latter definition covers what European enterprises have essentially become: enterprises which base their individual and global competitiveness on comparative advantages in terms of quality, expertise, continuous innovation, diversity, and capacity to meet demand more closely. For those that succeed and create jobs, control over costs is achieved by following a path of growth and investment aiming for absolute advantages on world markets beyond simply price. This is the only way for them to perform efficiently on the world stage.

The first two meanings of globalization are just bad literature. To believe in the war of all against all is the best way to make it happen and to suck European industry into a spiral of decline and loss of competence. Except for standard and bottom-of-the-range products where a pure price argument applies, relocation is sensible only if the enterprise finds, wherever it goes, a competent workforce and the appropriate institutional environment. As the DGII communication underlines, the rate of openness to imports in the European economy, taken as a whole, is just 8 per cent,[3] similar to that in the United States. The response to the challenges of flexibility therefore does not lie in such ideological commonplaces. Those who employ them are effectively aiming to set the national and regional economies which comprise Europe in competition with one another for the sake of a short-term individual profit differential. If generalized, such behaviour would lead Europe towards an economic model of low wage costs and low competence. It is not globalization which threatens the economic development of Europe, but the refusal to understand the nature of its opportunities and the inability to grasp them. What is needed, to understand and grasp how a flexible economy can guarantee security, whose scope is broader than the mere notion of protection, is an economic framework appropriate to the European economy and its present and future characteristics.

Finding an Economic Framework Appropriate to the Future of Labour Law in Europe

For the most part—following almost twenty-five years of continuous technological and organizational innovation in response to the shock of 1973— the work performed by the European workforce no longer has the status of a simple factor of production, and its products can no longer be seen simply in terms of price. Contemporary developed economies are becoming vast collections of ever-changing goods and services.[4] We are dealing with

---

[3] See also the report presented by the European Commission at the Dublin European Council in December 1996: *The mutually beneficial effects of strengthened co-ordination between economic and structural policies (Europe as an economic unit)*, ESC(96)8.

[4] Although the theory will not be elaborated on here, as that is not the aim of this chapter, note that there are problems posed by the scope of the changes, which is too vast to be addressed in economic theory. Economic theory tends to rely on the concept of commodities (or goods), which enables it to equate economic co-ordination with the general categories of the market and value of exchange, without getting involved in the varieties of use or co-ordination conventions which may exist between producer and user.

diverse, even heterogeneous goods and services which, in a complex and variable way localized in space and time, link the value of exchange to the value of use (in other words, price and utility). Company strategies seek to follow as closely as possible the dynamics of the market and production in their environment. In so doing, companies spur the restructuring of labour markets and the reorganization of the productive geography in Europe. What is sought are potential reservoirs of innovation, product and service quality differentials with no increase in cost, appropriate collective infrastructures, quality of life, skills in the labour force, and access to initial, lifelong, vocational, and higher training systems.

The definition of the necessary skills and products, rules, standards, and expertise have become an essential part of competitiveness. Unlike 'commodities', products understood in this way exhibit, to varying degrees, dimensions of creativity, commitment and uncertainty in the final result. We are leaving the realms of predictability to enter a world which is uncertain, to the extent that tomorrow we must do something different from what we are doing today, but precisely what we cannot say.

This requires us to define a relevant economic framework for flexibility on the basis of which we can evaluate, positively and negatively, the changes taking place in the world of work and draw up a realistic scenario for the future of labour law in Europe. We must draw up a framework for observation and assessment which is suited to economies that are becoming structured by the requirement for flexibility in the face of the uncertain. Certainly, it is a challenge for European social dialogue to reach agreement on this framework for the observation and assessment of flexibility. For workers' rights and systems of welfare protection will necessarily develop according to the form this agreement takes. A great deal of research agrees in concluding that an appropriate analytical framework could include the following four terms: opportunities, closer relationships, human capital, and territorial development. These are described briefly below.

Economic Opportunities

Europe will be a Europe of economic opportunities. Larger markets, and the security guaranteed by the strength of the euro, will make the production of a number of new products and services profitable, and provide a strong incentive to innovate. These products will find customers. The present proliferation of products and services illustrates the increasing diversity of use values which all of us, company or simple consumer, expect to find on the market and which make us more and more demanding and selective. This phenomenon has to accelerate. If we were to draw up a map of Europe's international specialization by adding the specialities from each constituent country which make it up, we would undoubtedly reveal a first-class world power, right in the front line for the vast majority of products, services and new technologies. European unification will multiply these effects, provided it uses this diversity as the basis for its future economic development and not as a pretext for financially-dominated restructuring by regrouping and 'cannibalization', which would have the opposite effect, destroying part of this potential.

Closer Relationships

Europe will be a Europe of closer relationships. The creation of closer relationships permits the specification of customized products, a necessary condition for taking advantage of the enlargement of potential markets. The ongoing intensification of economic exchanges within the European area is already accompanied by a strengthening of links between producers and users, of lasting co-operation in many forms, creating various closer relationships between economic actors. A territorial restructuring of the European economy against a background of the creation of closer relationships between producers and users is in progress. It will accelerate at the beginning of the next decade. All these factors are economically efficient, since they ensure the necessary suitability of products and services for their given uses.

Human Capital

Europe will be a Europe of human capital. To grasp the potentialities involved requires the mobilization of *true* capabilities for work, that is to say those based on apprenticeship, professionalism, expertise, capabilities incorporated in people, and communities of people. The economic strength of Europe in a world context resides not in the simple (though necessary) development of its technologies, not in a simple return to expansive macro-economic policies, but in the capacity to develop and reproduce specific human capital in order effectively to take advantage of these technologies, the enlargement of the market, and monetary stability. Policies addressing education, life-long learning, occupational mobility, standards of living and quality of life, or the struggle to work are thus also primary considerations in the development of lasting competitive advantages for the European economy.

Territorial Developments

Europe will be a Europe of territorial developments. Its different industrial, regional, and sectoral (sometimes transnational)[5] fabrics should be capable of the endogenous creation of their own resources (in jobs, skills, and financing) given their growing specialization in specific products. This will be furthered by the likely stabilization of exchange rates, demand, and income in the larger area unified by the euro. Given that this should bring about efficiency and ensure the reproduction of work competencies, the weakening of the national framework within which economic growth is defined is not necessarily unavoidable. What is unavoidable, however, is the disappearance of the 'nationalist' vision in these national frameworks.[6]

FLEXIBILITY IN PEOPLE'S WORK AND COMPETENCIES

Flexibility is often associated with a need to loosen the legal framework governing work, welfare, and codes of good practice. It is therefore assumed that flexibility and security conflict. Such an assumption would seem all the more obvious insofar as post-war social protection systems, based on steady jobs held by adult males whose wages covered the needs of a nuclear family, have become outdated in view of labour market

---

[5] Note, for example, that the economic areas of co-operation and integration between France and Germany, which are being established around a number of complex products (aircraft, motor vehicles and a wealth of associated components, or certain chemical specialties, etc.), are dominated by this type of product, which are the result of a diversified economy and a process of technological learning, and not by standard products (see Salais 1998).

[6] Investors who contribute to the financing of specific assets whose yield, whilst high, is initially uncertain, are particularly in need of an institutional framework which brings stability to medium- and long-term forecasts and generates confidence that they will actually be met. Hence the importance of the long-term stability of the euro.

changes. Must security, then, be forfeited for the sake of flexibility and efficiency? Such an approach overlooks the fact that people's competencies and productivity depend, essentially—as can be deduced from the effects of unemployment and its duration—on an assured quality of life and the ability they are given, and which they obtain from their work and social activities, to plan and implement meaningful life ambitions. This is in particular a key element of the growth in employment among women. It is at the core of equal gender treatment in the labour market. But more broadly, the reproduction and development of collective capabilities depend, in the long run, on community-wide agreements on the breadth and quality of social investments.

The point is, however, if we bear in mind what has been stated regarding the strengths that enhance the competitiveness of the European economy, that the nature of the positive relationship which exists between economic efficiency and flexibility should be ascertained. This positive relationship involves a new linkage between the social and the economic. Rather than making welfare a type of compensation made available after supposedly unavoidable economic damage has been done, it should be turned into something which gives individuals and intermediary groups their own resources, which, in turn, will enable them to equip themselves with active security to cope with risks. This active security would also place them in a position to learn about exposure to such risks and protect themselves in the long term.

It therefore follows that security in the form of guarantees of a minimum standard of life, as traditionally provided by social security systems, has to be supplemented, because of the need for economic flexibility, by the objective of shaping, maintaining, and developing people's competencies during their lifetimes. In a flexible economy aiming to maximize its economic growth and level of employment, human capital becomes central: its financing, its varied and developing characteristics (or competencies), its methods of training and updating, the nature of decision-making processes which affect it, and its efficiency. The nature of these competencies in the context of flexible work is considered below.

Whereas the post-war model was that the state should intervene through macro-economic employment policies, such action should now be part of labour market policy.[7] In this way, priority would be given to

---

[7] The concept referred to here and developed further in this chapter is essentially what used to be referred to in English as 'manpower policy', a concept which included the development of human capital and skills as well as matching individuals to jobs. However, this term has fallen into disuse and these wider issues are now usually considered to be part of employment policy. However, one of the key arguments in this chapter is that employment

improving the collective efficiency of the economic fabric established in different territories, and to the autonomy of deliberation and decision making by intermediary groups, in line with the principle of subsidiarity. The improvement of living and working standards should no longer be the direct and explicit target of policies, but the result of joint endeavours aimed at creating job opportunities and improving employability. This should bring about a new balance between legal innovation and political instruments which would once again make the creation of conventional frameworks for activity paramount.

From Passive Protection to Active Security

What is now relevant for economic co-ordination is no longer its reduction to predictable risk, but rather the management of all forms of uncertainty. One can manage risk by sheltering within a series of defined actions. The risk may be externalized in the form of protection founded upon actuarial calculation without it damaging economic efficiency. On the other hand, uncertainty must be controlled by an open, that is not predetermined, combination of freedom of action and a range of choices. Uncertainty must therefore be internalized. Thus, the paradox is that, to be efficient, flexibility must be based upon individual security. The governance of work within the context of uncertainty rests on a convention of trust between employer and employees.[8] Now, such trust cannot exist without giving each individual real freedom of action, in other words, freedom backed by the means for it to be effective. What is valid for entrepreneurs (guarantee of ownership of their assets, freedom to manage) is also valid for employees (guarantee of the development of their human capital, real freedom of action) in a context of flexibility under uncertainty.

Economic theory has now properly established that employment is not about exchange in the usual meaning of the word. Even when agreement has been reached and the job contract signed between employer and employee, the reality of the commitments made by the two individuals (wages and working conditions on the one hand, effort and quality of work on the other) remains uncertain. The contract does not settle the

policy (*politique de l'emploi*) is not enough, and what is needed is a more all-encompassing approach (*politique du travail*). The phrase 'labour market policy' is used in this chapter to refer to this latter idea, as this is closest to the underlying idea.

[8] The reader will note that this second section confines itself to drawing conclusions based on the Commission's Green Paper (European Commission 1997*d*).

exchange on the spot. Nor does it guarantee optimum adaptation to individual preferences. In reality, it opens up a mutual testing process which can only be settled, and perhaps not even then, by the completion of the product, its sale and the distribution of the proceeds. The central issue, as economists well know, is the uncertainty that surrounds work effort and quality.

Overcoming this uncertainty requires an institutional framework to cover the relationship between work and all those involved in it. To use a fashionable term, the accomplishment of work requires governance. Systems for the social and legal protection of labour are an essential part of this governance. However, there are essentially two views regarding the nature of this governance.

The standard approach considers that the rational individual will naturally behave in an opportunistic manner. According to this hypothesis, as soon as workers have a margin of action outside the control of the employer, they will tend not to live up to the standards of quality and effort expected of them. Similarly, if employers are the only ones aware of market demand for what they are offering, they will cheat on the exact value, so that they will then have more room for manoeuvre when dealing with the claims made by their employees. The standard approach therefore perceives social protection as a mixture of constraints and incentives to keep the opportunistic individual on the straight and narrow. The argument used is the same, for instance, as that which states that an unemployed person will only go job-hunting if the difference between welfare compensation and wages is great enough—an idea which ignores the value of work in itself in what it offers in terms of identity, social integration, and demonstration of one's own ability to do things. In the same way, businesses are too often considered to be concerned about little more than maximizing profit, as unmindful of the social needs and environments required by their companies as they are incapable of undertaking long-term commitments that determine the development of employment.

This is an inadequate view. Within a context of flexibility, the governance of work is more complex than a simple opportunism, since it must allow some latitude of action to the partners, in other words a space for freedom. This responds to a concern for efficiency. On the one hand, events at work or on the product market are interlinked: this is the characteristic feature of situations demanding flexibility. On the other hand, opportunities to effectively surmount problems will emerge if the decision to act is left solely to those in a position to act. There is no purpose in defining in advance what must be done, since the nature of these opportunities cannot be foreseen. The process will only be efficient to the extent that mutual expectations are established between the actors which leave each to act without interference, and, in co-ordination, to rely for their own action on the actions of others. The governance of work therefore rests on a convention of trust.

The existence of this mutual trust will depend on the system of social and legal protection in place. If it is supported by what the various partners consider to be legitimate principles of justice, forms part of an agreement based on such principles, and has already defined in advance the way in which the risks, costs, and responsibilities are shared out, if it sets out the way in which the anticipated gains will be distributed if risks are favourably resolved, then the co-ordination between the parties may proceed efficiently. The establishment of such trust necessarily entails the concurrence of a series of conditions, which is anything but easy and workable. Nevertheless, the achievement of full employment in most European countries in the post-war period shows that it occurred at that time and that it is therefore possible. One benchmark, possibly worth empirical investigation, for a good compromise between these different parameters might be the extent to which each planned reform or system promotes a virtuous circle between work competencies and effective freedom. After all, the most tragic observation that can be made about current systems is that they have not vanquished (indeed they have sometimes even maintained) the vicious circle between the deterioration of work competencies and confinement within casualization and dependence. Unemployment is the best illustration of this.

Unemployment and Loss of Collective Efficiency

Many authors explain the persistence of high unemployment rates and low rates of job creation in Europe in terms of the rigidity of the labour market and the 'overly generous' social protection systems which allegedly increase labour costs and undermine the competitiveness of European economies to below tolerable levels. Such arguments are not supported by a review of the national statistics available.

The study published by the Commission in 1995 in a paper on the future of social protection in Europe (European Commission 1995) shows a country-by-country comparison for 1993 of GDP *per capita* and the percentage of GDP earmarked to finance social protection.[9] It draws attention to the

---

[9] Similar statistical observations can be found in Chassard (1997).

dual nature of social protection expenditure. It is both a cost that must be financed by charges levied on the wealth produced and an investment in human capital which, like any other investment if properly conceived, generates greater wealth and creates jobs. GDP *per capita* is also an indication of a country's global productivity, and the percentage of GDP earmarked to finance social protection is an indication of the rate of investment in human capital (although, to be more precise, such expenditure should also be examined in terms of the expenditure funded by household income and free time given up). There is a positive correlation between the two; moreover, no country deviates very far from the correlation line. In other words, the richer Community countries can afford better social protection, but that is so because their large investment in human capital allows for greater productivity among the working population.

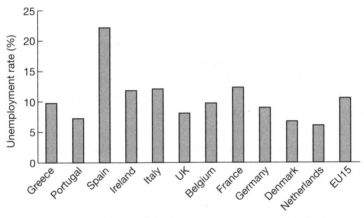

Figure 7.1. Unemployment rate (percentage of labour force) in 1996

Note: The countries are ordered from left to right on the *x*-axis in increasing order according to expenditure on social protection in GDP.

Source: Eurostat

Figure 7.1 shows unemployment rates by country in 1996. They range widely, from countries with high unemployment (Germany, Spain, France, etc.) to countries whose joblessness is substantially lower (the Netherlands, Portugal, the UK, etc.). There is no correlation between the unemployment rate and the relative weight of the cost of financing social protection; indeed, unemployment is low in the group with high social protection costs and, vice versa, countries with small social protection burdens are afflicted with high unemployment. The most striking examples are the Netherlands and Denmark in the former group and Spain in the latter.

The problem of unemployment, as indicated above, is related in only one way to systems of social protection. And it has nothing to do with their financial cost. It has to do with whether or not expenditure is geared to combating the vicious circle linking loss of work competencies and employment stagnation or loss of initiative and insufficient creation of business and enterprises. Far too often, funds have been siphoned off by social policies calling for passive solutions to unemployment (early retirement systems, public subsidies for restructuring, exemption from social security contributions to favour employment among specific segments of the population: young people, unskilled workers, etc.). While their effectiveness in achieving their stated objectives has never been soundly proven, such policies have none the less continued to draw on the available financial resources at the expense of potentially more productive applications.

Joblessness, moreover, is a wholly insufficient indicator to evaluate necessary redeployment. Connected with the capacity of post-war welfare systems to maintain an agreement of mutual trust between workers and employers and to restore the population's productivity levels, the unemployment characteristics that go hand-in-hand with the crisis such systems are undergoing differ qualitatively from one European country to the next and would merit a more thorough review.

In France, for instance, entry into the statutory system of employment is based on a generational queue. Employment levels increase more slowly than the population looking for a job, a phenomenon that automatically translates into long-term unemployment (1.1 million people in January 1997, or 34 per cent of the total looking for jobs). This is the prelude to exclusion, because not everyone who is working and becomes unemployed is ensured a place on the queue. The long-term jobless, of any age, represent a growing proportion of the beneficiaries of the *Revenu minimum d'Insertion* (minimum income for mainstreaming), which is not why that measure was implemented. Social justice, written into the labour machinery, is objective and general: a position, tasks, a pay schedule, a hierarchy, working hours stipulated and written down in advance, in other words, what in France is called a 'job'. Any economic risk translates into a divergence from a measurable norm. It sets off corrective effects. The social effect, total or partial unemployment benefit, materializes once the existence of a cause beyond the control of the actors (deterioration of the economic situation) is verified. The economic effect consists of the identification of a surplus of labour that has to be reabsorbed to re-establish apparent labour productivity. With such a model, obviously, any attempt at flexibility runs the risk, on the one hand, of being quantitative (which places undue constraints on economic decisions and hinders what would be efficient choices in the light of the circumstances), and on the other of translating into employment casualization. For only those who have a 'job' in the statutory sense are guaranteed social justice. All others are confined to tasks bereft of employment status, subject to very weak protection and, furthermore, only rarely providing a gateway to normal employment.

In Great Britain, the standard for measuring the effectiveness of a system of social protection is, for unemployment, the degree to which benefits preserve the unemployed worker's sense of personal responsibility. It is he, above all, who is expected to make an efficient effort to find a new job. It follows from this that the expression of the Welfare State crisis is the fragmentation of working lives in successive unconnected tasks. A sequence of tasks for an individual no longer constitutes a job that generates social rights (particularly income replacement or a pension) or human capital to be valued on the labour market. The rapid recourse to public assistance based on a means test breeds dependence and loss of competencies (particularly in terms of effort and responsibility). Private financing in the social protection market leads to growing and grossly underestimated economic costs. The restoration of individuals' earning capacity conceivably entails the establishment of collective support systems.

In Germany, where unemployment signifies deprivation of a job, interpreted as dispossession of social identity, mass unemployment threatens the existence of collective bargaining systems. The latter usually operate comprehensively in order, most particularly, to keep workers within their work community (company, town, sector) and protect them from the loss of identity that deprivation of a job represents. In lieu of being considered, as in France, as directly associated with macro-economic causes and therefore the responsibility of the State, economic risk remains at the company, sector, or regional level and is treated above all as a problem of economic efficiency. This leads to the possibility of agreements combining flexible working hours, work-sharing, and investment in training. In the name of excessively high real wage and labour costs, these systems soon fall prey to attempts at circumvention by relocating plants to other European countries or restricting social benefits.

Creating, maintaining, and developing work competencies becomes a primary concern in a flexible economy. Autonomy and flexibility are not innate qualities. They are learned, the result of training and experience. It is a fragile process which must be safeguarded by establishing an underlying legal and social framework. The discussion above of the kinds of unemployment stresses that a key feature in such a framework is the

204 LABOUR LAW AND ECONOMIC PERFORMANCE

extent of the actual, responsible freedoms at the disposal of the actors on the economic and labour stage. In France, indeed, the long-term unemployed and casual workers suffer the full weight of that loss of freedom of choice of life and work, which undermines their skills. In Great Britain, the difficulty of upward occupational mobility solely on the basis of labour market experience contributes to the same result. And given the impact in Germany of the feeling of belonging to a community on the delivery of a high quality of work (which is one of the strengths of German competitiveness), such losses of freedom may be expected to take unprecedented and economically unfavourable forms.

Competencies in the Context of Flexible Work and Effective Freedom

At the heart of the competencies required for work is the ability to master the uncertainty of markets and production situations. There are three kinds of uncertainty: in time (situations encountered are never identical, nor entirely repeatable); in space (the locations of exchange and production vary according to those who demand them); between persons (the identity and characteristics of persons with whom there must be efficient co-ordination vary from one situation to another).

Mastering uncertainty involves the practical resolution of the tension between two extremes. First, the risks that occur must be dealt with on the spot by the right person. That person's responsibility is total and is an inherent part of the particular market or working situation. The organization of production and hierarchical relationships are only a support, not a solution to the problem. Secondly, by virtue of the very variability and heterogeneity of possible situations, skills are acquired practically for life. True, they can only be within a given area of expertise, or in other words within one defined occupational status. But it is experience and repeated confrontation with constantly changing situations which provide the worker with his knowledge, enabling him to discover the appropriate action to take in the face of uncertainty. Furthermore, it is only the incorporation of this permanent requirement for immediate action which will permit the individual to learn the lesson of what happens in a working situation.

It therefore follows that, in the context of flexible work, we cannot necessarily equate work competencies with a high level of qualification, and that such competencies can only be developed if they are actually used (hence the overriding importance of getting into work and staying there).

Efficient deployment entails working situations which guarantee real free-dom of choice, and the latter can only exist if the definition of the jobs and tasks undertaken in an enterprise provide the people who carry them out with opportunities for learning and for mobility. In this way, the time spent working in the course of a life becomes permeable, permitting input from a combination of work in a variety of different forms (employee, self-employed, etc.) with vocational training and diverse social experiences. This is due to the fact that, on the one hand, the attachment to a given employer is jeopardized by the unpredictability of risks, whilst on the other, only this type of real-life experience can enhance the capabilities and efficiency of the capital invested in individuals.

In short, the best way to understand the difference in nature between protection and security in the face of risks is to see the latter as a con-stituent part of the former. To improve competencies in a flexible working situation, one must be in a position to learn from exposure to risks. A framework consisting of protection against risks is an obstacle to learning from these risks, since it is basically negatively oriented. If the flexible worker is to be able to learn, he or she will need a framework which pro-vides security in the face of risks. This framework would give the individ-ual the chance to anticipate the long-term, at any given moment. There can be no mutual trust in a working situation unless individuals have a guarantee that their life's ambitions which are close to their hearts, will remain feasible. Only then will they be able to form and embark upon life's more fulfilling ambitions, for themselves and their nearest relations, which contribute even further to the enhancement of work competencies which in turn lead to higher added value. It is in this sense that, far from being weakened by the need for flexibility, the securities of life linked to the respect for a minimum standard (for example, the effective right of every individual to a place to live and not simply to a minimum amount of income) are reinforced, or even more easily and more specifically defin-able, as a consequence of this need. But to the static dimension which takes note of or restores respect for a standard of living, we must add the dynamic dimension of the individual and collective paths of life and work.

Labour Market Policy and Subsidiarity

The only route by which a positive combination of flexibility and security is possible is within a labour market policy centred upon people's experi-ences and paths of life and work. The economic calculation associated with this is based on a simple principle: once the value added by the individual's work exceeds the cost of employing him or her, a surplus of wealth and utility is produced for the community. Admittedly, implementation of this is complex. It must incorporate modernization, temporal dynamics, and moments of critical evaluation, but it is nevertheless decisive. It is clear that labour market policy cannot be equated with engaging in social expenditure which simply lowers the monetary cost of putting people into work, either by paying the employer the difference in cost between the wages paid and productivity (assuming that this could be measured in the first place) or by lowering the minimum wage. The process element is paramount and gives active expenditure concrete content. The object is to produce the experience which improves the individual's human capital and increases his or her earning capacity. This may include different types of training, creating institutional mechanisms or improving the efficacy of those which already exist, making available shared facilities which would help put people into work,[10] and so on. In particular, the existence of specific social needs which are not automatically met by the marketplace constitutes an argument for such expenditure. These needs may be identified and met at the regional level under forms to be worked out by the social and economic actors (Lunghini 1997). There have already been a number of experiences of this kind with integration of the long-term unemployed or people on the margins of social exclusion.

Accordingly, the purpose of labour market policy is not limited to classifying problems in terms of target populations or specific social groups. It is more general. It concerns the redefinition of the principles of state action geared to the systematic and dynamic improvement of human capital, human capital that should be considered from two standpoints: the course of people's lives and careers and the collective competencies, in work, innovation, and productivity, needed for the economic development of European sectors and regions.

Seen from the standpoint of the individual, such a labour market policy aims to create continuities and not, as is the case with employment policies, manage queues and paperwork etc., after severance. Welfare ex-

---

[10] The same views were voiced long ago and more eloquently by Alfred Marshall when, as an economist anxious to help put an end to poverty, he considered the links between economic development, putting people into work and efficiency wages at the end of the nineteenth century. Part IV takes up once again the concerns expressed in Theme III: the creation of a new culture with the capacity for occupational integration as set out in the *Guideline proposals for Member State employment policies in 1998*, a Commission document dated 1 October 1997. In Theme IV, this same document puts forward the idea of the usefulness of refocusing state aid policies on promoting investment in human resources and adaptation capacity.

penditure, instead of being activated as a consequence of risk and managing its effects (with the familiar possibility of perpetuating the situation by stigmatizing the individual and placing him or her in a state of dependence), is then based on integrating and maintaining the individual in the sphere of work. The institutions in charge should act within a localized and delivery framework. Their task is to monitor the experience/career of the individual. The premise for their action is that each individual is free and responsible for his or her own life and ambitions. But rather than leaving individuals to their own devices (and opting out in advance from any supervision by paying out a minimum subsistence allowance), welfare institutions should act according to the principle of subsidiarity. A key area in their intervention is to assess the moment at which the risks taken in the context of work could cause the individual to meet with a risk which he or she is unable to control, in other words, not so much unemployment itself, but a more precarious situation, poverty or dependence. The thrust of their action, then, must be to provide individuals with the necessary conditions to exercise effectively their responsibilities towards themselves, and not to exercise this responsibility in their stead. This principle of subsidiarity, which is so essential in the building of Europe, has three consequences.

Social institutions should intervene as a matter of priority with those whose personal resources do not or no longer permit them to exercise full responsibility for their own path of life. This is why the guarantee of a standard of life remains imperative, as at the inception of social security schemes, but now, however, new problems are posed. It is not uncommon, for example, for a small employer who goes bankrupt to have no security to fall back on, to the extent that, in order to start up, he took personal risks with his own assets. Conversely, one may find it dubious that senior managers combine the advantages of being paid on the basis of capital returns—by way of share options or good redundancy cover—with generous salary and employee social security status, without also being forced to make high contributions, for example, through systems of capitalization. Social solidarity may be considered here as guaranteeing to all an effective capacity to exercise their own responsibility in building their lives, a capacity already seen to be one of the foundations of a flexible economy.

On another level, but related to the above, it follows that, mirroring the changes in labour law in Europe, there is some prospect of a swing from employment policies based on financial aid paid to employers under a general and predefined criterion of employment towards aid to individuals focusing on the development of their competencies in the context of flexible working (in the precise meaning set out in this report which, we feel, is adapted to economically and socially desirable trends in the European economy). There are any number of possible stumbling blocks in this approach, in particular the risk of contributing to stigmatizing individuals if they are subjected to narrow-minded institutional surveillance mechanisms instead of being engaged in a creative process to allow them to exploit new opportunities. But the possible benefits are no less impressive.

Several examples show that the existence of direct or disguised employment subsidies gives rise to competitive underbidding among European regions. This reinforces the role of low labour costs as the sole item considered by business concerns in deciding where to locate, which in turn leads to a static, short-term vision of economic development that reflects poorly on its advocates. It is, as we have seen, a conception that ignores Europe's real economic chances; if generalized, it would destroy those chances, which can only be maintained if their potential is exploited. Preventing social dumping is tantamount to combating unfair competition. It is merely a question, it must be realized, of applying the principles of equal treatment and prevention of anti-competitive practices laid down in the Treaty of Rome. This in turn draws attention to the need to give some thought to the way in which the application of the principle of equal treatment can be made consistent with structural policies aiming to improve, in the various regions and sectors, absolute competitive advantages on the basis of labour quality and specific skills. After all, by deprecating purely monetary and financial considerations of cost, the principle of equality steers inter-company competition towards the pursuit of such 'real' advantages as organization, quality, and adaptation to market demands. This, then, is also suggestive of a labour market rather than an employment policy.[11]

In the same vein, it may be noted that the exemption from or reduction of social security contributions to favour the creation of jobs should be carefully controlled. There is an understandable temptation in this regard with respect to unskilled workers. The macro-economic reasoning here, correct in itself, is nevertheless based on an inaccurate view of the way the labour market and companies actually operate. On the one hand, observation shows that the general scarcity of jobs makes selection processes more competitive: such subsidized jobs are more often than not taken not by unskilled jobless workers, but by other, better qualified candidates. For,

---

[11] These reflections are equally, if not more, applicable to the problems of tax harmonization in Europe.

if able to choose between two candidates for the same job, a company will tend, if the cost is the same and within certain limits, to recruit the one it feels will make the greater contribution, that is quite often the higher qualified of the two. And this is doubly detrimental: first, 'unskilled' workers continue to be excluded, and secondly, the potential skills of the qualified workers are not fully used. It is the European labour market as a whole that actually needs to be brought back into balance by increasing the job opportunities for skilled labour and thereby inducing an upswing in the labour market.[12] Moreover, the creation of skilled jobs in itself leads to the creation of other competencies and externalities, laying the grounds for a positive dynamic that would combine rising productivity and the creation of further business. Because skilled employment, in short, is efficient, it demands a logistic environment in which there is a need to cover a number of tasks requiring little or no skill and hence find the people to do this work.

Unskilled labour is indisputably overburdened by compulsory labour costs. This may be corrected by specific measures, such as for instance establishing funding solidarity for social protection systems between large capitalist companies—which create very few net jobs and, indeed, have settled into an ongoing process of downsizing—and small and medium enterprises that do create jobs (by relating the amount of contributions to participation in employment generation). In the case of unskilled labour, the priority should continue to be given to unemployed unskilled workers or workers who have lost their skills due to long-term unemployment: more broadly, people on the margins of social exclusion should continue to be the target for integration policies geared to individuals (see below).

One essential step advocated in the policies to be implemented, referred to at the beginning of this chapter, is to re-establish the grounds on which social protection system financing is based, rather than progressively sapping resources to fund overly generous policies involving the lowering or elimination of labour costs. Reaching such a balance is no easy matter. The re-establishment of financial balance calls essentially for the creation of socially profitable job opportunities, that is jobs in which the added value created is greater (eventually, at least) than the cost of putting the employee to work. The contrary, encouraged by the artificial profitability of government-subsidized jobs, occurs far too often. Another step—representative of a direction in which current British thinking is aimed—is to lay the groundwork for or to recreate the spirit of civil responsibility in

---

[12] This does not do away with the problem of adaptation of skills to needs or the problem of starting out on a career (acquisition of experience and rise in productivity).

people with respect to the social protection systems that protect them. Rights to which no duties are attached only rarely lead to responsible and efficient work. This stresses, once again, the importance of a system of rules that must be well understood, collectively discussed and sufficiently reliable to constitute the basis for mutual trust in the performance of work.

Considered from the standpoint of the community, the emphasis is essentially on the deterioration of work competencies and efficiency stemming from vulnerability to economic risks. Structuring the action of the social institutions concerned around employability calls for understanding that term from a versatile, broad and, above all, preventive standpoint. Employability and vulnerability need not be considered as contradictory terms, but it must be understood that the two are dynamically related and that 'good' employability rests on the reduction of individual and collective vulnerability to risks. The criticism that must be levelled against the notion of employability as the sole grounds for active policies is that it is based on increasing the rate of labour turnover on the labour market. In fact, even if it may be profitable for the individual employer in the short-term, it has never been shown that turnover of this type is collectively efficient, bearing in mind the losses in human capital that it entails. It is as if, when faced with the danger of a mountain avalanche, our first concern were to rebuild the houses that had been destroyed as cheaply and as quickly as possible, rather than trying to protect them by drawing up a land development plan which defined the areas that could actually be built on. The difference between passive protection and active security lies in the attempt to reduce financial costs by a policy of prevention.

The concept of social security should no longer regard the occurrence of economic risk as a natural phenomenon, a natural catastrophe. The central issue is its capacity to prevent it. Integration in employment comes first, followed by steps to tackle the vulnerability to unemployment of those who are in work, by improving their future employability in a preventive manner, that is to say by looking at work, its conception and its organization. In fact, many initiatives are already heading in this direction. Issues such as health and safety, occupational medicine, further education, or even apprenticeship provide a perspective for developing active policies. The economic basis for information and consultation of the employees of a business resides in the idea that getting their opinions is likely to improve protection against economic or technological risks. The additional requirement for employers to have an adequate workforce at any given time also responds to a preventive approach. One may multiply the examples.

Social institutions need to play a secondary role, likely to be restricted to supporting decisions taken by collective agreement at the pertinent level (business, sector, territory, Europe) and to ensuring a standard realization. This results from the 'political' content of the concept of subsidiarity and calls for a reversal in the respective roles of politics and the law. Collective bargaining conceived in this way no longer has a strategic nature (to act as little as possible against one's own interest and, in turn, to attempt to manipulate the other party without oneself making any true commitment). Such negotiation furthers European common benefits (the level of employment, social justice, the development of the competencies of individuals). It is constructive and comprehensive, transcending private interests. It comprises a social dialogue leading to joint agreements that include a mixture of rights, duties, and fundings. Without these conventions in fact, distrust would win in a social context of uncertainty. It would be impossible to assure the effective freedom and personal responsibility necessary for an efficient flexible economy.

Collective Frameworks for a Labour Market Policy

The more jobs and the more opportunities for work and earning there are, the more assurance there will be of a certain security in life and the lower will be its financial cost. The best security is therefore that which is based on job creation. This in turn depends on the creation of activity, skills, and new wealth. It therefore follows that a labour market policy cannot be limited purely to the optimal management of people's careers. It must also have adequate collective frameworks, which will need to be supplied by national and European policies designed to improve collective efficiency. The point is not to allocate existing resources in a different way by means of financial aid, but rather to encourage the creation of resources at the time and in the place where opportunities arise. Structural policies on research and innovation, occupational and continuing training, joint infrastructures, the setting up of networks of companies and representative groups, mechanisms promoting occupational mobility, and the creation of enterprise are all of paramount importance.

This is why any deliberation as to what should become of labour law in Europe must be placed in the context of developing European employment. But in turn, placing it in this context will help us to reformulate the employment issue. One thing is certain: employment is more likely to result from structural policies aimed at collective efficiency than if it is made the direct and explicit target of economic policies.[13] This is a direct result of the changed nature of economic development which we considered above: diversity, human capital, partnership, territoriality. It is not general, vertical policies, but close, long-lasting, horizontal co-ordination between the parties which will create networks and intermediary collective organizations that will generate and maintain employment. Furthermore, by addressing the company environment, these structural policies will improve collective efficiency and reduce the inequalities in labour productivity between different regions. This in turn will lessen the incentive to opt for relocation blackmail, rather than giving proper thought to the matter of what medium-term strategy to adopt.

It is essential that these policies should be placed in their territorial context. Let us return for a moment to the idea of globalization as an opportunity for European companies to make the world their individual sphere of action. We have already seen that this opportunity is based on the prospect of a steady increase in non-price-based competitive advantages. If these advantages are really to be obtained, the company must be a permanent part of its environment, which involves carving out a territory, the search for co-operation within a network covering the whole enterprise chain, closer relationships with the surrounding population (local groups, professional associations, public research laboratories and agencies, universities and systems of general and vocational training). These are the economic, social, and political territories within which the issue of flexibility, if it is to have any meaning or scope at all, must be defined. There and only there can we generate the collective dynamics which will positively link improved productivity with the creation of both resources and activity. This is where we will find the joint structures which legislation should help to update in Europe, in order to turn these into spaces for public deliberation to enable us to define the resources that can be mobilized and allocated. In short, these should gradually become the spaces within which the parties concerned can really exercise their freedom to act (in the way described above).

---

[13] Needless to say, a structural policy strategy aimed at collective efficiency entails a certain type of macro-economic environment if the effect these policies are to have on employment is to be maximized. Going into too much detail about the nature of this would take us outside the scope of the group's report, but it still needs to be done.

Individual Labour Force Membership Status and Intermediary Collective Mechanisms

Co-ordination between individual prospects and collective needs will be feasible as a consequence of a concept that needs to become a political imperative (and it can only become this if Europe acts to impose it as an agreement between the parties involved, thus making it a mutual expectation which can be relied upon).[14] This imperative is to ensure that people remain in a 'labour force membership status'[15] throughout their lives. It is this status that will then guarantee the efficiency and development of their work competencies. Since the exercise of real freedom and job changes are necessarily associated, the maintenance of such a professional status can only be conceived of within collective mechanisms. The proposal calling for the institution of social drawing rights (Supiot 1997) is an illustration of the argument for such collective mechanisms.

Such individual rights would be acquired gradually in the course of performing a job. They would bring about a liberation in terms of time, thus providing a space in which flexibility at work could be put into practice, provided that the idea of work-generating rights were to extend beyond waged employment to self-employed, charitable, and public service work and to the time spent acquiring continuing training, in whatever form. In this way, the individual would become a creditor who could lay claim to provisions which he or she could freely use (hence the notion of drawing rights) at different times in his or her life. The capital thus accumulated could take the shape of money or rights (for instance the right to perform a charitable activity or take a course, whilst at the same time retaining the resources required to continue living during this period).

[14] It cannot be emphasized enough that the principle of subsidiarity does not mean the disappearance, but on the contrary requires the exercise, of responsibility at European level. The responsibility in question, however, is not that of centralist intervention based on uniform, systematic criteria. The best definition is that it is a responsibility based on the premise that those involved are autonomous and can therefore themselves define the nature of what is in the common good, in such a way that it can be properly implemented in the situation in question. The responsibility involves a duty (but not a right) to intervene in those cases where the parties involved are unable to define the nature of what is the common good in this particular situation (see Salais and Storper 1993).

[15] *Statut professionel* in French. See footnote 1, Chapter 2 for a discussion of the difficulties of translating this concept into English. It was first proposed in Supiot (1997). From an historical point of view, it is striking that, once again, we come across the features, even moral features, developed in the occupational groupings of the second part of the nineteenth century. Codes of ethics and good practice, the development of professional associations, their advisory and training activities and placement of the self-employed and *professionals* in new jobs are all evidence of just how modern such intermediary groups really were.

We cannot fail to see, in each of these points, the need for a collectively established framework. Provision (of money or rights) could be supplied in a combination of ways: by the state or territorial collectivities, by companies through their contributions to the welfare protection of their employees, by individuals themselves through their savings (of leisure time and money), or by social security institutions through the benefits they pay out. There is a need to safeguard continuity over time—which is essential in the life of an individual—in the accumulation of these rights and the opportunities to draw on them in the face of changes in work, social systems, protection type, or European country. Similarly, thought should be given as to how we can define the initial allocations and subsequent increments which would give the cast-iron guarantee of an adequate base of rights and opportunities to those who, by virtue of their own circumstances or their social origin, have little in the way of property, monetary, or human assets. We must draw up procedures for collective deliberation to ensure the necessary reconciliation between the needs of the community to which one belongs (the firm, the region, etc.) and the individual's freedom to use his or her rights. The compilation of statistical indicators designed to gauge the degree of effectiveness and success of the rights thus defined is therefore all the more important.

8

Summary

In this survey, the expert group established by the European Commission's DG V has attempted to take a cross-disciplinary and transnational approach to the evolution of labour law. Its aim was to bridge the gap between legalistic surveys of the evolution of positive law and the sociological, economic, and cultural approach to the realities of the working world, in an attempt to produce a description from a normative perspective of the links between law and new social practice. It was ultimately an exercise calling for an understanding of trends as much as for the actual drafting of proposals.

GENERAL FRAMEWORK

The Classic Labour Law Model

The point of departure for the analysis was the observation that the socioeconomic regulatory model that had underpinned labour law since the beginning of the twentieth century is in the throes of a crisis. Important national differences aside, that industrial model may be ideally or typically described as a regulatory framework which depends on a standardized form of subordination, the widespread nuclear family and the institutionalization of the parties who have an interest in collective bargaining, all within a national state.

From an institutional standpoint, this model may be seen as a triangle whose three sides are companies, trade unions, and the state. Where internal organization is concerned, Fordist companies engage primarily in the mass production of fairly standard products. They systematically separate the design and implementation stages of production. Standard employment relationships are based on an employee–employer relationship (subordinate work), in which the former, whose training lasts for a relatively short period of time, is *pater familias* (a male breadwinner) and hired on open-ended terms to provide services defined by his job description. Fordist trade unions are active organizations centred not around specific trades (as in the previous corporatist model) but around business sectors. The key bargaining level is the industry (with the exception of the United Kingdom, where the company level has always predominated). The state is Keynesian—aiming primarily to maintain domestic demand (at the risk of inflation), national—protecting its domestic markets from foreign competition—and conciliatory—instituting machinery for social bargaining. Labour law, and the social protection deriving from it, tend to become standardized in the sense that they favour employment relationships that fall into a single pattern (based on a dual system of subordinate employment and self-employment) and guarantee workers passive individual security, uniform working hours, relatively independent collective bargaining and a special status for civil servants, associated with the notion of public service.

Current Trends

We cannot fail to see that all three sides of that triangle are collapsing. The internal reorganization of businesses has altered the distinction between design and implementation, particularly as a result of the emergence of production dedicated more to non-standard goods; as a consequence, employment relationships have become more flexible, involving long or continuing worker training. Women have entered the labour market *en masse*, thereby undermining the patriarchal Fordist model. Stable employment is being replaced by more casual working arrangements which are not defined exclusively in terms of job or position. Trade unions, in turn, in the face of the unemployment brought about by the economic crisis, have been obliged to redefine their role: no longer concerned solely with male wages and working conditions, they also deal with issues such as employment, company survival, and gender equality. Finally, the State has abandoned its Keynesian policies in favour of anti-inflationary strategies and budgetary control, turning its attention to maintaining competitive conditions. Its sovereignty, meanwhile, has been

curtailed to some extent by emerging regional movements and the
appearance of authority at European level.

Group Guidelines

In considering its approach to these changes, the group ruled out two possible courses of action: on the one hand, dismantling labour law and
bringing the employment relationship and protection against risk within
the scope of civil law and on the other, dissociation of social and economic interests via, first, flexibilization without the intervention of social
partners and the State and, secondly, the proclamation of social rights
regardless of whether or not the individual is involved in economic activity. The third course, which was the one finally chosen by the group, is
based on a diagnosis of socio-economic change and retrospective reference to the democratic demands that led to the institution of social law.

Diagnosis

The expert group took due note of the proliferation of production systems
which characterize the pattern of European growth at present. In this context, traditional employees and mass production still hold a relatively
important place, alongside other types of industrial organization. From
the standpoint of both individual and collective action, this proliferation
of alternatives leads to growing uncertainty. The notion of flexibility must
be interpreted in this context. Its economic reference point is not only the
need to optimize market relations (as if the market were the *sole* model for
economic co-ordination, and as such now taking the place of the welfare
model). It is first and foremost the need to optimize the numerous production relations, involving security for both workers and companies, the
development of individual and collective human capital, and the building
of local production relations based usually on geographical proximity.

Democratic Requirements

Labour law brought specific democratic demands into the socio-
economic sphere, and they need to be maintained and reformulated in

the light of present circumstances. The group paid particular attention to four of these.

- Equality must be maintained, but must incorporate the relatively new issue of gender equality.
- Freedom entails maintaining worker protection against dependence. But new forms of such dependence are emerging.
- Individual security, involving a wide range of social rights, must be reconstrued not as security against exceptional risk, but in the light of an ubiquitous risk associated with the inevitable rise in uncertainty. Coping with uncertainty must be made an integral part of the very definition of security.
- Collective rights guarantee the actual participation of the people concerned in the definition of the meaning of work, of both the purposes and means of economic development. It is for this reason that they must be maintained and at the same time expanded to take account of new kinds of collective representation, action, and bargaining, which should not, however, replace former practice altogether.

The group has worked on reformulating the conditions that would ensure the effectiveness of these four demands in different aspects of labour law. To that end, it has sought not to invent an entirely new model, but rather to selectively embrace tendencies already emerging in the evolution of European law and to propose an intelligible framework which may serve as a guide for future policies.

WORK AND PRIVATE POWER

Analysis

The notion of subordination has evolved along three lines. First, hierarchies appear to be flattening out. Greater operational independence may be observed even among workers involved in traditional employment relationships. At the same time, although self-employment is growing very slowly in European countries, from the legal standpoint the presumptions attached to the status of employee are losing ground. Both the courts and lawmakers appear to want to broaden the scope of self-employment. None the less, a second tendency may be observed whereby, despite greater formal leeway in subordinate relationships, the casualization of labour, mass unemployment, and new management practices may make subordination weigh more heavily in employment relationships in the form of informal pressure on workers, in particular younger, female, and less-skilled workers. Finally, the third trend involves more complex relations between employers and workers due to the appearance of third parties, namely sub-contractors or temporary employment businesses.

This evolution has important consequences for the protection provided by social law. The first consequence is, in many cases, increasing personal insecurity. Cases of 'false self-employment' or casual workers who are 'invited' to refrain from joining a trade union are eloquent proof of this. The second effect is the grey area between dependent employment and self-employment. Legally independent sub-contractors, individuals, or businesses are sometimes financially dependent on one or several clients or principals; conversely, the circumstances of legally dependent workers are increasingly resembling those of self-employed workers. Finally and thirdly, the employment relationship in networked companies needs to be addressed, in particular the principal's liabilities with regard to the health and safety of the sub-contractor's employees, protection of temporary workers or even companies' joint responsibility for compliance with working hours, etc.

Guidelines

In view of these trends, the group of experts is highlighting the need for a twofold choice:

- reassertion of the essential principle whereby the parties to an employment relationship are not vested with the power to establish the legal status of that relationship;
- a desire (with an eye to the future) to expand the scope of labour law to cover all kinds of contracts involving the performance of work for others, not only strict worker subordination.

From this perspective, the group advocates the following overall guidelines:

- The adoption of a Community definition of the notion of employee. Such a definition exists currently only within the area of freedom of movement for workers. By imposing it, the Court of Justice wanted to prevent any State from limiting the scope of this principle at its own discretion by way of a restrictive definition. This reasoning applies to all Community social law provisions.

- Upholding the power of the courts to redefine an employment contract. The technique of an array of possibilities, tried and tested in case law, must allow for the scope of labour law to be adapted to the new ways in which power is exercised in companies. At the same time it must ensure no restrictive definition of subordination is formulated on the basis of a single criterion (including 'economic dependence' or 'integration into someone else's company').
- Consolidation of a specific status for temporary employment businesses, along with the introduction of categories of employers' joint activity and joint responsibility, should make it possible to deal with the problems inherent in the growing complexity of employment relationships resulting from the increasing tendency to resort to dependent companies. In parallel, combating labour trafficking certainly continues to be a priority. All of this might form the subject, with due respect for the principle of subsidiarity, of European-scale intervention (modelled on directives relating to intra-European provision of services; or on the directive requiring different companies engaging in work on the same construction site or civil engineering project to co-ordinate all worker health and safety matters).
- The application of certain aspects of labour law to workers who are neither employees nor employers. The need for protection tailored to the special situation of these workers has been covered in labour law in several countries (the German notion of *arbeitnehmerähnliche Person* or the Italian *parasubordinazione*). Those workers who cannot be regarded as employed persons, but are in a situation of economic dependence *vis-à-vis* a principal, should be able to benefit from the social rights to which this dependence entitles them.

WORK AND LABOUR FORCE MEMBERSHIP STATUS

Analysis

In labour law, the concept of employment status establishes a bond between the various kinds of protection and the definition of the working circumstances prevailing throughout the worker's lifetime. But the Fordist model of employment status is disintegrating in four areas. First, continuity of status was typically associated with the continuity of a condition (employment) throughout an entire lifetime. However, such continuity has been called into question by internal (different jobs, same employer) and external (casualization of contracts) flexibilization, and also by high unemployment rates. Secondly, Fordist employment status was defined in terms of a person's occupation. It has, however, been noted that such a criterion has been giving way to other definitions, in particular, to the principle of attaching a monetary value to a job (see unemployment rules, for instance). Thirdly, the proliferation of different kinds of employment status makes a mockery of Fordist standardization. It should be noted that governments have contributed substantially to this disintegration through their policy of subsidizing jobs, in both the public and private sectors. Finally, the concept of a single employer is also at issue, both with regard to the entity concerned (groups or networks of companies) and over time (succession of employers).

Guidelines

In view of this situation, the expert group advises against maintaining the employment model within the confines of labour law. Given the inevitable flexibilization of labour markets, it believes that would encourage the working world to split into two. Rather, it advocates redesigning the notion of security, at three inter-connected levels:

- Employment status should be redefined to guarantee the continuity of a career rather than the stability of specific conditions. The prime aim is to protect workers during transitions between jobs. Particular attention should be paid to workers' rights to redeployment in the event of dismissal, changes of status (from employee to self-employed for instance), links between employment and training, between school and working life; access to a first job and the avoidance of long-term unemployment.
- New legal instruments must be developed to ensure continuity of status above and beyond different cycles of work and non-work. What is at stake is nothing less than the abandonment of the linear career model. Career breaks and changes of occupation should come to be considered a normal part of an ongoing labour force membership status. Such continuity may be ensured by law or collective agreement.
- Labour force membership status should no longer be determined on the basis of the restrictive criterion of employment, but be based on the broader notion of work. Social law may no longer disregard non-marketable forms of work. None the less, the group rejected the notion of activity as too imprecise. Work is distinguished from activity in that it

involves an obligation, voluntarily assumed or legally imposed, under onerous or voluntary terms, subject to a status or a contract. Work always has some legal connotation.

This broadened labour force membership accordingly covers three of the four circles of social law: the rights inherent in wage-earning work (employment), common rights connected with occupational activity (health and safety), and rights ensuing from unwaged work (care for others, voluntary work, training on one's own initiative, etc.) together constitute the three circles of rights associated with the notion of labour force membership. Universal social rights, guaranteed irrespective of work (health care, minimum social assistance), fall outside this notion and should therefore be protected under specific legislation. The principle of equal treatment for men and women, however, applies to all four circles.

Broadened labour force membership goes hand-in-hand with various kinds of social drawing rights. The specific social rights emerging today are new from two standpoints: they may be unrelated to employment in the narrow sense (time off for union activities; training credits; parental leave), even where associated with work which had led to the accumulation of credit; and they are exercised on a discretionary basis rather than in the unexpected occurrence of risks. As a supplement to traditional social rights, these optional rights allow workers to deal with flexibility on an individual basis. This is why the group recommends that thought be given to redesigning labour law in terms of the distribution of social drawing rights, a concept that seems an appropriate way of coping with the demand for 'active security in uncertain circumstances'.

WORK AND TIME

Analysis

Without prejudice to the genuinely important issue of quantitative working time, on which current debate is focused, the group concentrated on qualitative analysis. Three new factors are transforming the perception of social time. First, Fordist time, as a general work standard, made the regulation of time one of the system's primary regulatory tools. However, such a tool is appropriate only in Taylorist mass production contexts. The appearance of new production systems calls for new standards for measuring work, the subordination related to it and the insecurity generated by it. In particular, the transfer of many types of work to the tertiary sector, including those in manufacturing industry, involves qualitative changes in time-based relations. Thus, overburdening and keeping workers at the employer's disposal may paradoxically go hand-in-hand with a formal reduction in working hours. Maintaining a purely quantitative standard for time can easily conceal the diversity of work involvement, which calls for new kinds of protection. Secondly, flexibilization of the organization of work entails fragmentation of time, which should be reviewed from two standpoints. From the standpoint of the individual worker, part-time work and flexible working hours hold out both the promise of freedom and a threat of greater subordination. Women especially fall victim to this process. The key question in this regard lies in the conditions under which bargaining on flexibility and part-time work is conducted. Major differences are observed between countries where the process has been bargained collectively (Netherlands) and those where there are no collective arrangements. From the collective standpoint, the fragmentation of time entails new problems of co-ordination. Collective timing disappears and with it the conditions for social integration. The debate about Sundays off is revealing in this regard. Finally, a new issue related to free time that eludes Fordist patterns is clearly emerging. The latter wrongly define free time as non-working time. But such time is partly devoted to unwaged tasks (training, domestic chores, community life) which should be treated as actual work (see above). Work, furthermore, casts its shadow over free time (on-call work, unpaid tasks, etc.). This raises the question of the conditions under which workers can *genuinely* dispose of their non-working time freely.

Guidelines

Although there is no longer any such thing as standard time, the law can still ensure a degree of co-ordination for the different types of time. With this in mind, the group has drawn up certain guidelines.

- A comprehensive approach to individual time and collective time is required by law. We have to draw all the consequences from the general principle whereby work is adapted to human needs (and not the other way round). From the individual standpoint, it is important, for instance, not to limit consideration of the question only to the time services are provided, but to consider contract duration as well.

This affects the conditions under which certain elementary safety rules are learned, for instance. In the same vein, the different stages of life and the changing needs they entail (maternity, child rearing, training) should be protected in full. From the collective standpoint, the law should ensure respect for certain principles underlying co-ordination and social timing, with respect to both family and urban life.

• The overall idea is broken down into substantive principles. General principles, leading to effective subjective rights, should be guaranteed at Community level as well. For instance, the right to a family and social life is a principle enshrined in Article 8 of the European Convention on Human Rights; it is broader in scope than Directive 93/104, confined in turn to a Fordist definition of free time and addressing worker health and safety only. The issue of night work could be reassessed in the light of such principles.

• This overall approach is implemented through collective bargaining. Individualization of time should not be confused with changes in contract terms and conditions concerning time. Collective bargaining is the most appropriate platform to lay down rules governing time. Such bargaining should be systematically encouraged, subject to penalties as appropriate. But this entails a significant change in the ground rules on collective bargaining, as discussed below.

WORK AND COLLECTIVE ORGANIZATION

Analysis

The group of experts found collective bargaining, although in the midst of reorganization, astonishingly dynamic. The vigour of this Fordist institution is characterized by its expansion in three areas. First of all, more issues are being addressed under collective bargaining, insofar as it now deals with company management (time and work flexibility, social plans) and builds bridges between the world of those with jobs and the world of those without (maintenance of employment). Secondly, more parties are covered, insofar as such bargaining now also takes account of workers who are not employees and non-standard employers. Finally, the tasks of collective bargaining are expanding, and not only as regards the internal management of companies. Such expansion is set against a backdrop of increasingly complex relations between the law and collective agreements: collective agreements are vested with the enforcement of legal provisions, in addition to quasi-legislative functions, either because the law specifies that it is supplementary to agreements or because the legislative process includes social consultation (at Community level, this tendency is enshrined in Article 3 of the Maastricht Agreement on Social Policy).

None the less, this dynamism must be considered in association with two adverse factors related to social consultation which both result from and feed into it. First, there is the issue of representation: on the one hand, union membership is declining; on the other, representation is becoming more fragmented and complex both within and outside trade union circles, with the appearance of alternative representation (the unemployed and other groups such as consumer and environmental associations). This involves a dual shift: a reorganization within trade unions and/or realignment of their relative importance in bargaining. The same process may be observed on the management side, where manufacturing companies are over-represented compared with the new employers (essentially small and medium-sized enterprises). The second issue involves the institutions for joint consultation and action. On the one hand, there is a redrawing of the Fordist map: individual companies tend to acquire ever-greater relevance to the detriment of the central role traditionally played by whole industries (appearance of the *Öffnungsklauseln* in Germany, Italy, and other countries). Moreover, a second map is being drawn which tends to overlap the Fordist map. A new pattern of company/company networks (groups or geographical)/Europe-wide levels is being superimposed on the company/ industry/national hierarchy. Co-ordination of the various players involved is consequently becoming very confused and this confusion is particularly obvious in the difficulties arising around the interpretation of most favourable treatment, a fundamental principle of traditional labour law.

Guidelines

In view of such trends, the group of experts recommends:

- Active support from public (in particular Community) authorities for recasting collective bargaining: broadening the scope of bargaining and extending the parties covered and tasks involved should be encouraged as the only response to demands for flexibility that is consistent with the tradition of labour law. Such support may consist of rules on mandatory bargaining and procedural rules on representation.

- With respect to representation: the group finds the exclusive focus on representation at the company level risky. It is in this light that it undertook its discussion of the dual system of representation (works councils/union representation). The group feels that these two elements are more complementary than adversarial. Such complementarity should be regarded as reciprocal support. Trade unions need someone to liaise for them inside companies, someone whose legitimacy can be attributed to the election process; conversely, company representatives should be able to count on the backing provided by higher levels of organization to mitigate the effects of 'company corporatism'. Similarly, the group warns against neo-corporatist tendencies that refuse to acknowledge alternative forms of representation: the expansion of issues for discussion, the parties covered and the tasks involved automatically entails the acceptance of alternative forms of profiling collective interests by subject areas. In the light of the above, the group advises against the principle of simple trade union monopoly, in accordance with the trends in case law, particularly in France.
- With regard to the proliferation of bargaining forums: while acknowledging the relevance of other bargaining levels, the expert group stresses the importance of the role of networked companies (Directive 92/57 is a first example thereof) and territorial networks whereby businesses and other interest groups join forces (at local or regional level, for instance). This approach seems to be an appropriate way to meet the challenges deriving from business reorganization and, more generally, it may facilitate the transition from employment policy to labour market policy as mentioned above. As far as most favourable treatment is concerned, the group recommends that the interpretation of such treatment should not be confined to workers' individual and monetary interests, but should also include other collective and non-monetary criteria such as maintenance of employment or protection of the environment.

WORK AND THE STATE

Analysis

Like Fordism, the Keynesian nation-state is undergoing a crisis. The terms of regulation are affected first: the state faces increasing individualization of lifestyles and demands from civil society, and such individualization openly challenges the paternalistic traits that the Welfare State may have acquired. Moreover, the opening up of the European market, budgetary constraints and the need to combat inflation are putting an end to the continual expansion of State services. Secondly, the terms of public action are changing. The general trend in public services is to move from the State as manager (one that delivers services directly) to the State as guarantor (in which services are provided by private or mutual bodies, subject to the rules set by the State to guarantee all citizens equal access to such services). This entails new kinds of involvement in civil society. Civil servants have not been spared: there is a tendency to convert officials' special status into ordinary employment contracts (to varying extents, depending on the country). Finally, sovereignty in certain areas has been transferred to the Union.

These three trends threaten political society's potential for self-determination. The latter cannot be fully satisfied either by a minimal (neoliberal) state or by simply maintaining the welfare state. State intervention of a new kind should be developed, particularly in the socio-economic sphere.

Guidelines

The group of experts suggests that such recasting should be linked to an overall concept of social rights based on solidarity.

According to the group of experts, this solidarity should not be thought of as solidarity in the face of individual need. Such an interpretation would mean that social rights would be reserved for situations where a dearth of individual resources was established. This would convert the Social State into an aid-providing or even a charity State. Nor should its purpose be defined as the passive protection of individuals and companies on the basis of a closed list of risks. Instead, it should be regarded as solidarity guaranteeing individual and collective security in the face of risk as referred to earlier.

Two types of guarantees must be provided in this area:

- *Procedural guarantees.* Social rights entail the participation of the people concerned in determining them via collective mediation, notably through recognized representative bodies and a limited number of social consultation institutions. The law establishes the major objectives of the system, but the accomplishment of such goals is set out in terms of conventional logic. Accordingly, agreements are no longer merely ways of regulating the relations between the parties involved, but a legal tool that engages the parties in the pursuit of the objectives laid down by law. Independent agencies, managed by a wide range of collective players, would provide a common language for the State and individuals in this task of accommodating the general interest.

- *Substantial guarantees.* In terms of material content, the European Union must give priority to guaranteeing fundamental social rights at European level. These basic principles, which have already been partially acknowledged in the EU Charter of the Fundamental Social Rights of Workers, might usefully be incorporated into constitutional law. This approach fits easily into the Community dynamic, characterized by the prevalence of socio-economic factors at this stage of its construction. These fundamental rights must be worked into all the four circles defined above in accordance with the principle of subsidiarity.

Rather than the concept of social protection, social citizenship might synthesize the objectives of recasting labour law and social law in general. Despite the disparate national definitions of citizenship, this concept may be acknowledged as a suitable instrument for shaping European social law. The advantage it has to offer is that it is extensive (it covers many rights, not just social security); it links up social rights to the notion of social integration, and not just to the notion of work. Above all, it enshrines the idea of participation. Indeed, citizenship assumes the participation of the people concerned in the definition and implementation of their rights. In addition, it is worthy of note that social citizenship can be legally acknowledged, as in Germany.

COMBATING GENDER DISCRIMINATION

Analysis

The expert group felt that gender discrimination in the employment field is such an important, ongoing issue that it should be dealt with in a separate chapter. Their basic observation was as follows: current changes in work that give rise to discrimination on grounds of gender add to rather than replace the factors underlying discrimination that can be traced back to the organization of work deriving from industrialization. Such organization, which draws a distinction between reproductive female work and productive male work, was formalized under traditional labour law, which was strongly male-orientated, taking the male worker as its almost exclusive benchmark. Although women joined the labour market *en masse* in the 1960s and have continued to do so, labour law has not yet succeeded in ending such discrimination: the spread of the formal right to equality for women workers has helped to combat certain types of discrimination, but has not tackled the real discrimination factors arising out of the gender segregation of labour and the sharing of domestic responsibilities. Wage disparities and extra workload (the 'double working day') persist. Discrimination has since been made worse by two sets of circumstances. The first set is generated within the field of production itself, where changes in work in all the senses described above have had a very real and particularly strong impact on women: increasing subordination, greater insecurity, disturbances in private life on account of more flexible working hours. These all particularly affect women. In addition, external factors resulting from changes in family life often end up by increasing the economic burden on women, thus reinforcing the impact of the first-mentioned factors.

Guidelines

In view of such heightened discrimination, the expert group recommends:

- extending attempts to achieve formal equality for men and women to all areas where it is insufficient;
- backing up this protection through specific steps that cover situations particularly affecting women and persistent inequalities in the distribution of domestic chores: maternity leave, continuity of employment status despite breaks, training leave, etc.; these steps may even take the form of positive action, so it urges the Commission and the Member States to make full use of article 141(4) of the Amsterdam Treaty;
- paying special attention to the issue of representation of women's interests in collective bargaining. As trade unions and employers' organizations are still essentially male bastions, one option would be the introduction of special requirements for women's representatives in social consultation bodies.

APPENDIX

EXPERTS CONSULTED BY THE EXPERT GROUP

Robert Salais, Director, Laboratory '*Institutions et Dynamiques Historiques de l'Economie*' (CNRS-Ecole Normale Supérieure de Cachan) (M. Salais subsequently became a member of the Expert Group)
Giorgio Lunghini, Professor, Pavia University
Claus Offe, Professor, Humboldt University of Berlin

LIST OF PERSONS INVITED TO THE DISCUSSION OF THE INTERIM REPORT
(Nantes Conference, 25 October 1997)

Francisco Alonso, Representation of Spain to the EU, Brussels
Jorge Aragon, Foundation '*1º De Mayo*', Spain
Eric Aubry, Ministry of Labour, France
Paolo Barbieri, Trento University, Italy
Jacques Barthélémy, Barthélémy & Associes, France
R. A. C. Blijlevens, VNO-NCW, Netherlands
Marcel Bourlard, ILO, Brussels
Vasco Cal, EU Economic and Social Committee, Brussels
Erik Carslund, ETUC, Brussels
Albert Carton, CSC, Belgium
María Emilia Casas, Expert Group, Spain
Stefaan Clauwaerts, ETUC, Brussels
José De La Cavada, Confederation of Spanish Employers Organizations, Spain
Rudi Delarue, ETUC, Brussels
Jean De Munck, Expert Group, Belgium
Einar Edelberg, Ministry of Labour, Denmark
Eva Fehringer, Ministry of Labour, Austria
Concetta Ferrari, Ministry of Labour, Italy
Francesco Garibaldo, IRES, Italy
François Gaudu, Paris University, France
José Gomes Teixeira, Ministry Of Employment, Portugal
Rosendo Gonzalez, DG V—European Commission, Brussels
Peter Hanau, Expert Group, Germany
Joëlle Hivonnet, European Union Council, Brussels

Richard Hyman, Warwick University, United Kingdom
Bill Jestin, Department of Enterprise, Trade and Employment, Ireland
Anders L. Johansson, Expert Group, Sweden
Ingemar Jöranson, LO, Sweden
Emmanuel Julien, UNICE, Brussels
Juergen Kretz, Representation of Germany to the EU, Brussels
Michel Lafougère, Council of Europe, Strasbourg
Pierre Lanquetin, Cour de Cassation, France
Jouni Lemola, Ministry of Labour, Finland
Pamela Meadows, Expert Group, United Kingdom
Hilary Metcalf, Policy Studies Institute, United Kingdom
Enzo Mingione, Expert Group, Italy
J. Ott, Ministry of Labour, Netherlands
J. Jacques Paris, DG V—European Commission, Brussels
Anne Marie Pernot, Representation of Belgium to the EU, Brussels
Thierry Priestley, Commisariat Général du Plan, France
Odile Quintin, DG V—European Commission, Brussels
Chantal Rey, ISERES, France
María Isabel Rofes I Pujol, European Court of Justice, Luxembourg
Robert Salais, IRESCO, France
Claus Schnabel, Institute of German Economy, Germany
W. S. Siebert, Birmingham University, United Kingdom
Harry Staal, FNV, Netherlands
Alain Supiot, Expert Group, France
Adam Tyson, Representation of the United Kingdom to the EU, Brussels
Zigmunt Tyszkiewicz, UNICE, Brussels
Paul Van Der Heijden, Expert Group, Netherlands
Robert Villeneuve, Comité Européen des Entreprises Publiques, France
Margit Wallsten, Swedish Employers Confederation, Sweden
Siw Warstedt, Representation of Sweden to the EU, Brussels
Ulrich Zachert, Hamburg University, Germany
Jean Zahlen, Ministry of Labour and Employment, Luxembourg
José María Zufiaur, Carlos III University, Madrid, Spain

REFERENCES

Adam, G. (1990). Les syndicats sous perfusion. *Droit social*, December

Aglietta, M. (1976). *Régulation et crises du capitalisme. L'expérience des Etats-Unis.* Paris: Calmann-Lévy

Ballestrero, M. V. (1987). L'ambigual nozione di lavoro prasubordinato. *Lavoro e diritto.* 41

Barthélémy, J. (1994). L'aménagement conventionnel de l'organisation et de la durée du travail. *Droit social*, February

Barthélémy, J. (1997). Une convention collective de travailleurs indépendants? *Droit Social*, January

Bercusson, B. (1996). *European Labour Law.* London: Butterworths

Bercusson, B., Mückenberger, U., and Supiot, A. (1992). Diversité culturelle et droit du travail en Europe. *Convergences des modèles sociaux européens.* Paris: Ministère du travail, coll. Travail-Emploi

Beretta, C. (1995). *Il lavoro dramotamento [xxx or tra mutamento] e reproduzione sociale.* Milano: Angeli

Cartelier, L., Fournier, J., and Monnier, L. (1996). *Critique de la raison communautaire. Utilité publique et concurrence dans l'Union Européenne.* Paris: Economica

Castel, R. (1991). De l'indigence à l'exclusion. Précarité du travail et vulnérabilité professionnelle, in Donzelot, J. *Face à l'exclusion. Le modèle français.* Paris: Éditions Esprit

Centrale de l'industrie du métal de Belgique-FGTB (1997). *Un syndicat pour le 21ieme siècle.* Brussels

Centre Européen des Entreprises à Participation publique (1995). *Europe, concurrence et service public.* Paris: Masson-A.Colin

Chassard, Y. (1997). L'avenir de la protection sociale en Europe. *Droit social*, June

Commissariat général du Plan (1995). *Le travail dans vingt ans*: Rapport de la commission Boissonnat. Paris: Odile Jacob

Coriat, B. (1991). *Penser à l'envers. Travail et organization dans l'entreprise japonaise.* Paris: Christian Bourgois

Coriat, B. (1994). *L'Atelier et le chronomètre.* Paris: Christian Bourgois

Cross, G. (1993). *Time and Money. The Making of Consumer Culture.* London/New York: Routledge

Crouch, C. and Streeck, W. (eds) (1996). *Les capitalismes en Europe.* Paris: La Découverte

Deakin, S. (1998). Privatisation, transformation des entreprises et droit du travail en Grande-Bretagne. *Le Travail en perspective.* Paris: LGDJ

De Munck, J. (forthcoming). *How to regulate working time? From the homogenization to the proceduralization of time*

Entreprise et Progrès (1995). Inventer de nouvelles relations dans l'entreprise: Le contrat collectif d'entreprise. *Entreprise et Progrès*, January

Esping-Andersen, G. (1990). *The Three Worlds of Welfare Capitalism.* Cambridge: Polity Press

European Commission (1995). *The Future of Social Protection: Framework for a European Debate.* COM(95)466. Brussels

European Commission (1996a). *Employment in Europe.* Brussels-Luxembourg

European Commission (1996b). Employee Representatives in Europe and their Economic Prerogatives. *Social Europe.* Supplement 3/96

European Commission (1997a). *Cessation de la relation de travail. Situation juridique dans les Etats membres de l'Union européenne.* Luxembourg-Brussels

European Commission (1997b). *European Systems of Worker Involvement.* Brussels

European Commission (1997c). *Second Report on European Union Citizenship.* COM (97)230, Brussels

European Commission (1997d). *Green Paper: Partnership for a New Way of Organizing Work,* COM(97)128. Brussels

Eurostat (1995). *L'emploi non salarié en Europe (1983/94).* SSL no 768. Luxembourg

Eurostat (1997a). How evenly are earnings distributed? Eurostat statistics in focus. *Population and Social Conditions,* 15/97

Eurostat (1997b). L´activité économique des femmes dans l´Union Européenne. *Population and social conditions,* 1/97

Eurostat (1997c). Les femmes toujours sous-representées sur le marche du travail. *Population and Social Conditions,* 8/97

Favennec-Héry, F. (1997). *Le travail à temps partiel.* Paris: Litec

Ferrera, M. (1998). *Le trappole del welfare.* Bologna

Francq, B. (1995). Procéduralization et formation, in De Munck, J., Lenoble, J., and Molitor, M. (eds), *L'avenir de la concertation sociale en Europe,* Vol. II, Louvain-La-Neuve, Centre de philosophie du droit

Freyssinet, J. (1997). *Le temps de travail en miettes.* Paris: Editions de l'Atelier

Gaudu, F. (1995). Du statut de l'emploi au statut de l'actif. *Droit social,* June

Gaudu, F. (1996). L'application du droit du travail à des travailleurs non salariés. *Revue juridique Ile-de-France.* 39/40

Giugni, G. *et al.* (1994). *Codice di diritto del lavoro.* Bari: Cacucci

Hanau, P. (1997). Die Einwirkung des europäischen auf das nationale Arbeitsrecht—Ein Erfahrungsbericht aus Deutschland. In *Festskrift till Stig Strömholm.* Uppsala: Iustus Förlag

Ichino, A. and Ichino, P. (1994). A chi serve il diritto del lavoro? *Rivista italiana di diritto del lavoro.* 1994/4

ILO (1990). *Promotion of Self-employment.* 77th session of the International Labour Conference, Report 0074-6681 VII. Geneva: ILO

Kravaritou, Y. (1997). *Equal opportunities and collective bargaining in the EU.* Study sponsored by the European Foundation for the Improvement of Living and Working Conditions for DGV of the European Commission. Luxembourg: EU 9704201S

Lagala, C. (1997). Il contributo del 10%. *Dritto & Pratica del lavoro*, 1997/4

Laroque, M., Ray, J.-E., Doroy, F., Chauchard, J.-P., and Lyon-Caen, G. (1995). Sur la loi Madelin. *Droit Social*, July/August

Legendre, P. (1997). Remarques sur la reféodalization de la France, in *Mélanges offerts à Georges Dupuy*. Paris: LGDJ

Leibfried, S. *et al.* (1998). *Time, Life and Poverty*. Cambridge: Cambridge University Press

Lundgren, K. (1996). *Livslängt lärande*. Stockholm: Nerenius & Santérus

Lunghini, G. (1997). *Disoccupazione e bisogni sociali*, lecture delivered to the 30–31 May 1997 meeting of the expert group at Santiago de Compostela

Lyon-Caen, A. (1996). La Constitution française et la négociation collective. *Droit ouvrier*, December

Lyon-Caen, A. (1997). Le rôle des partenaires sociaux dans la mise en œuvre du droit communautaire. *Droit social*

Marshall, T. H. (1950), *Citizenship and Social Class*. Cambridge: Cambridge University Press

Maruani, M. and Nicole, C. (1989). *Au labeur des dames*. Paris: Syros

Méda, D. (1995). *Le travail, une valeur en voie de disparition*. Paris: Aubier

Mengoni, L. (1986). La questione della subordinazione in due trattazioni recenti. *Rivista italiana di diritto del lavoro*, 1986/1

Meurs, D. and Charpentier, P. (1987). Horaires atypiques et vie quotidienne des salariés. *Travail et Emploi*, 32

Ministre de l'Industrie (1997). *Mutations industrielles et relations de travail*, Étude publiée par la Direction générale des stratégies industrielles

Moreau, Y. (1996). *Entreprise de service public européennes et relations sociales.* Paris: ASPE

Morin, M.-L. (1994). Sous-traitance et relations salariales. Aspects de droit du travail. *Travail et Emploi*, 60

Morin, M.-.L. (1996). Sous-traitance et coactivité. *Revue juridique Ile-de-France*, 39/40

Mothé, D. (1994). Le mythe du temps libéré. *Esprit*, August–September

Mückenberger U. (1989). Non-standard forms of work and the role of changes in labour and social security regulation. *International Journal of the Sociology of Law*, 17

Mückenberger, U. (1995). paper in Hoffmann, R. and Lapeyre, J. (eds), *A Time for Working—A Time for Living*. Brussels: European Trade Union Institute

Mückenberger, U. (1997). Un temps pour la ville, in Obadia, A. (ed), *Entreprendre la ville. Nouvelles temporalités—Nouveaux services*. Paris: Éditions de l'Aube

Mückenberger, U. (ed.) (1998*a*). *Zeiten der Stadt. Reflexioned und materialen zu einem ninen gesellschaftlichen Gestaltimgsfeld*. Bremen: Temen

Mückenberger, U. (1998*b*). Democratization and Time in the Cities. *Transfer*, 3/4

Offe, C. (1984). *Contradictions of the Welfare State*. Cambridge, MA: MIT Press

Offe, C. and Heinze, R. G. (1992). *Beyond Employment. Time, Work and Informal Economy*. Cambridge: Polity Press

Olea, A. (1994). *Introduccion al Derecho del trabajo.* Madrid: Civitas. 5th edition

Panofsky, E. (1939). *Studies in Iconology.* Oxford: Oxford University Press

Polanyi, K. (1944). *The Great Transformation.* London: Gollancz

Priestly, T. (1995). A propos du 'contrat d'activité'. *Droit social*

Rodríguez-Piñero, M. (1996). La voluntad de las partes en la calificación del contrato de trabajo. *Relaciones Laborales,* 18

Rodríguez-Piñero, M. (1997). Igualdad de oportunidades y prioridad de la mujer en los ascensos en la Sentencia Marschall del TJCE. *Relaciones Laborales,* 24

Rodríguez-Piñero, M. and Casas, M. E. (1996). *In support of a European Social Constitution, in European Community Labour Law: Principles and Perspectives. Liber Amicorum Lord Wedderburn of Charlton.* Oxford: Clarendon Press

Sabel, C. and Zeitlin, J. (1997). *World of Possibilities: Flexibility and Mass Production in Western Industrialization.* Cambridge: Cambridge University Press

Sagardoy, J.-A. and Gil Y Gil, J.-L. *et al.* (1995). *Prontatuario de derecho del trabajo.* Madrid: Civitas. 2nd edition

Salais, R. (1998). *Identité économique nationale et échanges croisés entre la France et l'Allemagne,* in Didry, C., Wagner, P., and Zimmermann, B. (eds), *Le travail et la nation. La France et l'Allemagne à l'horizon européen.* Paris: Editions de la MSH

Salais, R. and Storper, M. (1993). *Les mondes de production. Enquête sur l'identité économique de la France.* Paris, Editions de l'EHESS (Published in English as Storper, M. and Salais, R. (1997). *Worlds of Production. The Action Frameworks of the Economy.* Cambridge, MA: Harvard University Press)

Soskice, D. (1990). Wage determination: the changing role of institutions in advanced industrialized countries. *Oxford Review of Economic Policy,* 1990/4

Supiot, A. (1995*a*). Temps de travail: pour une concordance des temps. *Droit Social,* December (published in English in as On the Job Time: Time for Agreement in the *International Journal of Comparative Labour Law and Industrial Relations,* 12/3, 1996)

Supiot, A. (1995*b*). L'avenir d'un vieux couple: travail et sécurité sociale. *Droit social,* September–October

Supiot, A. (1996). Work and the Public/Private Dichotomy. *International Labour Review,* 135(6)

Supiot, A. (1997). Du bon usage des lois en matière d'emploi. *Droit Social,* March

Teyssié, B. (1994). Sur le nouvel article L. 120-3 du code du travail. *Droit social,* July–August

Van der Heijden, P. (1998). *The flexibilization of working life in the Netherlands,* Paper for the 15th Congress of the Academy of Comparative Law

Vianello, R. (1997). La nuova tutela previdenziale per le attività di lavoro autonomo, libero-professionale e di collaborazione coordinata e continuataiva, in Cester, C. (ed.), *La riforma del sistema pensionistico.* Turin: Giappichelli

Winckler, J. T. (1976). Corporatism, *Archives européennes de sociologie,* 17(1)

Wood, S. (1993). Le modèle japonais: postfordisme ou japonization du fordisme? in Durand, J. P. (ed.), *Vers un nouveau modèle productif?* Paris: Syros

INDEX